# no excuses

# GLORIA FELDT

nine ways women can change
how we think about power

{ TOOLS FOR LEADING AN UNLIMITED LIFE }

SEAL PRESS

## *no excuses*
nine ways women can change how we think about power

Published by
Seal Press
A Member of the Perseus Books Group
1700 Fourth Street
Berkeley, California

Library of Congress Cataloging-in-Publication Data

Feldt, Gloria, 1942-
   No excuses : 9 ways women can change the way we think about power and leadership / Gloria Feldt.
      p. cm.
   Includes index.
   ISBN 978-1-58005-388-4
   1. Leadership in women. 2. Power (Social sciences) 3. Control (Psychology) 4. Feminism. I. Title.
   HQ1233.F45 2010
   305.42—dc22

                              2010014265


Cover and interior design by Domini Dragoone
Printed in the United States of America
Distributed by Publishers Group West

## Praise for *No Excuses*

"A knockout of a book, *No Excuses* hits the mother lode
by showing women how we deny our power. We serve and care
and rarely have the courage to take credit for it. Gloria shows us
how to work our 'power-to' and be stronger for it."
**—KATHLEEN TURNER**

"Gloria's redefinition of power is exactly what the world needs today."
**—PETER BUFFET,** composer, philanthropist,
and author of *Life is What You Make It*

"Feldt gives a comprehensive look at how far we've come and
how it's time to take it to the next level—time to move the
agenda forward for women and our nation."
**—SIOBHAN (SAM) BENNETT,** president, Women's Campaign Forum

"From personal to political power, *No Excuses* offers a clear
roadmap for women. But it's Feldt's relatable—and often funny!
—voice that makes the trip all the more fun."
**—JESSICA VALENTI,** author of *The Purity Myth*
and founder of Feministing.com

"*No Excuses* is loaded with fresh advice and uplifting stories.
As a businesswoman, I am inspired by Gloria's optimistic message.
**—DR. DEBRA CONDREN,** author of *Ambition Is Not A Dirty Word*

"We are no longer in the gender equity business but rather the
more sweeping societal transformation business. And, as Gloria tells us,
we must make changes to seize this historic moment."
**—MARIE C. WILSON,** founder and past president,
The White House Project

"*No Excuses* calls readers to recognize and pick apart our hesitation,
ambivalence, and a lack of surety that get in the way of our own ambitions. Feldt knows that women must understand and reshape their feelings
about power before they can grasp it. Now, she's saying, is the time."
**—REBECCA TRAISTER,** Salon.com, author of *Big Girls Don't Cry*

To the memory of my father, Max Feldt,
who told me I could do anything my
pretty little head desired.


To my second-wave sisters,
who showed me how.


And to all the amazing young women
leading the way to an unlimited future.

# contents

*"Together we're unlimited."*

**—ELPHABA** in *Wicked*

# your unlimited moment (and why there are no excuses for not embracing it this time)

*"If women want any rights more than they's got, why don't they just take them, and not be talking about it."*

**—SOJOURNER TRUTH,**
former slave, abolitionist, women's rights
advocate, and Methodist minister[1]

Kathryn Bigelow, the first woman to win an Academy Award for best director—for *The Hurt Locker,* which also won best picture of 2009—stood holding her two Oscars, looking completely flustered. Seeing her under the spotlight, one coveted golden statue grasped in each fist, I was struck by how accurately she mirrored where women in the United States stand today. We've got the evidence of success in our hands, and everyone in the world seems to be looking on, but we don't quite know what to do about it.

There are more ironies in this picture. Bigelow's film is a raw, violent portrayal of the war in Iraq, with no women as major characters—hardly a chick flick, despite some interpretations that it puts a feminist lens on masculinity and the senseless violence of combat. Yet it did not go unnoticed that Bigelow herself is gorgeous, gracious, and above all says not one word about the fact that she is a woman—indeed, she seems even more flustered when the obvious is called to her attention by inquiring journalists.

That she wasn't the first of her gender but the fourth to be nominated— the first was Lina Wertmuller in 1976—similarly speaks to both the progress women have made and the newness of our tangible triumphs. After eighty-two years of Oscars and over four hundred best director nominees, presenter Barbra Streisand was finally able to pronounce upon opening the envelope, "The time has come."[2]

Without question, the time has come. That's why *No Excuses* is foremost a book about hope and possibility. But it is also an urgent call to action.

I've had the joy of seeing women make stunning progress during my four decades of activism. Now I want to encourage women to embrace their power in this amazing moment when we can lead and live without limits. For the first time in history, as I will discuss in detail, we have the potential to do that. There are big challenges, to be sure. For example, the White House Project's Benchmark study, released in December 2009, documents that women are stuck at around 18 percent of leadership positions across the ten sectors they studied. Nevertheless, the biggest question is what we will choose to do with that information.[3]

We can start by changing the very meaning of power from an oppressive *power-over* to an expansive concept I call the *power-to*. And if we muster the courage to stand in our power and walk with intention, we can achieve our highest aspirations at work, in civic life, and in love for good—by which I mean we can transform power relationships for our own good and create good in the world for others.

But here's our predicament: Though insidious cultural barriers remain, we must face the fact that from the boardroom to the bedroom, from public office to personal relationships, no law or formal barrier is keeping us from achieving equality and justice except our own unwillingness to "just take them," as Sojourner Truth urged a century and a half ago.

There are many reasons why women have been held back or have stepped back from our power. But there are no excuses anymore. My intent is not to assign blame, but to inspire women to embrace our historic moment; not to dish up ancient history, but to envision a bright future, and to provide the tools to make it happen now while the opportunity is hot.

I'm incredibly optimistic about women, men, and the new expectations of equality I see in nearly every arena almost every day. I don't believe the ongoing chatter about gender wars or the media narrative that's rigged to make women feel like they can't have it all—or shouldn't even be happy about what they've got. This is without question an unlimited moment, yet we must see it, seize it, and take it over the top.


## UNLIMITED OPPORTUNITIES BECKON

Women have opportunities we have never enjoyed before, and our contributions to society are valued more than they have been at any time in history. Journalist and California's former First Lady Maria Shriver has proclaimed America "A Woman's Nation"[4]; Nick Kristof, *New York Times* columnist and coauthor with his wife, Sheryl WuDunn, of *Half the Sky*, has declared women "mistresses of the universe."[5] Hillary Clinton put those eighteen million cracks in the ultimate glass ceiling—the Oval Office. And Sarah Palin's rise shows that even right-wing Republicans are aware that this is a moment for women.

It's not just because women outnumber men in universities and that the numbers of men and women reached parity in the workforce during 2010, but also because women and men working side-by-side turns out to be a very good thing: McKinsey's "Women Matter" study is one among many demonstrating that when women are included in leadership, the quality of decision-making improves.[6] Not only that, but the World Bank posits as a result of a sweeping global study that more equality for women results in better governance and more women in public life correlates with less corruption.[7]

I see no limits and hear no excuses when I talk to the politically ambitious women in Emerge America's candidate training program who are determined to assume equal governing power.[8] Or in best-selling books like *Womenomics,* signaling that women are now so integral to the workplace that we can reshape its hard edges, if we want to apply ourselves to it, so that both men and women can have a personal life and earn a living.[9] And limitless vision is manifested in initiatives popping up everywhere, like the

National Council for Research on Women's plan "A Road Map for Achieving Critical Mass—and Why It Matters" to increase women's participation in fund management substantially.[10]

Concurrently, reproductive technologies that enable women to separate sex from pregnancy and, ironically, the economic recession have escalated the equalization of gender power in personal relationships and at work. The Council on Contemporary Families documents men's increasing involvement with their children, a trend that liberates men, too, from the stereotypes that have stifled them in the past.[11] And feminism has changed the culture so profoundly that young women grow up assuming they can do anything and young men don't doubt that women will. These trend lines are all converging in a positive direction.

I'm proud to be part of the vibrant women's movement that has pushed, prodded, pulled, and led these changes. But only in the last few years have I sensed we're at a place where we can change the underlying social and political structures that have been preventing a full-throated declaration of victory. If we give the fulcrum of parity one last heave-ho, it will very likely propel women to equal footing with men for good—ours and theirs.

## SO WHY IS THE DIAL OF PROGRESS STUCK?

With all that good news, why is there still a deep canyon between the promise and the reality? Why are women the majority of voters but only 17 percent of Congress; the majority of journalism school graduates but only 3 percent of top media clout positions; and why do we spend 85 percent of consumer dollars but control just 15 percent of the corporate boardrooms that determine what products we'll be allowed to spend our money on? Women earn 78 cents to every dollar men earn, in part because we still bear most of the burden for caregiving of both young and old. And women's reproductive rights are continuously under assault. Despite all the gains, every institution within society seems to replicate the same imbalanced gender dynamics—one where men predominate in leadership and owner-ship roles, and women struggle for equal representation at the top ranks of power—and right now they all beg for the skills and talents women bring. I mean, don't they always bring in the women to clean up the mess?

Plenty of unfinished business remains, to be sure. There are both exter-nal barriers of customs and laws to smash and internal barriers of resistance and co-option to be excised. Like columnist Ellen Goodman, I give the women's movement an incomplete. Yet, that's no reason to shrink from fin-ishing the job.[12] In fact, it's a clarion call to keep on pressing forward. And unlike in previous generations, opportunities for women today are bound-less. We're at a unique place in history—where we've blown open the glass ceiling but not yet swept away all the treacherous shards. Though we can find data to support many explanations about why we aren't at parity in elected office and boardrooms, we simply no longer have compelling justi-fications not to be taking up the responsibility to get ourselves there. It's a scary place to be, and an exhilarating one.

## LET US NOT SQUANDER THE MOMENT

For good or ill, what happens next will be of our own choosing. This moment could easily be squandered, just as women have failed many times before to catalyze other historic advances toward full equality.

Perhaps you're reading this book because, like me, you're puzzled, frus-trated, or downright angry about experiences of inequality or disrespect you've had, whether they're recent or buried deep in the recesses of your memory. Maybe you've encountered specific injustices, like Lilly Ledbetter, who sued Goodyear to get a paycheck equal to those of her male counter-parts. She won, then lost at the Supreme Court, then got a law passed to pro-tect other women's right to equal pay even though she herself won't benefit.[13] You could be one of many women I've heard from who are fuming that the much-needed health reform plan signed into law in March 2010 is tainted by anti-choice Hyde amendment restrictions. Or, maybe you're wrestling with internal roadblocks, such as difficulty negotiating a raise or reluctance to insist that your spouse share household duties. We'll look at why we continue to have these problems—and we'll propose solutions. What this book aims to do is encourage and inspire women to take the next step—to go boldly and with intention through the doors to equal power and leadership roles.

For the stunning advances we see today didn't just happen. People who saw injustices mobilized to make the changes happen. We'll celebrate those. But we'll also look at what all too frequently happened after major victories: Women voluntarily stepped back from the brink of power. Not this time!

Here's the hard fact that triggered my desire to research women's relationship with power and to write *No Excuses:* The doors to equal opportunity have been cracked wide open, but too few women are willing to push on through them. We have to stop putting boundaries around our own vision for what we can do. We must act now, with intention, to assume our share of leadership roles.

I've found a repetitive pattern of women coming to power and stepping back. I've done it, too.

## MY PERSONAL POWER RESISTANCE DEMONS

I had a startling confrontation with my own ambivalence toward power in 2005, when I left my thirty-year career with Planned Parenthood Federation of America—the final nine of those years as national president. Certainly not a minor role! There'd been many accomplishments I'm proud of, especially breathing an audacious new vision and activist energy into a movement long on the defensive. It's heady to work in the highest halls of power, and humbling to hear women say, as I still hear daily, "You saved my life."

But I had subsumed myself to the movement. I didn't know who I was. After I left, and the intense external pressures that had structured my life were removed, I felt like a woman made of jelly—amorphous, emotionally vulnerable, frightened by the wide-open possibilities for myself that I'd never confronted before, not to mention the chilling responsibility of choosing a new path. Unlike star quarterback Brett Favre, who retired but couldn't stand being out of the game, so he came back to play professional football at forty, I knew I didn't want to repeat the past. But what did I want for my future?

I found that having been the face of a high-profile organization meant others perceived me in a certain way—as an advocate for a narrow set of issues and not a bit more. I could change myself more easily than I could change who people thought I was. I had a long list of books I wanted to write. I shopped for a book agent and pitched my first idea. I proposed to investigate America's difficult relationship with sex, a topic I could write about with authority, but that would give me space to expand my expertise. My new agent urged me instead to partner with Kathleen Turner to write her biography. She persuaded me I'd be advancing the cause of women by chronicling the life story of a powerful sister, and I melted. It sounded compelling enough that I agreed to approach Turner and suggest it to her.

Kathleen Turner chairs Planned Parenthood's celebrity board, so I knew her professionally. We explored the book idea over tamales and margaritas at our favorite Mexican restaurant. She wasn't immediately convinced; she thought she was too young, at fifty-one, to be publishing a book about her life, and she fretted that she would seem egotistical. But during that meeting, we realized we were at similar stages in our lives, in transitions after achieving major heights. She'd reached the pinnacle of her theatrical career, playing Martha in *Who's Afraid of Virginia Woolf.* It was the role she knew at twenty she wanted to do at fifty, and she'd overcome enormous obstacles to get it. But what next? The question hit her hard. After thinking it over, and ever the practical activist, she decided to share her story and the lessons she'd learned that might be helpful to other women in similar situations.

I admired Kathleen's equal devotion to acting and community service. How many celebrities do you know who actually *deliver* meals on wheels? I sobbed over her struggles with debilitating rheumatoid arthritis that would have derailed a less gutsy person. I liked her when we started, and loved her by the time we were finished.

There was just one problem. *Send Yourself Roses* had to become a memoir rather than a biography to be marketable. That meant instant demotion for me. I might have legally been the coauthor, but to the publisher and agent, I became invisible as soon as the ink was dry on the contract.

One particularly humiliating experience happened as we sat around the conference table at our big meeting to review publicity plans. The publicist, who was directly across from me, turned his back to me and made the entire presentation to Kathleen as though I didn't exist. Needless to say, I threw a fit. While that did little to enhance the pecking order in his mind, the need for the confrontation was a wake-up call to me. Shortly after that, I roared with laughter when our editor accused me of making the book "too feminist," to which Kathleen retorted, "Who the fuck did they think they were getting?" Indeed, and proud of it.

I justified hanging in there when I read that historically eight autobiographies of men have been written for every one by a woman. That ratio is probably not as dramatic anymore, as women have increasingly found their voices through memoir, but regardless, there's no disputing that even women who have achieved great things rarely attribute their successes to their own agency or choices. Men, on the other hand, typically give themselves full credit for what they have accomplished and show no reluctance to claim they are fully responsible for their own success—and more. I could relate to this pattern, since, like many women, I'd always felt my own career had been serendipitous—just a matter of being in the right place at the right time—and I told my story that way.

When I was offered my first Planned Parenthood position as executive director of its fledgling West Texas affiliate in 1974, I felt seriously unqualified despite a glowing recommendation from my boss at Head

Start, where I'd taught for five years previously. But I was a woman who grew up in the choiceless 1950s and had bought the pervasive memo to girls: "Be nice, don't be smarter than the boys, marry young."

I didn't realize that the same circumstances that made me doubt my fitness for the job were actually my best preparation for it. I understood very well the struggles of too-young parents and too-frequent childbearing. I'd married my high school sweetheart—in the 1950s version of Bristol Palin and Levi Johnston you got married if you were pregnant—and given birth to three children by just after my twentieth birthday. This closely coincided with the (miraculous, I thought) advent of the birth control pill. During the dozen years between the pill and Planned Parenthood, I earned my college degree, bit by bit over twelve years, and was planning to teach—the default job for women then if, like me, you couldn't type and retched at the sight of blood.

Instead, I found myself in a tiny windowless office donated to Planned Parenthood by the local bank, staffed only by me and my big-haired assistant, Mary, who had given herself the title "sexretary." I broke out in hives from the stress of knowing how much I didn't know about running the five family planning clinics spread over a dusty West Texas expanse. Before long, I fell headlong in love with the movement to bring birth control to women, and with it, the power to chart the course of our own lives.

In four years, I grew the West Texas affiliate to eleven clinics. That was great fun. By then, my teenage marriage had sputtered to its predictable end. I was thirty-six. My youngest child was soon to graduate from high school, and I wanted to get the heck out of windswept Odessa, Texas, a town chronicled embarrassingly well—both its flat land and flat-lined possibilities—in Buzz Bissinger's *Friday Night Lights*. So I applied to run the Arizona affiliate, and was hired in 1978. I later learned their first choice (a man) had rejected their salary offer. It had never occurred to me to negotiate my salary.

Again, I expanded services substantially, on a mission to provide more options for all women. I had to learn on the job about virulent, sometimes violent, antiabortion politics, and how to ramp up fundraising to compensate for Ronald Reagan's assault on federal family planning funds during the 1980s. Eighteen years went by in a blink. The work was still rewarding, but I was starting to feel stale. Just as I was about to resign in 1996, I was recruited for the national presidency, into a public crucible where the challenges and controversies grew ever more intense.

People look at me like I'm crazy when I fail to acknowledge my own intention in this career path. "How did that happen?" they ask, incredulous at my claim that I didn't put myself forward for these amazing positions. I realize now that I sound as if I were a boat being carried by the current. To me, it felt I was just responding to what was needed of me rather than reaching for something I'd consciously sought to do. Only now am I coming to realize that women in general have been so invisible in society's halls of power for so long that we can hardly think of our own inchoate ambition as having intrinsic value; in fact, we've been cautioned that it could be dangerous to our love life to acknowledge such ambition publicly.

Writing Kathleen's life after unmooring myself from the formal leadership of the reproductive justice movement was like getting a year of free psychotherapy. It forced me to recognize my underlying pattern. The lack of personal intention that had led me to early marriage and parenthood continued through my career, however rewarding, and there I was doing it again: writing someone else's story, speaking in a voice that reflected my beliefs to be sure, but that I could never claim as my own. I was repeatedly giving away the power to define myself.

Though I had devoted half my life to enabling other women to set the course of theirs, I had yet to choose my own.

•   •   •

## WHY DO WOMEN RESIST
## THE POWER THEY DESERVE?

I began to discuss this with other women ranging in age from twenty to eighty. I soon learned I wasn't unique. I wanted to explore it further, and Hillary Clinton's hat in the ring as the first viable woman candidate for president was the perfect catalyst. My systematic research into women's conflicted relationship with power began during the 2008 election season, when I wrote an article for *Elle* magazine about why women do—or as I came to find out, more often don't—run for office.

What I found stopped me short: It's no longer external, structural barriers, though some do still exist, but internal ones that hold women back from fully embracing their political power. And I realized there are far more similarities than differences in how this dynamic plays itself out in the seemingly divergent realms of work, politics, and personal relationships.

I wanted to learn more: to understand what internalized values, assumptions, and beliefs about ourselves we as women haul around, like worthless cargo, hindering the full attainment of our potential as leaders and doers—what intricate personal and cultural constructs of power, the silent sinews that bind not only our political intentions, but our work lives and even our love lives.

Paradoxically, despite my cluelessness about my own power, I've spent most of my adult life working for social justice and power for others—African Americans, poor kids, women who don't have access to reproductive choices and healthcare. Not, as Jerry Seinfeld would say, that there's anything wrong with that. In fact, I feel blessed to have been able to make my life's passion for social justice into my life's work. Nor is my path so different from gendered behavior regarded (and rewarded) as laudable—being nice, putting the needs of others first, self-sacrificing, not caring about such "male" prerogatives as earning a high income.

Which is the point. Fighting for others seemed worthy. Fighting for myself, or something I wanted, did not. Defining my life from a place of my own intention was not in my mental repertoire. And many younger women tell me they experience similar problems today even as they seek role models and mentors to teach them differently. Yet both effective leadership and acts that create fundamental social change are rooted in the language of power. If women are ever to complete our staccato journey to equality, we must join the discourse and become deliberately fluent in power's meanings and nuances.

While the men around us operate as though they own the world—because, for the most part, they do—we have to work consciously to assume that place of intentional power and agency. Women's inner struggles parallel the pushme-pullyou history of our advances, and the intricate interplay between the social structures that can restrain or unleash one's power to approach life with intention.

It's this *relationship* with power—almost a spiritual factor, rarely acknowledged by the metrics or even the philosophers, which I've witnessed in myself and countless other women—that fascinated me and propelled me to undertake this book. For until we understand and redefine our relationship with power, we will stay stuck in our half-finished revolution. And I think that matters for two reasons.

First, we will remain able to excuse and justify our lack of progress by pointing outward rather than owning our part of the responsibility to take the harder road of pushing forward courageously. Second, until we can stand confidently in our own power, we won't be able to lead ourselves or others with intention. If we allow this to happen, if we miss this amazing moment, both women and men will remain constrained within lives of limited possibilities, lives that keep us from achieving our full human potential.

The Right Honorable Kim Campbell, former prime minister of Canada (and the first female head of that nation's government), put it this way: "Look, power exists. Somebody is going to have it. If you would exercise it ethically, why not you? I love power. I'm power-hungry because when I have power I can make things happen, can serve my community, can influence decisions, I can accomplish things."[14]

Why *not* you? How many women do you know who can say straight out that they are power-hungry? And yet we should be hungry to use our power—for our own gratification, as well as the benefit of the world.

## DON'T THINK LIKE AN ELEPHANT

Women should be flocking to the opportunities that are beckoning to us today in work, civic and political life, and on the home front. But herein lies the pattern: We've historically made leaps forward, only to step back. So here's what you'll find between the covers of *No Excuses*. Not theoretical discourse, but my unvarnished take on what I've seen and learned from life and leadership. Not dry statistics, but real-life stories from women who have courageously tried and even if they stumbled, picked themselves up and kept trying. Each chapter is matched with a Power Tool; collectively these tools offer specific advice and examples to help you lead an unlimited life.

It's said that when a baby elephant is being trained, she is tied to a post almost immediately after birth. During the first few weeks of life, she attempts to break free of her restraints, but she's not strong enough. So she comes to believe she can't get away from what is holding her back even after she has grown large and plenty powerful to uproot the post entirely. As a consequence, even as an adult, she remains tied to the post due to an internally motivated behavior that is no longer rooted in external reality.

If women want to embrace our power we must first reject baby elephant thinking and throw off the shackles of learned behavior that no longer serves us.

*Then we must dare to change other dysfunctional paradigms.* I don't want women to become men and repeat the same oppressive patterns of men's leadership; I do want to redefine power and its uses so we all have a place at the table of life and leadership.

To hold forth the vision of women who are unlimited with the courage to stand in our own power and walk with intention. To help women be brave enough and bold enough to hold high aspirations but offer no excuses.

To lead society toward a saner way of work, politics, and love.

To get the best of the masculine and feminine working together without the worst of them, found at the extremes, sabotaging our efforts.

I feel certain in my deepest heart that the doors to power parity in all arenas, if not wide open, are at least ajar. The locks that kept us out for so long are off; we are strong enough to break free of past tethers. Unlimited possibilities beckon to create a world that will be more equitable and healthier for both men and women. There are no excuses this time. Now it's up to us to step up and lead ourselves and our sisters through the threshold.

To take what we want and stop just talking about it.

# part**one**

## PIECES OF RESISTANCE

# CHAPTER ONE

# understand:

# you've come a long way, maybe

*"For a people is only as great, as free, as lofty, as advanced, as its women are free, noble, and progressive."*

**—SUSAN B. ANTHONY,**
nineteenth-century suffragist leader

*"You told us we could do anything. We heard 'You must do everything.'"*

**—COURTNEY MARTIN,** 30,
feminist commentator and author of
*Perfect Girls, Starving Daughters*

## HAVE YOU EVER?

- Waited politely to speak during a meeting only to hear a male colleague offer the very idea you had planned to suggest?

- Considered running for office but felt you weren't qualified yet?

- Found out after the fact that a man with the same qualifications holding the same job as you started at a higher salary because he asked for it and you didn't?

- Taken on the major burden of household duties in part because you know it'll get done that way—and then you felt resentful?

And if you answered "yes" to any of these questions, as I certainly have to all of them at one time or another, have you ever asked yourself "why"?

These are all examples of just some of the internal barriers that have slowed women's progress toward parity and still limit us today even as we have, Wonder Woman–like, demolished one external barrier after another. This ingrained mentality shows up time and time again among women, and portends how we've made such giant leaps forward, yet often, sometimes when we don't expect or intend it, we hang back from expressing ourselves, asking directly for what we want, or taking the lead when we know we deserve it.

As a practical activist, I'm just talking about what's going on. I'm exploring the topic to help women find a deliberate path to *un*limit ourselves. Now is the moment for women to expand our vision for what we can do and our will to do it.

Economic and political chaos—recession, crumbling of long-standing financial entities, gridlock when Congress and state legislatures try to make needed reforms on issues like healthcare—presents an enormous opportunity to break the rigid gendered role boundaries that remain. But progress won't happen on its own.

## "SIT IN THE HIGH SEATS"

When the late former Secretary of Labor Frances Perkins spoke about why she accepted President Franklin Roosevelt's call in 1933 to become the first woman member of a presidential cabinet, she said she did it because of her sense of obligation to other women: "The door might not be opened to a woman again for a long, long time and I had a kind of duty to other women to walk in and sit down on the chair that was offered, and so establish the right of others long hence and far distant in geography to sit in the high seats."[1]

Not all women today share Perkins's sense of obligation to other women. On top of the individual unwillingness to ask for the salaries and advancement they deserve, so many of the very women who have most benefited from advances in their education and employment opportunities—those elite women chronicled by Lisa Belkin in the influential *New York Times* article "The Opt-Out Revolution"[2] and admonished for doing so by Linda Hirshman in *Get to Work*[3]—are choosing not to sit in the high seats. Instead they take on traditional helpmeet and stay-at-home-mom roles, perhaps because it is easier and perhaps simply because they can afford to do so. As a result, just when women are on the verge of a seemingly unstoppable rise to genuine equality in all spheres, some substantial portion of those most capable of making the leap are taking themselves voluntarily back to a modern version of separate but equal— segregating themselves into the home. By claiming that having the financial prerogative of *choosing* to avoid going into the workplace justifies their doing so, they avoid the tough challenges of changing the childcare and workplace leave systems and cede leadership roles to men, who—no surprise—continue climbing the ladder uninterrupted.

With these two competing trajectories of enormous leaps forward and mincing steps back, coming face-to-face with the interruption of a recession that threw many people's plans into the air, the time is now to embrace the vision of an unlimited future for women. It's time to ask why such a future continues to be elusive despite all the signs pointing toward opportunity for progress.

The answer to why things happen is always personal and it's always political. A look at how we got here may be helpful.

## "WHAT'S A TOMBOY?"

There are no limitations so far for Emily, my friend's eight-year-old soccer ace. When my occasionally impolitic husband, Alex, asked Emily whether she was a tomboy after she came bounding home from a winning game, Emily replied without a trace of self-consciousness: "What's that?"

You can be sure women have made serious progress when even the language that would have defined an athletic girl as an aberration from her gender just a generation before has disappeared from the lexicon. Emily learned a bevy of leadership skills from the team sport, and has had the sort of experience that boys have been learning as a matter of course forever but only recently have been available to girls. Physical mastery, for starters. How to be competitive and collegial at the same time. Building a team and the power of teamwork. How to win gracefully, and that losing isn't the same thing as defeat. Strategic thinking—just to name a few. That girls who play sports are somewhat more likely to get higher education and to work in high-skilled but previously male-dominated jobs suggests that these leader-ship competencies pay off over the long haul.[4]

We've passed many mileposts heading toward equal opportunity on the road to Emily's soccer game. Sometimes a seemingly mundane improvement makes a profound difference. Take the comfortable clothing championed by nineteenth-century women's rights activist Amelia Bloomer, who became so identified with loose trousers, allowing women freedom of movement, that they were named for her.

One hundred years later, sweeping legal changes leveled the playing field. Emily gets to play soccer in school thanks to Title IX of the Education Amendments of 1972, later renamed the Patsy T. Mink Equal Opportunity in Education Act to honor the late congresswoman who authored the law banning gender discrimination in federal funding of educational programs, including, for the first time, athletics. The impetus for this legislation came about when Bernice Sandler was turned down for a professor's position. After a male faculty member told Sandler she hadn't been hired because, "You come on too strong for a woman," she realized she had no recourse against such discrimination unless new laws were written. A woman who would not be limited, Sandler researched the laws and then located a supportive congresswoman to draft the remedy.[5]

## SOCIAL NORMS AND SELF-LIMITATION

Gaining the *right* to an equal opportunity to play soccer is one thing. Choosing to *take* the *opportunity* to play is another. Self-limitation despite social and legal advances can be the result of many factors: social norms that are hard to overcome, particularly those that overemphasize the qualities of niceness, deference, and attractiveness to the opposite sex, individual personality traits, or, more likely, the relationship between the two and how they interact with one another. Studies show that boys and girls already have incorporated a clear sense of their own genders and what behaviors are assigned to each gender by the age of two. Which doll likes to clean the house? The child of either sex typically points to the female doll. And who is more likely to go to work or play action games? The male doll. That internalization is hard to shake.[6]

As a countervailing force, the increasing number of girls who play organized team sports statistically have lower rates of teen pregnancy and higher self-esteem than those who don't participate in these activities. Today, one-third of girls play organized sports as compared to one-half of boys, and the disparity continues to lessen.[7]

But as Emily enters adolescence, she's at risk for becoming a "female impersonator," to use the descriptor coined by therapist Mary Pipher, author of *Reviving Ophelia: Saving the Lives of Adolescent Girls.*[8] A female impersonator is someone who makes her personality smaller rather than larger, and girls, particularly adolescent girls, often do this to be attractive to boys, to get attention from friends both male and female for things that are perhaps considered more cool (i.e., girls who play up being bad at schoolwork even though they aren't, or downplay their skill at something for the sake of getting attention for their deficits rather than their smarts). Take a girl who has a tendency toward these behaviors and add in those ubiquitous hyper-sexualized female media images she'll inevitably encounter. It's easy to see how girls start to relinquish pieces of their power at a very early age and how the cumulative erosion, like water on stone, eventually reshapes the self-assured girl into a young woman who is insecure about her body and her capabilities during the process of going through puberty and entering her teenage years.

Dr. Louanne Brizendene, author of *The Female Brain,* concluded from her research that these teenage physical transformations often knock a girl like Emily off her emotionally even girl-keel and into an unpredictable adolescent personality. Brizendene says this personal transition can put a "gash in her self-esteem," causing the young woman to question her abilities and recoil from the sense of conflict and chaos such dramatic changes in body and brain can bring.[9] Few adult women can fail to remember those periods of insecurity, of obsessing over whether she was too thin or too fat, whether her breasts were the right size, and whether or not she was regarded as one of the cool girls by the girls she thought were cool. All this worry about what others think gets in the way of focusing on what impact she might want to have were she to assert herself into a leadership role. I don't subscribe to the hormones-are-destiny school of thought, though the mind-body connection can't be overlooked (not as excuses but as contributing reasons for choices girls make during these critical junctures). And certainly the process is different for each girl-to-woman.

But because of these complexities, we can't predict with any certainly the extent to which Emily will remain the physically empowered girl she is now once she reaches puberty and young womanhood. Nor can we pluck conclusions from delightful individual anecdotes such as Emily's without examining our collective roots in the fertile earth of the culture(s) that created and nurtured our identities.

Because we're still in the process of changing to a new paradigm of gender power, we must continuously ask: How can we help to ensure Emily makes it through her passage to adulthood with her ego strength intact so she will relate to the world from a place of her own agency rather than reactively molding herself to what she thinks others want? How can Emily and women of all ages get their fair share in the three most important power grids of our lives: work, love, and politics?

The sum of women's collective struggles to achieve parity and power is far greater than its disparate parts. There's not a straight path, but a kinetic relationship with many moving elements. We are shaped by the structures we live in at the same time we're changing them by individual efforts and through social movements. That's why there often seem to be multiple (and sometimes contradictory) cultural narratives, each inevitably ringing true to some substantial percentage of the population. For example, consider the following:

- Women support one another's advancement; OR women have "catfights" and sabotage one another.

- Women are happier today than in the past; OR women are unhappier today.

- Women are better leaders than men because they consider more options before they make decisions; OR women aren't tough enough to lead because they are too risk averse to make quick decisions.

- Add your own examples. I'll bet you encounter them every day.

What a bundle of contradictions! No wonder women both approach and avoid power, often simultaneously.

## A REASON IS NOT AN EXCUSE

But this push and pull is a reason, not an excuse. Moments of opportunity like this have come around before, and they don't last forever—for individual women or for women collectively. And so we find ourselves in a place similar to others where we've been before, on the historic brink of a new breakthrough for women, if only women will lead their own way forward. Will we choose to make it happen this time? We must glean what we can from the lessons of our history before we can hope to create the future of our choice. Here's my CliffsNotes version of highlights that illustrate the pattern.

# powertool number one

## know your history and you can create the future of your choice.

NOTE: I primarily deal with U.S. women's history because it's my own primordial soup. I hope women in other cultures find helpful reference points, but I make no assumptions of universality. And I encourage you to share your stories at www.gloriafeldt.com if I've missed something important to you.

## THEN AND NOW:
## STEPPING FORWARD, STEPPING BACK

American women have collectively been on a roller-coaster ride toward equality not unlike the typical girl's individual journey to womanhood ever since 1776, when Abigail Adams threatened her husband John that the women would rebel if the men drafting the new nation's laws failed to "remember the ladies and be more generous and favorable to them than your ancestors." Abigail added, "Do not put such unlimited power into the hands of the husbands."

The men didn't comply with Abigail's demands; in fact, John lovingly if cleverly mocked her outright, allowing as how the men would never accept this "despotism of the petticoat." Though not legally held in bondage, women might as well have been slaves since they generally had no property rights, no means to support themselves, or even the right to protect themselves physically from husbands' "unlimited power."[10]

The ladies didn't rebel. Too bad.

It's a pattern often repeated by women: a habit of taking the boniest parts of the chicken and leaving the meatier parts for others to feast upon. A lack of organized, persistent resistance to power techniques, such as when men mock and belittle women's legitimate concerns and the women don't push back or foment that promised rebellion. An inability or unwillingness to risk losing security. A walking up to the brink of power and stepping back voluntarily.

One consequence is that women have been all but written out of history. Take the story of Sybil Luddington. At age sixteen, on April 26, 1777, Sybil rode through towns in New York and Connecticut warning that the British were coming. She gathered enough volunteers to beat back the British army the next day, and her ride was twice as long as Paul Revere's. Yet, unless you live in the small Connecticut town named for her, it's doubtful you've ever heard of her.

Women were everywhere, giving birth to everyone, and yet invisible. How many women did you learn about in high school history classes? Bet you can count them on one hand without using all your fingers.

Little wonder: until the mid-nineteenth century, as a result of the advent of the women's movement, husbands were legally allowed, and even to some extent expected, as a component of retaining control over their wives, to chastise and control the women by inflicting corporal punishment as long as they didn't kill or permanently injure them. And women had little recourse, since their identities were legally merged with their husbands' at marriage.[11]

Women would not get the right to vote for 144 years after independence was declared.

Until June 26, 1918, the Texas constitution specifically said that anyone could vote except idiots, imbeciles, aliens, the insane, and women.

You could say the American women's movement began in London at the 1840 World Anti-Slavery Convention, when women delegates were denied seats. Two delegates representing the United States, Elizabeth Cady Stanton and Lucretia Mott, met there; probably because they weren't allowed to participate, they came away sparked with the idea of holding a women's rights convention back home. Their plan came to fruition at the first Women's Rights Convention in Seneca Falls, New York, eight years later.[12] But the uneasy relationship between abolition and women's equality had already begun.

Like most social change debates, there was constant tension between incrementalists and those who wanted to go for broke from the beginning, between those who thought it smarter to narrow the issues versus those who wanted to move the entire social justice agenda concurrently. This type of debate over strategy would be seen later in the civil rights movement when Booker T. Washington argued for post-slavery African Americans to assimilate into American culture and accept gaining equal liberties step by step, whereas W. E. B. DuBois believed that blacks should challenge the establishment and push for fundamental structural change in law and customs. The women's movement carried on a very similar internal debate even as they were fighting opponents of equal rights for women publicly. How far to move and how fast is always the strategic question.

> **1866:** The American Society for the Prevention of Cruelty to Animals is formed. It predates the Society for the Prevention of Cruelty to Children (1875). Both predate any organization preventing cruelty to women.

> **1882:** Maryland passes first law that makes wife-beating a crime.

> **1979:** President Carter establishes the Office of Domestic Violence. President Reagan dismantles it in 1981.

**1994:** Congress passes the Violence Against Women Act, creating for the first time a federal right to sue an assailant for gender-based violence.[13]

Adding to the fray, the very concept of women voting was so unthinkable that it was considered absurd even by many who supported advancing women's equality in other spheres. Lucretia Mott said of Stanton's wild idea that women should have the right and the responsibility to vote: "Why, Lizzie, thee will make us ridiculous." But Stanton later reported, "I persisted, for I saw clearly that the power to make the laws was the right through which all other rights could be secured."

Though their intention to secure equality for women was inspired by their commitment to abolition, these early nineteenth-century suffragists were also fighting a big internal battle about whether or how to keep their coalition of abolitionists and feminists together. They argued about whether the two causes would advance best by fighting for both simultaneously with a united front, or whether it would be more advantageous to work for the two issues separately. White women's rights activists couldn't agree on a unified strategy, creating a fissure between the two oppressed groups that festers to this day. This was despite charismatic African American orators like Sojourner Truth and Frederick Douglass, who implored both groups to realize their fates were intimately joined and their power would be multiplied if they stuck together.[14]

Perhaps still stung by having been rejected at the London abolition conference, Stanton refused to support black emancipation until women were given the right to vote. She hoped that withholding support for African Americans' voting rights would give the female suffragists greater leverage to get their share of the attention from reformers in the abolition movement. Her closest colleague in activism—Susan B. Anthony—worked tirelessly for civil rights on behalf of both women and African Americans, attempting to bridge the two; however, during the Civil War a great many white women deferred to the idea that slavery must be abolished first and then women's rights to vote and own property could be taken up again. In one stratified belief held by both North and South, women were inculcated with the idea that they were not worthy of being the priority. Another voluntary stepping back.

Once the conversation had begun, and the idea of women's suffrage had been planted, it eased away from being perceived as such a radical idea; even so, there were many in both the women's groups and the mixed-gender African American groups who thought securing voting rights for black men should take precedence over women's. Such repetitive self-abnegation by a significant portion of women, though certainly not all of them, kept women's power splintered and allowed gender equality to be moved to the bottom of the priority list over and over.

Instead of building an ever-larger coalition with a broad agenda, women's rights leaders become increasingly conservative and single-focused on passing a constitutional amendment giving women the right to vote; they abandoned much of their progressive agenda. They even made a practice of dressing in white to symbolize purity in order to signal that they were not so radical after all, and their sashes and banners were often the royal color of purple. The idea of women's moral superiority began to take root and make them appear less threatening to the status quo that they were of course bent on dismantling. But then, once they were (finally!) successful in passing the suffrage amendment to the U.S. constitution in 1920, the movement dissipated rather than consolidating its gains and pressing forward for more advances.

## SETTING THEIR BANNERS DOWN

I'm sure the suffragists felt they were entitled to a little rest. They'd been carrying their purple protest banners for many years. A few leaders, like Alice Paul, who drafted the Equal Rights Amendment in 1923, understood that suffrage was just a starting point for equality, not an end in itself, and that to be a political force, women needed to keep advancing other progressive initiatives. Mostly, however, the remaining activists either felt their job was done or morphed their efforts into political educational organizations like the nonpartisan League of Women Voters, formed in 1920. Regardless, when viewed from today's vantage point, this was a breathtaking step back with serious ramifications for the future.

Groups like the League of Women Voters and the American Association of University Women, founded in 1881 to advance women's higher educational attainment, played a very important role in teaching women how to participate in the government from which they had been historically excluded. But by taking a neutral electoral stance, they failed to capitalize on their new authority. They forfeited the chance to be a respected and feared political power. Had they stayed together as a movement to push a broader social justice agenda—like those issues advanced by early twentieth-century progressive political reformers, including public health programs, daycare, birth control, better working conditions, economic justice, and even universal healthcare—a more seamless trajectory of progress for women during the subsequent century most likely would have followed.

I'm personally indebted to the League of Women Voters. They taught me much of what I needed to know about how the government works when I was a desperate housewife and fledgling activist in West Texas. And, in the last few decades, that organization, too, has become increasingly willing to take stands on issues, including controversial ones, once they have gone through their thorough, if ponderous, consensus process.

But instead of the fiery passion for the advancement of women that had propelled the early suffragists, the good gray nonpartisan, everyone-should-vote-as-she-wishes approach that permeated most of the post-suffrage women's organizations squandered what could have become women's mass voting power for change. If they had organized to deliver or withhold their votes from politicians who failed to support their progressive agenda after they got the vote, they might have brought women to our just portion of leadership roles long before now.

To be sure, the debate about what constitutes "women's interests" was hot then and continues to be argued to this day across wide religious and cultural divides—Sarah Palin and Hillary Clinton being clear current examples of the range of opinion about what's good for women. But real power comes from taking action rooted in a point of view, coalescing around a forward-looking agenda even if you lose some constituents along the way. It's also about visibly mobilizing constituents to support policies or policy makers or both. A movement has to move or it starts immediately to ossify.

Ironically, while opponents of women's suffrage lost their battle, they won the war by exploiting this weak spot in the women's movement. Besides charging that voting would cause women to become masculinized, promiscuous, and possibly even crazed—because, after all, voting was against the delicate female nature and heaven help us if we used our brains as well as our uteri—the anti-suffragists had argued that women didn't need to have the right to vote because they'd just vote like their husbands anyway.

Turns out that's pretty much what women did—voluntarily stepping back once more, even though they had just won an enormous victory in the defining equality issue of their time. And the consequence? Women's voting power was quickly co-opted by male hegemony in the realm of ideas and in the reality of what gender the candidates and office holders would remain.

Women had achieved voting power, but as a result of their self-limited influence, it would be many years before they began to achieve any measurable governing power.

**1887:** Susanna Medora Salter becomes the first woman elected mayor of an American town, in Argonia, Kansas.

**1916:** Jeannette Rankin of Montana is the first woman to be elected to the U.S. House of Representatives.

**2007:** Nancy Pelosi (D-Calif.) becomes the first woman speaker of the House of Representatives

**2011:** The U.S. ranks 85th among the 195 nations in the percentage of women serving in national parliaments.[15]

## WOMEN'S WORK REDEFINED, AND REDEFINED AGAIN

During the 1930s well-to-do women took another step back from activism even as they found new outlets for activities in the public sphere. They turned their energies away from trying to change the system to initiating community-based social services such as mental health programs, infant feeding, and family planning clinics that solved the problems caused by the system. They did this largely through volunteerism rather than paid employment.

Some women have always worked outside their homes, of course. Many African American and other minority women, as well as low-income white women, have worked outside of the home out of financial necessity. And farm women have traditionally worked alongside their men, albeit for egg money rather than crop profits. But the culturally sanctioned division of labor placed middle-class white women in the home, with men in the workplace supporting them. And with this new social ideal came the standard to which all women were told they should aspire.

Women who wanted occupations traditionally held by men were denigrated for taking jobs from genetically ordained male breadwinners. Still supplicants asking the men to remember them, "the ladies" were often denied by law as well as custom the right to attend universities or to be considered for such positions. There were always women like Amelia Earhart, the first woman pilot to cross the Atlantic solo, who were willing to leap through enough hoops to become qualified for the posts they were seeking. They were just few and far between.

With World War II, that all changed. Suddenly, women's labor was needed to fuel the economy. Rosie the Riveter, the iconic "She can do it" avatar for women working in jobs previously advertised in the "men only" column, was created by the government's War Advertising Council in 1942, the year I was born soon after my father went into the army and my mother dutifully planted her victory garden where I would crawl around munching the tops off her scallions and asparagus.

Rosie was a highly effective propagandist. She recruited millions of women who had never worked outside their homes and convinced them it was now their patriotic duty to work in arms factories and other endeavors essential to wartime production. But though she grew to enjoy the freedom of wearing pants to work and drawing a paycheck, for the most part Rosie donned her gingham apron again and went dutifully back to the kinder and kitchen after Johnnie came marching home. Together, they settled back into their gender-segregated roles and started the Baby Boom.

But the seeds of a bigger vision for women's liberation had been planted (are you beginning to pick up on a pattern here?). Many women who had tasted of the Pierian Springs of education and known the pleasure of having their own money began to get restless in their gilded domestic cages. Author of *The Feminine Mystique* and feminist leader Betty Friedan called their malaise "the problem that has no name." Such labor-saving devices as washing machines and dryers were only serving to give them more time to fulminate about the limitations of their pedestals.

* * *

## REAWAKENING TO PRY OPEN THE DOORS TO POWER

Feminism's second wave roared into the 1960s and 1970s royally ticked off at injustices formerly known as "just the way things are." These women were determined to shatter every glass ceiling they could find and to raise the consciousness of other women who had not yet experienced the click moment of liberation. This is where I came into the picture. I wasn't among the first of these feminists—it took a few years for the good news to travel to West Texas—but I was an early adopter.

I had, after all, been repeatedly confronted with discrimination that affected me personally. First, I became furious when I applied for a credit card in my own name and was told it had to be in my husband's. Then I had a major click moment about gendered unfairness when the bank required my husband's co-signature on a car loan, even though by that time I was earning more money than he was.

But the biggest click of all was a more positive one: the birth control pill. Approved by the FDA in 1960, it made reliable family planning possible for the first time in human history and freed women like me from the tyranny of biologically determined destiny. Five years later, the Supreme Court caught up with the reality of people's lives and legalized birth control as a right of marital privacy, in *Griswold v Connecticut;* eight years after that, the *Roe v Wade* decision legalized abortion, also based on the right to privacy.

This is almost unbelievable for young women like Courtney Martin, the thirty-year-old author I quoted at the beginning of this chapter. When she interviewed me for a Women's eNews profile several years ago and heard what my life had been like before the pill, her eyes popped and she put her pen down momentarily; she couldn't imagine not having reliable birth control with the autonomy it gave her to plan her life. Reproductive choices are to her like the air and water—simply there when you need them.

The 1960s and 1970s were a heady time of many firsts for individual women. The defining slogan, "Sisterhood is Powerful," codified by Robin

Morgan's 1970 book of that name, with the iconic symbol for female with a clenched fist inside on its cover, tells the story: Concerted action for social justice was back. The movement was moving again. And while it was known for shedding bras (they never burned them—that's a media myth—but they did throw them away) and trashing girdles (thank goodness!), the second wave accomplished many, more substantive, changes.

**1961:** President Kennedy establishes a Presidential Commission on the Status of Women.

**1964:** Title XII of the Civil Rights Act bars employment discrimination on account of race or sex.

**1966:** The National Organization for Women is established.

**1970:** Groundbreaking women's health resource book *Our Bodies, Ourselves* publishes as newsprint booklet, sold for 35 cents through the burgeoning campus women's centers. Over 4,000,000 copies have been sold since then.

**1972:** *Ms.* magazine launches.

**1977:** The Equal Rights Amendment—first introduced in 1923 and every year thereafter—finally passes Congress but fails by just three states to be ratified into the Constitution before the 1982 deadline.

Things were already rocking along for this new wave of feminists by the time the Baby Boomers arrived. My sister is five years younger than I am and was in the first cohort of Boomers who had the pill when they came of age. We have marveled at what completely different perspectives and life experiences we had despite coming from the same parents.

New activist organizations were forming daily. "Coalitions like the National Women's Political Caucus took us out of the dark ages," said Deborah Siegel, author of *Sisterhood Interrupted: From Radical Women to Grrls Gone Wild*, a highly readable history of second wave feminism, when I questioned her about their significance. The Caucus was formed in 1971 to "increase the number of women in all aspects of political life—as elected and appointed officials, as judges in state and federal courts, and as delegates to national conventions," according to the NWPC website. In 1974, The Women's Campaign Fund became the first organization to support women candidates financially.

Once again, when it came to exercising political power, each step forward brought us at least a half step back. These first efforts assumed, perhaps naively, that if only training in the basics of the political structure were offered, more women would assume their places in the governance panoply. But the culture was not prepared for women to hold political power, nor were women prepared for the shock of navigating an entrenched power grid in a political system almost devoid of female role models.

The first wavelet of women in public office were those like Maine Republican Margaret Chase Smith, initially elected to Congress in 1940 to serve out her late husband's term. The second wave were women like Nancy Pelosi, who came from political families and developed their interest in politics around the dinner table but waited, usually serving as envelope-stuffing worker bees in men's campaigns, until their children were grown before they ran for office themselves.

Karan English, a Democratic former Coconino County supervisor and state senator, was elected to Congress from Northern Arizona's swing District 6 in "The Year of the Woman." No, not 2008, but 1992, the year the number of women running for Congress almost doubled from the previous year and the number of women in the Senate increased fivefold— from one to five.[16] 1992 was a political moment similar 2008 in other respects, too. The nation was ready for change, tired of a president (George

H. W. Bush) who took us into war while taking the economy downhill for personal greed. People were disgusted with Jerry Falwell's Moral Majority right-wing wedge-issue politics that kept the country fighting about abortion and homosexuality rather than solving their bread-and-butter woes. Even Arizona's "Mr. Conservative," the late Senator Barry Goldwater, endorsed English because he so disliked her fundamentalist Christian-right opponent Doug Wead. The Republican senator had opined in his famously frank way that all good Christians should kick Falwell in the ass. Goldwater's endorsement had nothing to do with the fact English was a woman, but it marked a moment when the nation thought the misnamed religious right's political power was on the wane, and the ascendancy of women in politics was touted as one evidence of that.

Just two years later came the backlash—the (Newt) Gingrich Revolution with its "Contract with America" determined to slam the country back to a reactionary definition of "family values," including gender roles straight out of the 1950s and the end of Karan English's political career as an elected official.

Far from being passé, conservative political strength had come back with a vengeance to capture a congressional majority and scare the bejeezus out of Bill Clinton's still wet-behind-the-ears administration. Not insignificantly, in Texas that year, George W. Bush defeated Governor Ann Richards in 1994, setting in motion his 2000 race for president, which became the most devastating ever to twentieth-century advances in civil rights, women's rights, and reproductive justice.

How had this happened? Ironically, it wasn't because women changed their minds about the issues. The 1994 elections were lost by almost exactly the number of women who had voted in 1992 but stayed home from the polls two years later. Did they think the job of citizenship was done after one election cycle?

The pace of progress toward gender parity continues to be excruciatingly slow because women stepped back once again in 1994, failing to use the power that resided in their hands.

Only in the last decade have an appreciable number of women run on the basis of their own desire to serve in political office. Finally, in 2006 the beginning of a potentially critical mass of women was elected to Congress, at ages young enough that they are likely to have the staying power (biologically speaking) to earn the seniority and agenda-setting authority of someone like the late Senator Ted Kennedy.

New York's Senator Kirsten Gillibrand and Arizona Representative Gabrielle Giffords were both elected to Congress while in their thirties. Giffords told me shortly after her swearing-in in 2007, "I grew up thinking I had certain rights. I think in today's terms about what a feminist is: a woman who is strong, self-sufficient, moves beyond gender focus and is a successful person. . . . I'm on the Armed Services Committee because I want to be. But women are more likely to see issues like health and education as important too."[17]

When Nancy Pelosi took the speaker's gavel in January 2007, she declared she'd "broken the marble ceiling." Yet her very novelty speaks volumes about what women have not yet accomplished. Between Victoria Woodhull's quixotic race as the first woman to run for president in 1872 and Hillary Clinton's 18 million cracks that shattered what she called the "highest and hardest" glass ceiling in 2008, plenty of treacherous shards remain for the next aspirant to finish off.

## IF WE DON'T CREATE THE FUTURE, SOMEBODY ELSE WILL DO IT FOR US

To illustrate how far women have progressed, Clinton was fond of observing during her presidential campaign, "My mother was born before women could vote. My daughter gets to vote for her mother for president."

Yet when I interviewed her in 2003 for my book *The War on Choice,* the ever realistic then-senator told me: "It's human nature that when the established order is changed, there will be a reaction, and the magnitude of this reaction shouldn't surprise us. The advancement of women in the last fifty years has been breathtaking. There has been no comparable advancement in human history. There are victories along the way, but none of them is secure because of the pressures that undermine women's rights and advancement. . . . So now, women who value their autonomy have to step up and take action."[18]

We limit ourselves most when we don't step up and take action, and not just when women's advances are threatened. We must also continue to break boundaries where they exist, and to take an expansive view of what the agenda for the future can be.

During the last fifty years, thanks to women's and other civil rights movements, the leadership of extraordinary women like Gloria Steinem, Irene Natividad, Robin Morgan, Byllye Avery, and so many more, because of reliable birth control and an economy that now requires more brain than brawn, women have broken many barriers that historically prevented them from partaking as equals at life's table. But though we've smashed many corporate glass ceilings and marble barriers to political leadership, women remain far from parity in any sphere of political or economic endeavor. Look at the numbers: Women hold 25% of state legislative offices; just 3% of clout positions in mainstream media corporations, and 15% of corporate board positions. Even after the 2008 election, whose outcomes were in large part determined by women voters, U.S. women increased their percentage of seats in Congress by a mere 1%. Today, women make up 17% of the Senate and 16% of the House. Considering that since 1789, women have been only 2% of members of Congress, you could call that progress, but at the current rate of increase, it will take us seventy years to reach parity.[19]

And despite gender equity laws and the separation of biology from reproductive destiny, women earn three-fourths of what men do while shouldering the lion's share of responsibility for child-rearing. These factors—reproductive and economic justice—are interrelated, which is why the phrase "barefoot and pregnant" has resonated through much of human history.

> **1847:** Elizabeth Blackwell is the first woman accepted into medical school. The student body votes her in, thinking it was a joke.

> **1853:** Antoinette Blackwell (Elizabeth Blackwell's sister-in-law) becomes the first woman ordained to the ministry in a recognized denomination (Congregational).

> **1963:** Valentina Tesreshkova, a Russian cosmonaut, is the first woman in space. Sally Ride is the first American female astronaut in 1983.

> **1984:** Geraldine Ferraro is the first woman to run for vice president on a major party ticket.

> **1997:** Madeleine Albright becomes the first female secretary of state. A child of elementary school age today might think one must be a woman to hold that position, as Albright's successors have included Condoleezza Rice and Hillary Clinton.[20]

The second wave women's movement's remarkable advances certainly opened many doors for women in all kinds of leadership roles. That's why women's complaints today tend to be like Martin's, about the challenges of having to make complicated choices rather than having no choices at all. Even the many women who demur, "I'm not a feminist, but . . . " generally assume they have a perfect right to do and be whatever they choose. And many of the current crop of smart, ambitious young women see the world like twenty-four-year-old social media consultant Jen Nedeau, who says confidently, "Getting to do what I want, following my dreams and standing up for myself isn't selfish in my book—it's what the boys have been doing for years."

Still, Siegel, forty-year-old daughter of a second-wave feminist, says she found in her research that while much had changed since her mother's generation told men to stop pinching their asses and demanded equal pay, far more remained the same in the gender relationship area.

## ARE WOMEN TODAY STEPPING BACK AGAIN?

Today the favored media narrative holds that "elite" educated women are back-to-the-kitchen 1950s Rosies redux by choice. Though the reality is somewhat less retro, it's still a fact that many women are opting out of the very career paths that could shift those highest clout positions to gender parity within a decade or two if these women took them and kept climbing the workforce ladder.

Shockingly, Leslie Bennetts whipped up a stormy controversy in her book *The Feminine Mistake* when she urged women to make these important life choices with their own financial interests in mind—in other words to keep working so they could always support themselves and retain their power in their relationships. She actually elicited so many blistering emails from viewers when she appeared on the *Today* show to discuss her book that they crashed NBC's website. In the book, she warns women in the strongest of terms, backed up with very compelling data, about the perils of giving up their careers when they marry and have children.

Bennetts told me in a lengthy interview for this book in fall 2009, after her book had already been out for several years, that whenever she makes a speech, women in their fifties and sixties inevitably come up to her with tales of how they are impoverished because they chose to leave their careers and stay home when they married and became mothers. "They're just completely screwed," she laments. "They have no power and no options. They figured it out only in retrospect and too late."

What especially astonished Bennetts, who interviewed hundreds of women all around the country in her research, is the number of younger women who don't get the importance of acting in their own best interests: "What they want to believe is that Prince Charming is going to come along and take care of you. Baby Boomers saw their mothers screwed by the Feminine Mystique," she told me. "Their marriages blew up. And the women had nothing in that era. So the Boomers said, 'I saw that didn't work for women so I was determined never to have that happen to me and to have a career so I'd always be able to take care of myself.' But somehow there was this regression in younger women. Partly, it's just historical cycles. They're far enough away from what happened with women in the '50s and the divorce revolution of the '70s. They didn't see the carnage. And the culture of capitalism plays a huge role. The Disney Princess line is selling billions of dollars worth of products a year. These are the aspirations we are cultivating in girls. This is not about power; this is about pink dresses and being on the arm of a man who gets power."

Every generation needs to push against its parents' generation. Children of second-wavers missed the fun, sisterhood, and adrenaline rush of breaking big barriers, and they chafe when they come face-to-face with the challenges of having choices—like having to take responsibility for them. Feminism never disappeared or died, as those who wished it would were fond of saying, and the flame has been held aloft by "third-wavers" like Jennifer Baumgardner and Amy Richards (now pushing forty), who teamed up to write such groundbreaking books for young feminists as *ManifestA* and *Grassroots*. They formed their own speakers bureau and funding networks, and now lecture widely at universities around the country. In fact, the basic precepts of feminism's quest for equality for the female half of the population, at least when it comes to removing barriers to education and employment, have come to permeate the thinking of most people in American society today, whether they articulate them in those terms or not. At a minimum, the overt opposition to women taking new roles is all but gone, if for no other reason than the pressures of political correctness in public discourse.

Significant "firsts" continue to remind us we have come very far at the same time that we have a long way to go: In 2009, for example, Elinor Ostrom became the first woman to win a Nobel Prize in economics, which in the past had been an all-male bastion. Ostrom was the fortieth woman to receive a Nobel.[21] Marie Curie was awarded two, so Ostrom received the forty-first Nobel Prize given to women. That's just forty-one out of the 829 Nobels in total that have been awarded. Still, the sight of women in the sciences is no longer unusual and serious efforts are under way by groups such as the Association of Women in Science to smooth the path for more women to enter the field and to have more opportunities for advancement than previous generations once they get there. I doubt that men who take the credit for a woman's discoveries, as DNA researchers and Nobelists Francis Crick and James Watson did when they usurped Rosalind Franklin's work without her knowledge in the 1960s, would be tolerated today; no doubt the feminist bloggers would expose them in short order.

Best of all, today's youngest generation of women in their twenties seems more balanced to me, and much more into taking the feminist torch forward, even if they do wear pink dresses, with cleavage yet. (Courtney Martin tells of having her epiphany that she could comfortably be a feminist after seeing Baumgardner speak at Barnard wearing fishnets and heels.) Young women like Jessica Valenti, founder of the widely read blog Feministing.com, Shelby Knox, who became nationally known as the subject of a PBS documentary on her journey from the West Texas fundamentalism so familiar to me to a leading advocate for sex education, and the thousands of participants in the Feminist Majority's Campus Leadership Program are bound to rise to the top and become the trailblazers for women in the future.

## TEACHING THE LESSONS

We must teach young women their history if we don't want them to repeat the less uplifting parts of it, and certainly if we want to inspire them to greater things. Whenever I speak to groups of young women in universities and social gatherings I find them hungry for such mentoring. In part I imagine this has to do with the fact that they're not sure where to look for role models and mentors, even if we are indeed out there. But also it is because as we have seen, women still don't learn their own history as a matter of course as they go through school.

I teach a course called "Women, Power, and Leadership" at Arizona State University. During one class, I showed pictures of about twenty significant women leaders from Susan B. Anthony through the present. The students, mostly women's studies majors or minors, didn't recognize Bella Abzug, Alice Paul, Toni Morrison, Amelia Earhart, or Margaret Sanger. They did recognize Oprah Winfrey, and I loved that they recognized Danica Patrick, the feisty twenty-something racecar driver. But the simple fact is that men still write most history books, and they cast themselves as the actors and heroes.

While universities now by and large have women's studies departments, it is the rare middle or high school that teaches women's history, and few colleges make even one women's history course a prerequisite. The lessons of the women's movement and its heroic struggles aren't typically taught, with the possible exception of a photo of Gloria Steinem in her aviator glasses and perhaps a protest march. There are no holidays to remind them of their heritage as women, no symbols, no anthems to stir their souls. They probably don't realize they got to play basketball if they wanted to—and full court at that—because of Title IX, and that they have the liberty to reject career options their mothers couldn't even have thought about seeking.

Once we take over our share of the top roles in government and business, fix the economy, get universal healthcare, and pass the Freedom of

Choice Act to guarantee reproductive freedom—advances that are at the top of my list—we need to redo the teaching of history to write women into it, top to bottom. And not just through the male lens of wars. Who knows, maybe if women were writing the history books, children would sing of the midnight rides of Sybil Luddington *and* Paul Revere. But meanwhile, it is incumbent upon older women to tell our stories to younger ones, to mentor them, and to build out our own networks of women of all ages in a vast New Girls' Network that can lift up our sisters and ourselves. As twenty-four-year-old budding activist Jenna Mellor said in a note to me last year, "I'm desperate for mentorship! I feel disconnected from older women and I think they feel that the feminist movement of my peers is disconnected from them. There are real tools we need: the power to publish an op-ed, to negotiate for a higher salary, to navigate the work/life balance. I'm jealous of older women who I feel had the opportunity to be part of an at least somewhat cohesive feminist movement, who had clear objectives and the so-called 'Man' to fight against. They did a lot of really amazing work. I think it's harder to know where to start the work now and to avoid being marginalized doing it."

So here women are today, at this moment of unlimited possibility, ours for the taking. If we choose to take it, that is. If we choose to break the patterns of the past. There are challenges, yes. Roadblocks, yes. Impediments, yes. Injustices and unfairness, yes. But there are no limits to what we can envision ourselves doing and no boundaries to what we can dream and achieve.

And with each door one woman walks through it is incumbent upon her to bring another woman through it with her.

By far the most confounding problem facing women today is not that doors aren't open, but that women aren't walking through the open doors in numbers and with intention sufficient to transform society's major institutions once and for all.

So what are we going to do about it?

By studying our history, we may avoid the mistakes of previous tipping point junctures, such as after we won the right to vote, after World War II, and after the many advances made in the workplace during the last thirty years when the so-called opt-out generation took the notion of choice to mean that they had the choice to withdraw from the movement to advance women. All these were times when women made extraordinary leaps forward only to fail to consolidate around an agenda, lose momentum, and relinquish power once again.

And by learning about our past, we can once and for all overcome the invisible, almost primal, cultural barriers to women's equality. We can choose to break the old patterns within ourselves that hold us back, and we can make new ones. We can step forward and keep on stepping yet further forward instead of continuing to take steps back every time we advance. We can refuse to allow our power to be dissipated by victory or diminished by defeat. We can create the future of our choice.

We will always experience backlash when women make these significant advances. Because when you change the world there is always backlash. Deal with it. For there is no greater power shift in the world than the movement to equalize gender power. And the benefits of participating in that movement are well worth the risks. As writer Vivian Gornick said, "[T]he question of equality for women, each and every time around, opens a Pandora's box of fear, hope, and confusion that is existential in its very nature . . . But to live one's life in service to that ultimate clarification—whether in a period of quietude or of activism— seems to me a privilege."[23]

Now is the simply right time for women to equalize gender power in politics, work, and love. It's a moment that can change the lives of both men and women for the better. And it's this moment—when public conversation reveals a fascination with women in power and a readiness to support equality—in which we must establish true, lasting gender parity because it is the good and just thing to do.

It's in your hands now. You're no victim. Your personal choices matter. You have the responsibility to yourself and other women. And you have the power. Use it.

Does this sound scary? Impossible? Inspiring? Ridiculously simple? Whatever, the first step is to define power on our terms.

# margaret**sanger**

Margaret Sanger opened the first American birth control clinic ninety-three years ago at 46 Amboy Street, in Brooklyn, New York. I've often turned to her life for inspiration, courage, and practical examples of leadership, and you will recognize many of these leadership lessons as the basis for the Power Tools I share in this book.

Sanger must have been standing beside me during my first Congressional testimony as president of Planned Parenthood in 1997, when the late Representative Henry Hyde thought he'd attack my credibility by asking whether I was troubled by the number of abortions taking place in this country. I retorted, brandishing his voting record, which I had reviewed in advance and brought with me, "If that troubles you, Mr. Hyde, why have you never once voted for family planning?" The *Today* show played that clip along with Hyde's flustered look the next day. Just taking one small step to challenge authority publicly breathed new energy into the prochoice constituency, starting with my staff, who gave me a T-shirt that declared, "Feldt-1, Hyde-0."

Sanger was visionary and practical, courageous and cranky, idealistic and pragmatic. She was a redheaded, green-eyed feminist socialist who died a registered Republican. She was a mother, a grandmother, a sexual adventurer, and a woman of many contradictions—but aren't we all?

Here are eight leadership lessons I learned from Sanger's life and work.

**ONE:** All worthwhile accomplishments start with a vision. Not a small, incremental vision, but a bold, audacious, bigger-than-yourself vision.

While Nick Kristof and Sheryl WuDunn are lauded for saying women's rights are the great moral imperative of the twenty-first century in their book, *Half the Sky*, Sanger said essentially the same thing one hundred years ago.

Born Margaret Higgins in Corning, New York, in 1879, the sixth child of eleven living siblings, her earliest memories were of crying beside her mother's bed after a nearly fatal childbirth. Anne Higgins, a devout traditional Catholic, did die at age fifty, worn out from frequent pregnancies.

Sanger's father was a charming freethinker, a stonemason who loved to drink and spin a tale, but was less than a dependable provider. Sanger knew poverty; she identified with the struggles of women.

She enrolled in nursing school. But a few months shy of finishing, she resigned to marry a handsome architect, William Sanger. Three children followed. Sanger began to take special-duty nursing assignments after Bill's widowed mother moved in with them in 1910.

Women needed a great deal of nursing care. According to the 1900 census, the eighteen wives living in the small Orchard Street building that is now New York's Lower East Side Tenement Museum had given birth to 111 children, of whom 67 were alive—a 40 percent infant and child mortality rate. Maternal mortality was astronomical, too: Forty percent of mothers' deaths were caused by infection, half from unsafe back alley or self-induced abortions.

Birth control, such as existed, was illegal, too, largely because of Anthony Comstock, the one-man sex police. Comstock formed the New York Society for the Suppression of Vice. Named a special investigator for the U.S. Postal Service, he personally enforced the 1873 law named for him, making it illegal to send information or devices for birth control or abortion through the mail. Many similar state laws followed.

Comstock bragged that he had seized sixty thousand

"obscene rubber articles" and tons of "lewd and lascivious material." Like today's abstinence-only zealots, he didn't distinguish healthy, responsible sexual expression from promiscuity, pornography, prostitution. But Comstock was about to meet his match.

**TWO:** A leader is someone who gets things done.

The defining moment came when Sanger was called to an overcrowded tenement to nurse a twenty-eight-year-old mother of three, Sadie Sachs. Sachs had been told another pregnancy would kill her. But when she asked her doctor how to prevent pregnancies, he callously replied, "Tell Jake to sleep on the roof." Bitterly poor, weak from her last pregnancy, Sadie self-aborted. She got a raging infection (pre-antibiotics). She begged Sanger to tell her how to prevent pregnancies. Sanger shared what knowledge she had, but it wasn't much.

A few months later, Sanger was called back to the same house. Again, Sachs had self-aborted. This time she died. Sanger walked for hours afterward, immersed in grief. She resolved: *Women would have knowledge of contraception.*

**THREE:** There's power in your story.

Sanger told Sachs's story over and over. Dramatically. Using all media at her disposal, connecting the personal story with the call for political change.

She wrote a sex education column, "What Every Girl Should Know," for a Socialist newspaper; Comstock censored it. The following week, the paper ran an empty space with the headline, "What Every Girl Should Know: Nothing by order of the U.S. Post Office." She ratcheted it up by publishing a periodical, *The Woman Rebel,* to challenge Comstock directly.

About this time, a friend coined the term *birth control.* Sanger ran with it.

Arrested in August 1914, she went to Europe and researched homemade birth control methods prevalent in France. In England, she began an affair with sexologist Havelock Ellis. She visited a clinic in the Netherlands, where family planning advice, diaphragms, and contraceptive jelly had been dispensed for thirty years. This gave her the vision of a network of clinics all over the United States.

● ● ● **FOUR:** Timing is key.

She sensed the tide turning in her direction the next fall. Bill Sanger had been arrested for distributing birth control pamphlets with much media fanfare, and her rival leader in the birth control movement, Mary Ware Dennett, had started the National Birth Control League.

Returning to the States, where charges against her were still pending, Sanger gave a speech—her first—on January 17, 1916. She would repeat it 119 times across the country: *"Women from time immemorial have tried to avoid unwanted motherhood. I found wise men, sages, scientists, discussing birth control among themselves. But their ideas were sterile. They did not influence the tremendous facts of life among the working classes or the disinherited. . . . I felt myself in the position of one who has discovered that a house is on fire and it was up to me to shout out the warning."*

Outmaneuvered, the prosecution dropped the charges against her.

● ● ● **FIVE:** Use what you've got. What you need is usually there if you can see it.

On October 16, 1916, Sanger opened America's first birth control clinic. Her sister, Ethel Byrne, was the nurse. Handbills in English, Yiddish, and Italian advertised the clinic. Police closed it down ten days and 464 patients later. But Sanger had founded something much larger than a clinic: She had ignited a great movement for women's reproductive freedom.

Ultimately, she was arrested nine times for her civil disobedience. Each time, she used what she had—not money, and certainly not the law. But she had the power of an idea that touched a deep human need.

**SIX:** Controversy is your friend.

She used controversy especially brilliantly. In 1929, she was banned in Boston, so she got the esteemed Harvard professor Arthur Schlesinger Sr. to read her speech while she stood gagged beside him. This made major papers across the country.

"Dear Mrs. Sanger" letters flowed: *"DMS: married at 20 to a laboring man, in 11 years I have five living children, one stillborn, and 5 miscarriages . . . I am desperate . . . "*

She compiled these stories into a book, *Motherhood in Bondage,* which inspired my own first book, *Behind Every Choice Is a Story.* Even in the twenty-first century, there is no end to the heartrending stories.

Successful legal challenges began to convince doctors they could provide birth control to their patients. Sanger crisscrossed the country to help start clinics; increasingly, prominent women joined these efforts.

In the mid-1930s, she moved to Tuscon, Arizona, for family reasons. Her second husband, Noah Slee, the millionaire founder of Three-in-One Oil company, was so besotted with his wife that he smuggled diaphragms illegally for her clinic, staked the Holland–Rantos pharmaceutical company to increase the supply of diaphragms and condoms, and provided her with separate living quarters to live as she pleased—her condition for marrying him.

Sanger was far from perfect.

She was egotistical. She rarely credited others' contributions. Though unwavering about her mission, she changed her argument based on what was selling at the time. Her strategy was to seek the locus of power to advance birth control.

That's how she came to align with the eugenicists—who believed in improving the human race through selective breeding—during the 1930s when that sentiment was at its height and supported by most of the nation's leaders. She saw through it sooner than most and broke away publicly; still, this remained a stain on her personal narrative that those opposed to women's equality in any form use unfairly against her and the movement she founded. To her credit, she was among the first U.S. leaders to denounce Hitler's eugenics, far ahead of Franklin Roosevelt, for example.

Sanger's argument also morphed variously into women's health, poverty alleviation, population control, and "every child a wanted child." These are all valid benefits of birth control. Still, the feminist crusade for women's biological and sexual liberation, where Sanger started, was always her core principle.

She loved parties, especially international theme parties with costumes, and threw them often. She slept with the most interesting men of her time, including the writer H. G. Wells, who later called her the heroine of the twentieth century.

In less than a century, the movement Sanger launched won so many victories that most people couldn't believe they could ever be reversed. Instead, the backlash against such sweeping change in the gender power balance was fierce, and the war on choice rages on.

**SEVEN:** A movement has to move. Power and energy come from moving into new spaces, not from standing still.

Our great challenge now is to shift the moral and legal framework from the right to privacy to the human rights of women to make their own childbearing decisions. We need to connect reproductive justice with economic justice and to say clearly that it's time for women to have an equal place at life's table.

Sanger said so many times, "No woman can call herself free who does not own and control her own body. No woman can call herself free who cannot choose for herself whether and when she will become a mother."

This was her conviction. But she understood that convictions, alone, are not enough.

**EIGHT:** This is the leadership lesson I hold most dear, for it's a good summation of Margaret's life: "Life has taught me," she said, "we must put our convictions into action."

Well after her place in history had been assured, Sanger continued putting her convictions into action. When Planned Parenthood was formed in 1942, over eighty local clinics were already in operation. She founded the International Planned Parenthood Federation in 1952 and raised the money to develop the birth control pill. She was convinced that an effective pill would be the transformational, woman-controlled method to free women from "Motherhood in Bondage" at last.

Birth control was finally freed from state laws banning it by the U.S. Supreme Court in *Griswold v Connecticut* in 1965, and then abortion in 1973 with *Roe v Wade*, both based on a right to privacy. Then government started financing family planning for low-income women through Great Society programs. Today, more than 95 percent of Americans of reproductive age or older have used birth control.

Not long before Sanger died in a Tucson nursing home in 1966, nearly eighty-eight, her granddaughter and namesake, Margaret Sanger Lampe, asked her how she'd like to be remembered. She said she hoped she'd be remembered for helping women.

*Help women.* Margaret Sanger and her brave leadership most surely did.

# CHAPTER TWO

# redefine:
# not power-over, power-to

"When I dare to be powerful—
to use my strength in the service of
my vision, then it becomes less and less
important whether I am afraid."

**—AUDRE LORDE**

"If you wait until the Frogs and Toads
have croaked their last to take some action,
you've missed the point."

**—KERMIT THE FROG**

- What would the world be like if women held most of the positions of power and leadership? What do you think would be different? What do you think would be the same?

- If you ran the world, how would you define *power*?

- How does "power-over" feel different to you from "power-to"?

Kermit the Frog knows what he's talking about. The little green puppet's homespun advice says a lot about the nature of power, and how the simple act of speaking, and speaking early in the conversation, bestows the power to define the terms of engagement on any topic.

If women don't want others to have power *over* us in ways that we might deem bad, then we have to claim our own power to construct and define what is good about having power: the power to make positive things happen.

To stay within the childhood mind-set conjured by Kermit, did you ever play the game called "Chicken"? When I was growing up, this often played out in the form of a dare, where we'd do a standoff on our tricycles and wagons, or sometimes just with our eyes: Who would blink first? When I was in high school, the boys loved to play a more dangerous version of Chicken in which two of them would face off in their cars, squeal out racing toward one another, and the first one to swerve to avoid being killed was dubbed the "chicken."

Funny, I don't remember any of the girls driving in these mechanized tests of will. In fact, they were more likely to stand on the sidelines and watch with clenched teeth than to ride in the cars during the competitions. No, women are more likely to engage, or be engaged by, not screeching vehicular feats of daring, but rather equally intense though too often silent tests of their personal agency.

## CHICKEN GAME THEORY

I call Linda Hirshman my tough-love feminist friend because she pulls no punches about what's at stake for women today. Hirshman, a retired Brandeis philosophy professor and author of *Get to Work: A Manifesto for Women of the World*, wrote about the deeper meaning of Chicken for women in an article for *Double X*. She describes the consequences of the power play to the loser like this:

> He or she survives that time, sure, but after that? They're stew. Nobody swerves when playing Chicken with someone they know is a chicken. So in every successive race, the chicken has to keep on swerving. Every time he swerves, he sinks a little lower.[1]

Hirshman then shows how playing Chicken works in relationships, even when played by two ostensibly well-matched professionals:

> Here's how the legendary misogynist novelist Philip Roth played Chicken with his wife, the British actress Claire Bloom: Early in their relationship, Roth insisted that Bloom's sixteen-year-old daughter, Anna Steiger, move out of her London home. "It wasn't about hatred for my daughter," Bloom reminisced years later in the November 1996 Vanity Fair. "He knew I would make any compromise to support our relationship. If I was willing to jettison my daughter in this manner, what could I ever deny him? I know I was diminishing my own character with each successive act of capitulation. These confrontations left me debilitated and unsure, and were to shape many of my future decisions."[2]

By blinking instead of staying clear-eyed in her own power to define herself, Bloom relinquished her capacity to set the terms of the debate from then on in their relationship, and that gave Roth unmitigated power over her. That Bloom ultimately acted of her own volition to relinquish her child is the most heartbreaking part. She missed the point. She blinked on a pivotal issue; she weakened her power to choose her own fate in future confrontations.

Indisputably, Roth had exerted his power over his wife in a domineering, coercive way. That kind of oppressive power over women's lives is something we have increasingly come to reject in theory even while we are still engaged in the transformational journey toward equality. This is our moment to shift the tectonic plates of power on both the personal life and the leadership levels. We can't afford to play Chicken this time.

To put this chapter into perspective, let's do a cursory overview of the four questions we're going to be looking at: (1) What is power and who wants it? (2) Why is it important that we redefine power? (3) How can we redefine power so women can embrace it on new terms, our own terms? (4) Why is *now* women's moment to lead the change?

## POWER—WHAT IS IT AND WHO WANTS IT?

Power, through most of human history, has been a concept rooted in brute force, the *power-over* something or someone. Because women have usually been among those over whom the powerful rule, it's no wonder that when we think about power we imagine negatives. Women's bodies have been restricted, raped, and beaten by more physically powerful males high on the testosterone rush of hunting or battle. Why would anyone want to emulate that kind of cruel brute force?

Talking about women and power, the 1970s feminist leader Florynce Kennedy once said, with trademark feistiness: "Women are not afraid of power; they're afraid of the oppressor. 'Cause the oppressor is very ruthless with people in power from oppressed groups. Also, women tend to do things that are safe. And what's safe does not put you in a position of power. . . ."[3]

Moreover, when physical strength is the measure of power, power is seen as a finite pie: If I take a slice that means less food for you. While we're well past the time when brawn alone rules the social order, the notion that if women have more power, there would be less for men still lurks in the recesses of our prehensile minds. Therefore, *power-over* must necessarily be power that is a limited resource. And because the predominant power-over framework has imprinted many women as well as men, it is not surprising that some women model behavior similar to men's and carry out the agenda of the patriarchy to a fault. Think Ann Coulter at the extreme, but also women like Margaret Thatcher and Sarah Palin.

We've named the current iteration of power, specifically power over women, "sexism." Sexism is merely a form of humiliation used to assert *power-over*. It belittles and diminishes based on gender whether by denying (the right to vote, seats in the corporate boardroom) or falsely elevating (the gilded cage, the pedestal).

The most virulent form of sexism is rape and intimate partner violence. Those are obvious; they can be identified and must be combated head-on. But even terms that diminish, like *honey* or *sweetie,* when generically used to address women (remember John Adams's mocking "tyranny of the petticoat" retort to Abigail?) are a highly effective, if more subtle form of power over women. And the pre–women's suffrage adage, "The hand that rocks the cradle rules the world," exemplifies how women have been doled out power in the domestic and child-rearing realms when in fact they had no formal power to rule anything. This type of moral puffery is equally sexist—merely gilded daggers aimed at the heart of women's stature.

And if all else fails, there's sexism as feigned concern: In *Mad Men,* Don Draper asks Roger Sterling the famous Freudian question, "What do women want?" to which Roger replies more honestly, "Who cares?" Roger's underlying *power-over* brand of sexism is further revealed when he plays the sexual power card and counsels his pal, "Remember, Don, when God closes a door, he opens a dress."

Back in the 1960s, the time in which *Mad Men* is set, men could laugh at such a line with impunity. Socially sanctioned power-over always seems to be justified as the natural order of things. "Was there ever any domination that did not appear natural to those who possessed it?" is the prescient question, posed by a male feminist, nineteenth-century British utilitarian philosopher and economist John Stuart Mill, in his book *The Subjection of Women*. It was published in 1869, just four years after the American Civil War ended with the emancipation of slaves—but, as we have seen, when women remained without their most basic rights to vote or own property.[4]

## Power: The Classic Definitions

The most often referenced definition of power-over (pardon if I get a bit academic here—it won't last long, I promise) was first summarized by social psychologists J. P. R. French Jr. and B. Raven. They said a person could have five distinct methods or "points of power" over someone else.[5]

- As you read the power methods that follow, think about how people you know use them—whether in work, politics, or personal relationships.

- What do you like or dislike about each one of these methods, or points, of power?

- Can you think of times when you have used each of them? What happened when you did?

## COERCIVE POWER.

Power based on fear and intimidation. This is power-over of the most direct and potentially harmful sort. A person with coercive power can make your life hell through physical violence or the threat of it, or more subtle abilities to coerce through laws, policies, or withholding necessary resources. Think Hitler. Think the schoolyard bully. Coercive power isn't likely to engender deep loyalty, but it can certainly influence observable behavior. The late President Lyndon Johnson, whose masterful wielding of power during his Senate years was legendary, used to offer this salty formula for getting his agenda through Congress: "If you've got 'em by the balls, their hearts and minds will follow."[6]

Sounds ominous, but remember he's the guy who finally was able to get the Civil Rights Act, Medicare, and the Public Broadcasting Act passed.

## REWARD POWER.

Power based on the ability to distribute rewards valued by others—salary, grocery money, compliments or other emotional support, letters of recommendation, votes—any sort of benefits or rewards that people want in exchange for desired behavior. In politics, there are often exchanges of reward power based not necessarily on principle but on a pragmatic calculation about how to get something done—good or bad. I have a friend whose job used to be persuading people to let his company dig up their land to put pipelines through. Once I asked him how he did it. "I just hit them over the head with a checkbook until they smile," he chuckled. And what parent hasn't used reward power to influence a child's actions?

## LEGITIMATE POWER.

Power stemming from one's position in the formal hierarchy of an organization, the culturally sanctioned hierarchy of a family or group, or the legal or social power of a professional status. Think police, teacher, military officer, school crossing guard. People comply because of socially sanctioned position. So on the positive, we all know what a red light means and for the most part willingly stop when we see one. Legitimate power helps to prevent social chaos. But when carried to extreme, we have a Fascist state where some people carry out horrendous acts because they were ordered to do so by others holding "legitimate" power.

## EXPERT POWER.

The power of influence because of skills or knowledge one possesses. Doctors, lawyers, hairdressers, plumbers, and IT managers have power because of their experience and knowledge. Expert power can be power-over, but more often it's exercised as the power-to get something done in a positive way.

## REFERENT POWER.

Charisma-based power. Some people just have "it." Celebrity power falls in here, too. It is power based in respect for someone's personal traits or the resources he or she can bring to the table. People respond to this person's influence because they like her, or he inspires them. Think Oprah and her ability to catapult anything to bestseller status by featuring it on her show (and oh, how I hope that will include this book!). Think about political races: In the 2008 Democratic primary, more people just liked Barack Obama better than Hillary Clinton. Referent power sounds all good, but don't forget that cult leaders have often used it to get their followers to cause harm to themselves or others.

These five methods of power can be used in an infinite variety of combinations. As gangster Godfather Al Capone once put it, "You can get much farther with a kind word and a gun than you can with a kind word alone."[7]

Looking back at what I've written here, it's instructive to see I've just quoted a number of people on the subject of power, and they are all men. So here's what Roseanne Barr, whose comedic portrayal of a working-class wife and mother on the sitcom *Roseanne* mirrored her own experience, has said, Sojourner Truth–like: "The thing women have yet to learn is nobody gives you power. You just take it."[8]

Will we ever learn that lesson?

## IN WHICH I LEARN A LESSON ABOUT WHY WE MUST REDEFINE POWER AND HOW KERMIT'S ADVICE CAME IN HANDY

Lars Larson is a conservative radio talk show host. His tagline—I couldn't make this up—was "culturally incompetent white man"; his website, www.larslarson.com/site, shows photos of himself with cigar, guns, and fishing gear. He has a following of four million listeners. His producer, a courteous young woman named Heather, asked me to talk with him in a phone interview about the Supreme Court's *Roe v Wade* decision legalizing abortion. "Lars will disagree with you, but he'll be respectful," she said. "No problem," I said, "as long as I can speak my piece."

See, I'm a sappy patriot. I think democracy requires us to speak our piece—to argue vigorously, then either reach a consensus or take a vote and move on. This is perhaps the most important power a citizen has.

It turned out that using my power to "speak my piece" is exactly what Lars couldn't stomach.

I answered his questions in the way I think the debate should be framed: as a woman's human right to make her own childbearing decisions. In my experience with this topic, it's not about abortion per se. When you dig down an inch or two, the argument becomes about defining women's place in the world and who controls the means of reproduction. At one time, especially in agrarian societies where having many children to work the fields equaled wealth, a woman's ability to bear children was the sole measure of her worth, and even today motherhood remains a metaphor for a woman's worthiness in some conservative circles. No wonder men would want power-over this asset. I get that. But Lars apparently did not. When he couldn't exercise his power-*over* me, he lapsed into bullying.

Every time Lars was unable to keep the conversation within his preferred framework of pitting innocent baby against murderous woman who "stupidly didn't use birth control," he started spinning. He even lectured me in stern-father tones during the commercial break. I could practically see his finger wagging at me across the phone line from his studio in Portland, Oregon, to my small bedroom office in Scottsdale, Arizona.

This is not to disrespect him; as I said, I firmly believe Lars is entitled to his view. But what so vexed him, I suspect, was that he and I were looking at the world from diametrically different vantage points. Worse, I had the audacity not to back off of my point of view when he pressed his. I was the uppity woman who challenged his righteous power. Everything I said disturbed his very sense of who he was and where he fit into the universe. What seemed like simple justice to me was clattering dissonance to him.

Was this conflict rooted in gendered perspectives on the world? Yes—at least part of it was. For Lars, having a woman stand up to him must have felt frightening and infuriating, particularly since he and people who look like him have always been the ones in charge.

No surprise then that Lars used verbal weapons to defend his worldview. Minutes into our debate, he shifted from challenging me about abortion to peppering me with denigrating statements about women, based on assumptions that put all responsibility and blame for unintended pregnancy (not to mention other evils of the world) on women. I in turn felt I had the responsibility to speak from the integrity of my beliefs and values—honed by thirty-five years in the crucible working with these issues.

Still, despite countless talk radio interviews, many full of this type of animosity, I have to confess that I experienced with Lars a small, involuntary twinge of fear when his deep voice of authority and power thundered at me. Remember Claire Bloom's breathtaking acknowledgment of the consequences of failing to speak one's piece early in the game? Perhaps that's how she felt and why she capitulated so readily to the male voice of authority.

But wait a minute, I thought. Why is it that men don't question their worthiness or their perfect right to challenge others? Why did I feel Lars had power and authority in the first place? Why did I feel I needed to "answer" him? I managed to avoid being the chicken that blinked first, but why didn't he seem to feel the same need to answer me?

Imagine, if you would for a moment, what it would look like if the world were turned upside down. What if women held the majority of power and leadership positions? What if women controlled the microphone? What if this had been true for, say, several dozen millennia?

Would peacemaking rather than war be the primary subject of recorded history and the evening news? Would abortion become a sacrament if men could get pregnant, as the inimitable Florynce Kennedy[9] famously opined?[10] Would most Fortune 500 companies have female CEOs and would men be carrying at least half the child-rearing load? Would men, not women, wear high-heeled shoes so that they couldn't run away, and would older women who lust after younger, less accomplished men be called not "cougars," but just "normal"?

Would angry misogynists like Lars and Rush Limbaugh still dominate talk radio, for heaven's sake?

●　●　●

# **power**tool

define your own terms—*first,*
before anyone else does. Whoever
sets the terms of the debate
usually wins it. By redefining
power not as *power-over* but as
*power-to,* we shift from a culture
of oppression to a culture of
leadership to make things better
for everyone.

## Power Giveaway:
## The Deadly Wages of Waiting to Speak

It's intriguing to speculate, but we'll never know how the world might be different if gender power had been reversed, or even equal, through the millennia. We do know the problem remains this: Women too often hesitate to embrace their power to speak their piece. With good reason, to be sure, but oh, at such a cost!

Because women have borne the brunt of the raw, abusive side of power-over us for most of human history, it's no wonder many women don't just eschew power—some even say they dislike it altogether. That's a common reason why some women resist taking it. But the upshot, as Kermit the

Frog wisely observed, is that when we don't use our power to speak first, we miss the point. We miss the moment of opportunity to define the terms of the debate. We cede the intellectual framework within which everyone's thoughts will be constructed. We limit our future choices.

An axiom I love illustrates how the same principle applies to politics. It was coined by Boss Tweed, who controlled New York's Democratic party machine in the nineteenth century: "I don't care who does the electing as long as I get to do the nominating."[11] And every high school debater learns that whoever defines the question is likely to win the argument.

Writer Katie Orenstein, whose wonderful book *Little Red Riding Hood Uncloaked* is a fascinating look at what this popular fairytale has to say about sexuality and culture, started the Op Ed Project[12] when she noticed that about 85 percent of the commentaries in the nation's newspapers were written by men. And because the opinion pages of newspapers and major online news media outlets shape the rest of the media discourse, it's no wonder that 85 percent of influential Sunday morning political talk show guests are men, 85 percent of the nonfiction books on the *New York Times* bestseller lists are by male authors, and the same gender imbalance is perpetuated and exaggerated throughout the media world.

But, says Katie, the problem is that women submit nine times fewer op-eds than men. So it's not surprising the ratio of published commentaries remains skewed. You can't wait for the Frogs and Toads to croak their last punditry and still expect there to be space left on the op-ed page for you. In fact, you can never expect pundits to croak their last, ever.

"No wonder the *Washington Post*'s op-ed page clocks in at 90 percent male authors—90 percent of the opinion piece submissions they get come from men," Katie observed. When I saw her speak last it was at the 2009 BlogHer conference, where she addressed a crowd of one hundred or so women who'd come to her workshop eager to find out from her how to get their opinion pieces published.

BlogHer is a giant women's bloggers' community that's listed as number four in *Forbes's* top seven media powers. Take in that last factoid, please. BlogHer is a huge portal where thousands of women bloggers post and millions read every day. Their alliance with iVillage, owned by NBC, has made them giants in both new and mainstream media. Their annual conference attracts over 1,200 women and a small but growing number of men, called BlogHims, all courted assiduously by sponsors who pay for meals and lavish on the swag in tribute to their buying power. But still . . .

"Women are afraid to use their voices," bemoaned a workshop participant upon watching the women in the room, one after the other, demur when Katie asked them to state aloud to the group their particular expertise that qualified them to write op-eds.

At the outset of her presentation, Katie had a small wardrobe malfunction. Her gray jersey wraparound dress didn't have a pocket where she could clip the base of her lavalier microphone. This now seemed like a metaphor for the frustration swirling about the room: the frustration that occurs when people feel like they can't make themselves heard. Once the mic problem was solved through female ingenuity, by slipping the cord through the wrap and hooking the base on her sash in the back, Katie responded that she constantly observes this reticence to assert their qualifications from the women who take her training. They question whether they are worthy of having their commentaries published, especially by major media outlets; they seem to feel that if they don't have certain formal credentials, what they have to say lacks value. And they are reluctant to keep submitting their work once it has been rejected. In contrast, men don't take rejection personally, and it doesn't deter them from being aggressive about submitting pieces.

Then Katie confronted us with these unminced words: "If you had the cure for cancer, would you hesitate to share it with the world? No! You'd feel responsible to tell people about it. Think of it as the potential to help someone else. Consider it social responsibility. Let the driving context be the value of what you know and say to other people. You will never be on the op-ed page if you are not willing to accept the value of yourself to other people."

Later, Katie told me via email that her challenge, and what she finds gets women to jump that hurdle of reticence at last, is to "provide a scenario where women think the stakes are so high—for *others*—that it forces us to see our knowledge and experience as a potential resource. That it's something that could help the world or even save lives, and if we don't share it, it is actually very selfish."

## The Half-Million-Dollar Price
## We Pay for Failing to Speak

Not everyone wants to write for the op-ed pages. But even if you're a woman who has no interest in having your commentaries published, then consider the consequences of not speaking your piece in the workplace. Your reluctance to ask for what you're worth, for instance, could be costing you a cool half-million dollars over your earning lifetime! Lower earnings today also mean that your retirement funds and Social Security will be lower, so you'll feel yet more pain from lost wages in your dotage.[13]

We know that much of the wage discrepancy—currently 78 cents for women compared to men's dollar—can be traced to the fact that women are four times less likely to negotiate higher compensation at hiring. The Center for American Progress think tank looked state by state at how the "career wage gap," as they dubbed it, affects women and men who are employed full-time, projected over a forty-year work life.

The same thing took place when it didn't occur to me to negotiate a higher salary when I was offered my position with Planned Parenthood in Arizona—the one that had been rejected by the male candidate because the pay was too low. I was so thrilled to have the chance to continue work I loved in a larger city that I didn't research comparable salaries in the community or what the previous (male) director had made. Partly this was a lack of negotiating skills, but the larger factor was completely underestimating the power of my own worth to my prospective employers. If I didn't place a high value on what I brought them, why should they?

Failing to "speak her piece" to negotiate wages equal to men at her first hiring costs a woman an enormous amount of financial power—enough cash to pay for her 2.5 children to get an Ivy League college education. To unpack the $500,000 average a bit more:

- Women at all education levels lose significant amounts of income due to the career wage gap, but women with the most education lose the most in earnings.

- Women with a college degree or higher lose $713,000 over a forty-year period versus a $270,000 loss for women who did not finish high school (who, of course, start with a lower pay base).

- Women in all occupations suffer from the career wage gap, but the gap ranges widely from one occupation to the next, with the widest gap in finance and management and the smallest gap in construction and maintenance.

- Women lose hundreds of thousands of dollars from the career wage gap no matter where they live.

- The gap exceeds $300,000 in fifteen states, $400,000 in twenty-two states, and $500,000 in eleven states.[14]

If you're an unmarried woman or a woman of color, the disparity is even greater. As I've noted, women overall earn 78 cents to a man's dollar, but unmarried women earn just 56 cents, according to Women's Voices, Women Vote, an organization devoted to engaging unmarried women in political life. The fact that college-educated women of color earn less than white women with college degrees—black women earn about 67 cents on the dollar, and Hispanic women make 58 cents—shows that some of the discrepancy is clearly due to overt or covert discrimination (black men make 78 cents to each $1 earned by a white male; Hispanic men make 66 cents on the dollar), as reported in a fifty-state 2009 study by the American Association of University Women.[15]

Still, because these systemic barriers are now based in cultural bias rather than laws, it's up to those affected to press for change at every turn. The more often women speak our piece, not as supplicants but by presenting our value to the enterprise compellingly, and the more women define ourselves to hiring bosses before we become defined as less worthy than male employees in the same job, the sooner we can revise these dismal data in favor of fairness and gender equality.

Women must learn these skills and practice them intentionally because men have been primed to pursue their self-interest from childhood. Economist Linda Babcock found that men are far more aggressive when they negotiate raises and promotions, because women often don't know the market value of their work—they report salary expectations between 3 and 32 percent less than men in the same jobs.[16] Babcock says in this article entitled appropriately, "In the Office, Nice Girls Finish Last," that men "are encouraged to go for it growing up. The world is their oyster, they're in charge, they're encouraged to take risks, and they just have so much more practice initiating negotiations growing up and with so much more encouragement from our society that this is an acceptable thing for them to do."[17]

Recently, when I spoke to the University Career Women at Arizona State University, I asked the audience of professionals, who handle many of the university's human resource administrative functions, why they thought men are so often paid more than women for the same job. "Because they ask for it!" came the resounding reply from several dozen women in unison. I take that as a good sign that at least women understand the consequences of failing to define the terms of their own lives. Courses like the one designed and taught by University of Akron women's studies professor Paula Maggio are being created to teach young women the basic purse power skill of salary negotiation, because, Maggio pointedly says on her blog intended for the young women who take her courses, "the idea of negotiating either doesn't occur to them or scares them to death."[18]

The same aversion to negotiating for their own good percolates through power struggles within personal relationships. We need to be aware of how, after a concession like Claire Bloom's, defining the debate on our terms will always elude us and we will live on the defensive ever after. We must commit to use the power-to on our own behalf so that we can translate it into the power to help others and ourselves.

## POWER-OVER IS FROM MARS, POWER-TO IS FROM VENUS—OR HOW WOMEN CAN REDEFINE POWER AND EMBRACE IT ON NEW TERMS

Okay, lecture over. Now comes the fun part: throwing the classic definitions into the air and reorganizing them in a completely new way to create a healthier relationship with power. To borrow another phrase from the archetypal "Mad Man" Don Draper, "If you don't like what's being said, change the conversation."[19]

What if we *could* turn the world upside down and define power differently?

We can. Power-over is passé; power-to is the next iteration of leadership.

Almost anyone can employ power-over, but it takes skill to employ power-to. It takes skill to lead others rather than to force, require, coerce, or lord over them. Leadership power is much different from the use of force to gain acceptance of a goal. Power-over does not require that people aspire to the same goal, but successful power-to, or leadership, does require goal congruence, by consensus, trust, or government of the people.

Power-over focuses on tactics for gaining compliance, while leadership focuses on getting answers and solutions in order to be able to accomplish something for mutual good.

Power-over makes people feel power*less*. Even if it isn't force or brute power, but a manipulative power such as political dominance, the feeling that one has no control over one's choices makes her disgruntled, angry, or passive-aggressive.

Power-to supports and enhances whatever power the individual brings to a project, workplace, relationship, or civic activity. It abhors coercion. It opens up the possibility of choices; the ability to choose is what makes us human. Choosing is the basis of morality.

Power-over is amoral. Power-to is responsibility.

This is the type of revolution in the definition of power that has the potential to change the world for good; for good in the sense of making life better and for good in the sense of changing it for all time.

The previously cited economist Linda Babcock's research, for example, also reveals that despite our unwillingness to bargain for higher salaries, women are actually great negotiators after all—just not for themselves. "It's not as if women are missing a negotiation gene or something!" she says. "[Women] negotiate for their family members, they negotiate for the causes they believe in. So it's not that we don't have these skills. It's that society has told us that it's not appropriate for us to use them for ourselves—because that would be selfish or greedy."[20]

A close colleague of mine recently conducted a focus group of executive women for a leadership program we were developing. The women interviewed were by all measures leaders who hold significant power within business and nonprofit sectors. When possible titles for a women's leadership program were floated for discussion, titles with the word *power* in them drew the most controversy. One participant said, "I don't like the word *power*. It speaks to dominance." Another said the program shouldn't use the word *power* because "it is highly offensive to some people."

But once we define *power* as the power to accomplish something for others, or for the good of us all, women become much more willing to embrace their power. The use of power is legitimated, taken out of the realm of the power-over. Every time I propose this definition to women, I can see jaws relax, breath going out. Tension relieved. Power-to makes one power*full*.

In practical terms, the value of this definition of power-to in business, politics, and relationships becomes more evident daily as studies and comparisons to power-over hierarchical models of leadership and governance are made.

McKinsey and Company management consultants published a study in 2007 called "Women Matter." Female managers, they observed, "are more likely than men to make collaborative decisions, to behave as role models and to consider the ethical consequences of their acts. Men, on the other hand, are more likely to make decisions on their own and then order the troops to carry them out."[21]

But gender diversity doesn't make a significant difference when there's only one woman, or just a token few, in the mix. From looking at the metrics of what constitutes a critical mass of women to bring about cultural change in the organization, the McKinsey study, and others like it, have concluded that companies employing at least 30 percent female executives or board members perform better than all-male organizations. They even generate better returns on investments.

The best little nugget in this news is that at last, there are enough women in powerful positions that the 30 percent critical mass theory can be tested for the first time ever.

Political scientist James MacGregor Burns predicted the change in 1978 when he coined the phrase "transformational leadership," and wrote: "Transforming leadership occurs when one or more persons engage with others in such a way that leaders and followers raise one another to higher levels of motivation and morality. . . . Transforming leadership ultimately becomes moral in that it raises the level of human conduct and ethical aspirations of both the leader and the led and, thus, has a transforming effect on both. Transformational leaders are concerned with substance and truly empower others."[22]

That's the power-to. It's a way of conceptualizing power that women are particularly suited to and adept at using. It's the positive side of all those years of taking the boniest parts of the chicken for ourselves to make sure our children were nourished first. It's the happy consequence of all those years of honing the skills to calibrate nuances of a situation before taking a risk, the times we didn't play Chicken—necessary behavior for the gender with lesser physical strength.

Burns wasn't just talking about women, but he was way ahead of his time when he said back in 1978 that leadership had in the past meant power and control over others to make them do things you want done "whereas, today, leadership is about a mutual relationship where each can transcend to a worthy purpose and behave with moral fibre, courage, integrity and trust."[23]

I think we can safely say that "today" has finally arrived, and today turns out to be women's moment to embrace the power-to for good in life and leadership.

Republican political consultant David Gergen wrote in the foreword to *Enlightened Power: How Women Are Transforming the Practice of Leadership*, published in 2005: "Think of all the words we use to describe old style leadership: aggressive, assertive, autocratic, muscular, closed. When we describe the new leadership, we employ terms like consensual, relational, web-based, caring, inclusive, open, transparent—all qualities that we associate with the 'feminine' style of leadership."[24] Is this exciting or what?

And when it comes to politics, the online political site *Politico* posted a piece appropriately called, "Study: Women lawmakers outperform men," citing a Stanford University study that found women members of Congress introduce on average three more bills per session, attract more cosponsors for their legislation, and bring home more money for their districts than their male counterparts. A congresswoman interviewed in the article said of herself, as well as her observations of others considering a run for office, "Women seem to wait for someone who plants the idea and gives them confidence. I had individuals who shared their confidence in me, and it helped erase some of the self-doubt."[25] Once that doubt is gone, watch out!

## Embracing the Power-to:
## Jennifer Buffett's Responsibility

Jennifer Buffett, the forty-four-year-old president of the billion-dollar NoVo Foundation, sat ramrod straight and looked totally centered when I interviewed her in her environmentally correct New York City office with its warm natural wood tones, unpretentious and authentic as Buffett family philanthropy has typically been.

Jennifer is married to Peter Buffett, one of three children of Warren Buffett, who ranked number two on *Forbes* magazine's 2009 list of the world's wealthiest people, and his late wife, Susie. The elder Buffett has vowed to give most of his wealth to charity and part of that transition was endowing a substantial foundation for each of his offspring to control.[26]

In my work with Buffett, who also cochairs the foundation's board along with Peter, I'd been impressed with her clarity of intention. We met first through the Women's Media Center, where I serve on the board and the NoVo Foundation has funded its Progressive Women's Voices Program. Buffett later invited me to participate on an intergenerational panel of women that she organized for New York's Culture Project. I wanted to talk with her because I hoped to explore her thoughts about how women who control substantial philanthropic wealth relate to the enormous power in their hands. What I found out went substantially deeper. Buffett took me into the kinetics of masculine and feminine power and how she and Peter had redefined their foundation goals to focus on improving the status of women and girls globally, as a direct result of first confronting and, after thoughtful reflection, changing the gender power paradigm in their personal relationship.

A slender, chestnut-haired woman who speaks with steely passion, Buffett told me she'd been born the second and smaller of twins. Always faster developing than her brother, she was told to hold back in favor of his efforts, to be quiet and supportive, not to make waves, "yes, even growing up in the '70s when we should have been over that stuff."

Then she realized that she'd been doing the same with her husband. "I was running on empty. I felt invisible, like I didn't matter. A little voice inside me said, 'Well, isn't that great! You're such a good person because you're selfless and egoless.' Then I realized, no no no no no. You will be invisible, and you won't be powerful, and you won't be effective at what you believe in. You have the right to take up space, have a life, have an identity.

"But it got that bad for me. Before that moment, I kept getting smaller, quieter, more deferential, and more powerless. I started to lose weight and to disappear, literally. I thought that would earn Peter's love, to be very honest, but it wasn't working. And Peter was just mirroring my belief about myself. It wasn't fun for him either. It was borderline abusive, very dysfunctional. Because I wasn't standing into my power.

"And then I knew. I woke up the day after my thirty-ninth birthday and had no voice. Could not peep out a whisper. It scared me. I remembered my mother-in-law, Susie, who had passed away the year before (from oral cancer). I kept getting a message from her, I could just hear her saying, 'I bit my tongue in deference to my father and my husband and what I knew in life. Don't do what I did.' It was time to process that pain she must have felt and that grieved her."

The big awakening for Jennifer and Peter together came when she finally brought her new awareness to his attention. It was an act that must have taken a good bit of courage, though she says simply, "We just got conscious about it."

The way they took those conscious steps led them to question the very basis of the institution they were creating and changed their personal relationship. In the process, the couple said "no" to power-over as Buffett took her power-to. They changed the focus of their future philanthropy from giving to various worthy causes as proposals were presented to them to "looking at the foundation as a clean slate and trying to come up with what we envisioned for the world as the core of our work. What we realized is that the world is out of balance between the masculine and feminine forces on the planet. We're living in a hypermasculine, punitive, competitive, dominator, Empire society. Power is held at the top control and then it seeps down. I had to go do research to find another way. Kind of embarrassing, but it shows how we're trained not to think in terms of the feminine and nurturing. I did a simple paper on feminine principles, and we talked about it. It gave us our frame in terms of ourselves as individuals, and then in our relationship, and in life. That gave us more choice and more ability to have individual power."

Buffett calls this "paying attention to the dashboard of life." When the alarm system goes off, she says, you have to pay attention to it or it gets louder and louder and finally knocks you on your can.

## PUSHING THE FULCRUM TO LEAD THE CHANGE

The alarm from the dashboard of life is sounding for all women today. We must pay attention to it, and we must have the courage to take the actions that can change the world for good.

Buffett pressed a thick blue paperback book into my hands as I left her office, saying, "Please read this. It influenced me a lot." The book was David Hawkins's *Power vs. Force*. In the following quote from the book, I've added the bracketed words, but the author clearly articulates something very close to what I'm proposing about the need to redefine power: "Power [to] gives life and energy—force [power-over] takes these away. We notice that power [to] is associated with compassion and makes us feel positively about ourselves. Force [power-over] is associated with judgment and makes us feel poorly about ourselves."[27]

So how is it another man sees this and women still have to be persuaded?

Every fiber in my mind and body tells me this is the moment when we can redefine power from power-over to power-to, and that will position women to make the next great leap toward equality and parity.

True, despite our extraordinary gains, we stand within a half-finished revolution. We've been backlashed and told feminism is dead; for all our educational attainment and shattered glass ceilings, we remain stuck to the floor—doing over 50 percent of the work but far too little of the decision-making. We're still shaped by a predominant media narrative that makes us dislike our bodies and question not only our capabilities, but even our ambitions. We have yet to define our individual and collective futures or to commit to gathering up the courage and practical tools we'll need to get there once and for all this time.

Yet this is the moment when all that can change.

Every day brings another report that women are about to take over the world, or perhaps already have. As noted, California's First Lady Maria Shriver declared that it's a "Woman's Nation." Journalist power couple Sheryl WuDunn and Nick Kristof rediscovered the Chinese proverb that "Women Hold Up Half the Sky." *New York Times* op-ed columnist and former editorial page editor Gail Collins has written a magnificent history of women's progress from the 1960s to today, accurately named *When Everything Changed.*

Much ado has been made of the fact that in October 2009, women topped 50 percent of the workplace. Whereupon we were informed "boys are the new girls," as *Lilith* magazine's Fall 2009 bright red cover screamed.

This is all to the good. But deep down, I think we understand that cheering is premature. We're well on the road, but we haven't arrived yet. These pronouncements are based in the faulty assumption that a trend once started will continue its trajectory indefinitely, on its own. Malcolm Gladwell's influential bestseller *The Tipping Point* made the case that ideas are like epidemics. Those that take root in the cultural psyche grow by a contagionlike process, exponentially, until they take over completely.

We are, without question, at a *potential* tipping point moment for women, despite all the starts, stops, and backward steps I described in chapter 1. But what will happen next is in no way inevitable. History has seen countless trends that were once declared definitive fizzle before they had a chance to make a dent in our cultural memory. And even an epidemic eventually burns itself out from the weight of its own entropy.

When it comes to expanding social justice and equality for women, a moment like this one today is more like a fulcrum than an epidemic. A fulcrum can shift weight in any direction depending upon who's doing the pushing and from what direction. When pushback from groups fearing loss of power becomes ever more fierce, as Susan Faludi described in *Backlash*, forward movement can splinter, unless leadership emerges to regroup the energy and create a bold new vision that inspires people to keep working deliberately for that better future. And we have seen women take those giant steps forward only to step back from pushing the fulcrum, resisting the responsibility that comes with having the power-to.

Still, women today can truly unlimit ourselves if we keep moving forward, persistently pressing the fulcrum's weight toward fairness and equality. Consciously defining our own terms so that we can change the meaning of power from power-over to power-to is the first big step.

That process of changed thinking has already begun to shape how younger generations look at gender roles. My grandson Millan was eleven in January 2007, when I went to Washington, DC, to witness and write about the swearing in of the first woman speaker of the house, Nancy Pelosi. Afterward, I told him about the event, and putting two and two together, he replied, "Yes, and did you know a woman is probably going to run for president?"

"I did know that," I told him, and then I asked, "Would you vote for a woman for president?"

"Well, yeahhhh!" he responded, as though I had three heads even to pose the question in the first place. Then he thought about it for a split second. "But I guess it would matter what she said."

Millan is a smart kid, not just because he's my grandchild. It certainly matters a great deal what she says. Women who use today's opportunities to assume powerful positions by merely adopting male models of power and leadership don't advance the cause of equality very far.

That's why it's important for women to change the very meaning of power to one we can embrace wholeheartedly because it is the power to define our own lives and leadership, for good. We have the responsibility to use the power to speak our truth without delay. And when we do, that will change the nature of this conversation in profound ways.

As Katie Orenstein says so passionately, "Self-abnegation is irresponsible." Jennifer Buffett points out that to her, power is itself a responsibility, "the ability to respond."

Women are generally smart enough not to be interested in attaining power for its own sake—to wield power over others just because it's there for the taking. By redefining power to mean the *power-to,* we release the negative connotations that make many women wary of power and we give ourselves the freedom to envision a world where women are equal opportunity leaders and doers, and where we can lead with integrity, intention, and confidence.

Forget *power-over*. In today's world what we need is the *power-to*.

Some, like conservative talk show host Lars Larson, will always think we're turning the world upside down. What we're really doing is setting the world aright.

# nina**simons**

Nina Simons's twin passions, for the plight of women and the planet, draw strength from her conviction that our better values, restored to a more natural harmony, can save the world. But learning to find the locus of power within herself has required a journey of self-awareness. Since I first met her at a conference early in 2009, I have been struck by how the metaphors she uses for embracing her power and using it ring the same notes as those that have enabled me to see and accept mine. Perhaps these are universal chords that can inspire you, too.

As a cofounder with her husband, Kenny Ausubel, of Bioneers, a visionary organization that works to find and disseminate breakthrough solutions to environmental and social problems at the global to local levels, Simons has worked for years to promote sustainability, with women's leadership of that effort becoming an increasingly significant part. The need for women to fully embrace their power-to and use it impressed itself on Simons as she came to see the self-limiting, power-unused tendencies in herself. "For most of my career," she writes, "though I had many accomplishments and successes, I didn't consider myself a leader. I have worked in the arts, as a social entrepreneur, in the corporate world, and co-leading a nonprofit organization. The way my path meandered and changed embarrassed me." Conventional metrics, Simons found, blinded her to the success of her unconventional career, the strength of her unconventional abilities.

The awareness that her power was no less real for coming in a nontraditional form signaled for Simons a need to rethink how we understood such qualities as competence and leadership. At the same time it pointed to a larger systemic issue. "I saw a pattern of imbalances of 'masculine' and 'feminine' qualities everywhere I looked," she explains. "Rational, linear, goal-oriented, quantitative, short-term, and competitive approaches were consistently front and center. Concerns about future generations, emotional intelligence, subjective experience, process, relationships, aesthetics, qualitative, and cooperative efforts were hard to measure, and therefore generally discounted as 'soft,' or irrelevant.

"I began to see an insidious and largely invisible cultural legacy of devaluing or even demonizing those human characteristics relegated to the domain of the 'feminine,' and elevating and institutionalizing those associated with the 'masculine.' I realized that it was not only women who have been systemically culturally devalued, but the 'feminine' qualities within us all. This legacy of cultural bias has damaged everyone." And she had devalued it in herself.

Whether or not you are comfortable divvying up traits by gender, Simons's experience and insight are bound to resonate. How many of us have undervalued what we bring to the table by judging it against a narrow or oppressive conception of power? The great power-to that Nina has wielded as an organizer and teacher has come from shedding a self-limiting narrative and making room for a new one. "I loved to orchestrate diverse groups of people to work together toward a common goal," she writes. "Rather than diminishing my inclusiveness and ability to inspire cooperation as having little value, I have come to appreciate them as leadership skills."

Unleashed to see that what she needed was there in her own hands, Simons's talents have brought together and inspired many who share her ideals, her hope for greater balance in our world and our lives. Since its inception in 1990, Bioneers has hosted an annual conference, which connects a diverse group of leaders and innovators in a supportive community. After she realized two-thirds of the activists who participate in Bioneers are women, she began to hold retreats for "disparate women leaders," the first of which, called "UnReasonable Women for the Earth," birthed the now well-known women's activist group Code Pink. A subsequent retreat, entitled "Cultivating Women's Leadership," lies behind Moonrise, an anthology of stories about women and leadership that Simons is currently putting together. The book's goal, Simons explains, "is to ignite the power and capacity within us all to create change by leading in ways that are joyful, healthy, and whole."

A key element of igniting and using that power is explored in the book's section called "Leadership Sourced from Inner Authority." It describes "how women have found all the authority and power they needed to face adversity by tapping into their hearts, their souls, their bellies, and their convictions. None of these women required or sought the support of any power outside of herself, but rather they were ignited to act and strengthened from a knowingness that came from deep within." What follows is a shortened version of an inspiring speech Simons gives about her own journey from recognizing how much of her own power was unused to making a conscious decision to use it from a place of her own intention:

> Of all the ways we might cultivate our leadership to address this intensely changing time we face, for me, increasing my awareness, will, and compassion seem the most essential.

> How might a heightened awareness of all that currently threatens life inspire us to act more boldly, more purposefully, and more courageously to shift our collective course?

> I believe the way through is by reclaiming the underworld parts of ourselves.

> Emotions that have been banished, trained away, and anesthetized—the anger, loss, and grief we have no rituals for anymore are needed to heal our relations with ourselves, each other, and this endangered and sacred Earth.

> Stories are medicine for our false isolation; a way to forge connection and community and help shift our course.

> Stories are the seed forms of culture we carry around within us. They define how expansively or tightly we offer the

*gift of our lives. We decide how far we can go, how large a stand we're willing to make, or what risks we're willing to take, based upon the stories we tell ourselves.*

*Sometimes they stem from our family and social conditioning, and we carry them unwittingly, unaware of how they shape our lives.*

*About ten years ago, I began unearthing my own hidden stories. I discovered that I thought of myself as "the woman behind the man," (And, as you may have heard, "behind every great man is a woman, rolling her eyes.")*

*It was shocking to realize how self-limiting my inner narrative was.*

*It required the reflection of a colleague, friend, and mentor, a savvy man whose opinion I trusted to help me believe in a new story to replace it.*

*He told me that he saw my contribution as being of equal value in co-creating Bioneers's uniqueness. It took me a while to wrap my mind around this new narrative. Once I did, I understood that I held the keys to my own liberation.*

*We're all indigenous to someplace, and have community embedded in our cellular and ancestral memory. In some deep corner of our hearts, don't we all yearn for it?*

*But in a quest for certainty, seeking an illusion of "safety," criticism and judgments reinforce our separateness.*

*The invisible stories embedded throughout our culture lead us to ruthlessly rank ourselves, and each other, hardening our hearts to empathic connection.*

*May the soil of our souls be sown with seeds that expand our capacity for compassion,*

*Watered with the grief that strengthens our commitment, and fired by the outrage that fortifies our will.*

*May our roots entwine underground like aspen trees or seven sisters oaks, whose underground networks of connection offer the resilience to weather hurricanes and storms.*

*May we leave with stories carried like seeds in our feathers, to sow them wherever, and with whomever, we next connect.*

*May we savor together some visceral taste of beloved community—so nourishing, so enlivening and desirable that our hearts and hands take it on, and the flaming light of our purposes will not be quenched.[1]*

CHAPTER THREE

# unblock:

# power unused is power useless

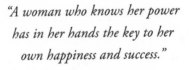

*"A woman who knows her power
has in her hands the key to her
own happiness and success."*

**—RAFAELLA BARKER,**
journalist[1]

- What is your vision of what you want to happen as the next step in your professional or personal life?

- What are the power blocks that are standing in your way?

- What are three steps you can take using your power to make your vision happen?

In my dream I'm holding on to the steering wheel for dear life as the family car, a white Chevrolet Impala, hurtles down a winding dirt road, churning up so much reddish-brown West Texas dust that it streams like rocket exhaust in the car's wake. In the back of my mind is the puzzling contradiction that the car keeps going faster even though my foot isn't on the accelerator. And something very odd: The key isn't in the ignition.

Where the heck is my key chain?

Fortunately, there is no other traffic on the narrow road, because I can't see around the hairpin curves. My heart is racing faster than the engine.

It dawns on me in slow motion that my keys, on my familiar metal key chain, are in my hand—the very hand that's clutched tight to the steering wheel.

At first this disjunction doesn't register. All I can think about is the car, which seems to have a mind of its own, started without the key in the first place. Finally, I pay attention to the instinct I had been consciously ignoring. *You idiot!* the little voice inside me screams. *You have the key! Put it into the ignition and you can stop the car!*

As though it were all perfectly natural, I look at the keys, put them into the ignition, and take control of the car. The brake responds. The car slows down and gradually rolls to a stop.

I woke up in a cold sweat, still able to feel the hard metal of the keys pressed into my palm. I started laughing. I didn't need a shaman to interpret this dream.

I was at a crossroads in my life. I was thirty-three years old and ready to leave my sputtering marriage. And yet I was continuing to speed along the path I had chosen eighteen years before, when I was too young to make mature relationship decisions and devoid of the personal aspirations that had lately begun to uncoil like tendrils of an unruly vine that knows just where it wants to climb.

I didn't think I would be able to halt the inexorable momentum of daily-ness in order to reroute my course for the long haul. And given the fact that I'd never been on my own before, a part of my resistance was simply not having an alternative life model to follow; venturing into the unknown felt particularly daunting. But the solution was in plain sight. As is so often the case, however, I was oblivious to it.

I knew what I needed and wanted to do. But what made me hesitate to use my power to change my life was a long history of self-sacrificing like I had observed in my mother and grandmother before me, and that so many women absorb from the cradle onward. I was so programmed to respond to the needs and expectations of others, I didn't even realize at first that I could act on my own behalf, to take charge of the vehicle and drive my own life. Was I afraid to use the power in my possession? Looking back on that time, I used powerlessness as an excuse to defer action. In truth, I was afraid of assuming responsibility for making my own decisions about life's big questions.

## FINDING THE POWER SOURCE

The decision to leave a marriage, no matter how much we want to leave, forces us to come face-to-face with a confusing set of emotions. I had to ask myself whether I had the courage to give up the familiarity of the known, however insecure and unsatisfying my situation was. Tears welled as I processed what I would be relinquishing by stopping my metaphorical car, getting out of the marriage it symbolized, and walking away, alone, into uncharted territory—and that was long before we had GPS to guide us.

I would be changing directions, and I knew that would transform the way others saw me. I was getting ready to step away from the role of traditional homemaker-wife-mother I had truly believed I wanted when I entered my marriage. I had to face telling my children, owning up to my parents, feeling an almost overwhelming sense of failure when I told the rest of my family and friends that a divorce was imminent.

But *I* was the real unanswered question. I was about to have to figure out whether I was prepared to become a woman on my own, fully responsible for my own fate and the consequences of my choices.

With the wisdom of the years since then, I now understand that changing any paradigm can be terrifying. We can't change the context of our lives without changing ourselves, too. The flip side of every choice is sacrifice. It means giving up something. And then getting what we want is like that old Toyota jingle: "You asked for it, you got it." Okay! Now what?

After we've begun to drive our own car and, in the larger social justice sense, after we've begun to set the world aright, there's still a great deal of work to do on ourselves. Gloria Steinem talked about this in her book *Revolution from Within.* Today Steinem holds iconic status as a feminist leader because of the way her activism has changed the course of history for women. But she once said she only gradually began to suspect the existence of her own internal power's "pinpoint of beginning" because she had always been encouraged to locate power as though it existed entirely outside of herself.[2]

That mistaken tendency to locate the sources of power outside of ourselves so that we respond rather than initiating action is the essential challenge women still face today, despite the many doors that have been opened and barriers that have been smashed. Even young women, who grow up being told they can do anything and be anything, often don't make the necessary connection between their ability (potential) and their willingness to act on it (intention). Nor do they have a clear sense of their responsibility to themselves and to other women to utilize their abilities to the fullest so that the female half of the world can continue to advance toward full justice and equality.

Let's take a look at two women, over a generation apart, whom I interviewed to get their take on why women resist their own power: Leslie Bennetts—author of *The Feminine Mistake,* a book that takes to task women who don't remain in the workforce and stay capable of supporting themselves—is sixty. Jen Nedeau is twenty-four, a social media consultant and the former director of digital strategy for the recently defunct liberal radio network Air America. In separate interviews, both women (who don't know each other) referenced the potency of the Disney princess mythology in shaping young women's perception of where their power sources reside.

As I've previously noted, Bennetts excoriated the multibillion dollars worth of product sales the Disney princess line reaps for instilling unhealthy aspirations in young girls to be rescued from having to take charge of their own lives by "being on the arm of a man who gets or has power."

Nedeau was a little more forgiving of the pop culture princess narrative, but her point was the same: "I don't blame Disney for giving us a concept of fantasies. I think that fantasy and imagination are wonderful things and a wonderful starting place. But there's a lack of ownership that I see among young women, where they expect for certain things to just fall into place. Their life path is defined by society's life path and, therefore, the goal setting gets shifted onto what's *supposed* to happen versus what you *want* to happen."[3]

While individual women might be in various states of recognizing the power-to they already have within themselves, women collectively are still negotiating the sources of power in our social and political lives. Some are aware of recovering from the intoxicating fantasy of the handsome prince or other sources of power outside of ourselves. And the truth is, all the intelligence, education, opportunities, antidiscrimination laws, and open doors in the world won't change a thing if we, as women, don't see our own potential and seize what's ours for the taking, to unlock the next set of doors and then go through them to the next level. It's well past time to get beyond that pervasive 15 to 20 percent barricade where we're stalled in the leadership of almost every profession.

Though the power to define our own lives and the power to accomplish whatever we want to achieve might be right there and available to us, the fact remains that power unused is power useless.

## FIRST, KNOW WHAT YOU'VE GOT

To be able to use power, first you have to know you have it. Then you must be courageous enough to use it intentionally to go toward goals that you have set and that align with your true passions, aspirations, and gifts.

Journalist and former *Washington Post* syndicated columnist Marie Cocco told me about a speech she'd delivered at a conference put on by the White House Project, a nonpartisan organization that works nation-wide to recruit, train, and support women to run for political office. In her talk, she'd highlighted the discrepancy between the large number of women in the talent pool of educated, capable professionals and their scarcity in political and corporate leadership roles. She presented data from a study that had identified women's internal reluctance to own their qualifications as the greatest barrier to their running for public office or aiming for high corporate executive roles.

After Cocco finished her speech, she was milling around with some of the other participants when she witnessed a conversation that illustrated depressingly well the point she had been attempting to get across to the audience. She was standing with Marie Wilson, founder and president of the White House Project, when a participant approached them and said to Wilson, "People often tell me I should run for office, but I don't have a college degree."

Unfazed, Wilson asked, "So what?"

"It turned out," Cocco relayed with palpable frustration, "that this woman was the highest earner in her real estate firm. She had demonstrated her leadership ability many times over and had a keen interest in running for public office. Yet, what she focused on was what she did not have—a college degree."

Cocco stopped and then emphasized: "So in addition to having their qualifications downgraded in the public eye, women downgrade themselves." Then she gave an example of self-imposed humility that is doing women harm: "When Cheerios advertises, they don't say, 'Oh, I'm not cornflakes,' do they? That is cultural. That is the legacy of our work having been diminished for so many years. Women as a group have internalized this. Our work has been viewed as outside the lifeblood of the economy. And we have internalized that we are not good enough. And how can you not internalize this if you go through your career as I have, getting awards and commendations for your work, only to find out you are earning $125 a week less than the men in the same job?"

The woman who thought she couldn't run for office reminded me of that dream I had when I was propelled along by forces I didn't try to control or even think I could. Yet my power to define my own life in a new way turned out not to be elusive at all, but to reside in my own hand. And many women have told me that's the kind of problem that has kept them from taking steps into leadership roles, or from trying to accomplish something they really want to do in their lives. They genuinely can't see the keys in their own hands.

This phenomenon is particularly striking when we see women who already hold incredibly powerful positions, whether in public office or the private business sector, who are unable to see what they could accomplish if they used their power in a more purposeful or strategic way—if they used it to push the fulcrum for women just a little bit further toward gender balance.

# **power**tool number three

## what you need is almost always there, in your hands or within reach, if you can only see it and have the courage to use it.

The following stories are three recent examples of power unused that I have witnessed. The first demonstrates the unused power of female consumers to shape what products are sold in the marketplace. The second showcases the dismal failure of women to mass their political strength in 2008, and the consequences for perceptions of women's political clout in the foreseeable future. The final example represents women's tremendous economic power on a global scale, and demonstrates how we have long held the ability to push women's corporate executive and board membership to parity within a relatively short time—and yet it took a man to figure it out and initiate a strategy to accomplish this.

## Do Swag Bags Equal Real Consumer Power?

I've noted in an earlier chapter that BlogHer's founders made number four on *Forbes*'s list of most influential people in new media for good reasons. BlogHer was created by three visionary women in 2005: Lisa Stone, a journalist who came from the mainstream corporate media world; Silicon Valley marketing executive Elisa Camahort Page; and author and media strategist Jory Des Jardins. What these three women created is a wholly new model for a media company. They're in excellent company on the *Forbes* list, along with giants like Google founders Sergey Brin and Larry Page (#1), Federal Communications Commission Chairman Julius Genachowski (#2), Arianna Huffington (#3), and Craigslist founder Craig Newmark (#5).

The twenty million women who write for, read, and/or attend BlogHer events run the socioeconomic gamut but collectively represent enormous economic and social power. As of March 2010, the popular web portal boasted over 2,500 affiliated blogs that carry their advertising to many millions of their own readers; 22,000 blogs total listed by thirty topics ranging from food to feminism, cars to careers, global to local; and 51,000 community members, who log in to the site and return to it regularly. In all, a strong platform for both millions of interested female readers and writers, and for the advertisers who desperately want to reach them.[4]

In 2005, the blogosphere was abuzz with people asking where the women bloggers were. "Here!" these women answered, and they proposed what became the first BlogHer conference in 2005. BlogHer's mission statement, which the website says was written around the kitchen table, is to create opportunities for women bloggers to pursue exposure, education, community, and economic empowerment.

Word of the first conference's success quickly spread, particularly among the so-called mommy bloggers, who were seeking community, and women blogging about politics who by and large felt ignored by the newly ascendant male-dominated political blogs. They were also soon joined by food bloggers and women who covered any number of other topical issues.

I began dipping my toes (or fingers) into blogging in 2006, when a young intern advised me I must have a blog of my own and then proceeded to set me up on Google's simple blogger platform. I immediately took to the delicious freedom of writing without constraints. A blog is the ultimate personal reality show where one can say whatever she wants; no one is there to edit you, censor you, dismiss the importance of your topics, or throw you off the island. I began to cross post occasionally to BlogHer and joined as an affiliate.

The idea of a portal, or "hub," as the founders prefer to call BlogHer's website, was exactly the right idea at the right time, and its growth has been so explosive that by 2007 it had become the largest blogging site on the web and had launched the BlogHer business conference; by mid-2008, the site entered into strategic partnership with iVillage, "the leading online destination for women." This teaming brought a $5 million infusion of capital to BlogHer. A significant aspect of the partnership is that iVillage—started in 1995 and now owned by NBC Universal—was once as groundbreaking an idea, also conceived and implemented by women (Candice Carpenter and Nancy Evans), as BlogHer had become a decade later. That both enterprises are now owned by a corporate conglomerate is part of the success story, but also part of the reason that the phenomenal power-to that BlogHer could have to shape the consumer marketplace has morphed into phenomenal power unused.[5]

After hearing raves about it, I was excited to attend my first BlogHer conference in July 2009, The Year Everything Changed, according to blogging colleagues who had attended previous years.

Some things, they said, remained the same. There were power strips to trip over everywhere, and women curled up in chairs in every nook and cranny of the Sheraton Chicago's public spaces, tapping away on their laptops. There was a lactation room, babies in slings, babies in Snuglies, babies in strollers. Despite these ubiquitous reminders that women bear children and this was quintessentially a women's conference, many of the women in attendance regarded the BlogHer conference as their big annual escape from children and husbands. The half-dozen women with whom I shared an airport van to the hotel seemed intent on packing in as much child-free activity as possible, largely involving drinking and late-night partying.

And the sponsors—all five dozen of them, if you count gold, premium, platinum, and exhibiting—from Walmart to Ann Taylor to Procter & Gamble to Microsoft's Bing.com—underwrote most of the booze at the daily cocktail hours and end-of-evening parties. And then the drinking at the after-that parties. Meals were also entirely comped by the sponsors, as were the cookies and fruit in the afternoon. This largesse kept the registration costs reasonable for participants, certainly a boon for those on a tight budget.

If you were still hungry after all this, you could go into the exhibit hall where Disney provided free-flowing Mickey Mouse ice cream bars, Walmart dished out Paula Deen's sickeningly sweet apple cake from her new line of desserts (yes, I tried almost everything), and Pepsico offered soft drinks and flavored vitamin waters.

But the real stars of the conference were the swag bags: gift-filled, logo-carrying inducements to attend this consumer product's party or that commercial purveyor's exhibit booth. In previous years, such loot had apparently been pleasantly plentiful. But this year it was swag on steroids: huge bagsful of valuable goods that included digital cameras, plush stuffed animals, games for the kids, food products, makeup galore, giant-size cleaning supplies, jewelry . . . it was easy to be seduced. I stopped picking it up not from inadequate greed but because I simply had no more room in my luggage even after I gave one humongous bagful of kids' toys away to a friend of mine who lives in Chicago. (All right, I do like my Bing.com T-shirt's V-neck and close fit, great for the gym, where I am a sweating, treadmilling billboard for them, heaven help me.)

Most amazing, even with General Motors on the verge of bankruptcy, the company still knew where its bread of hope for a viable future was buttered: Chevrolet provided "an entire fleet of fuel-efficient carpool vehicles for transportation to and from the conference."

I don't know how many women got free rides as a result of their perceived market value, but clearly the lure of "free" anything is like an aphrodisiac. And the resultant behavior bordered on crass. People shoved into the lines outside the parties reputed to have the most or best gift bags. Many cruised the exhibit hall multiple times, stuffing their bags to bulging.

To be fair, sponsorship, especially at that level of excess, was recognized as a two-edged sword by many of the bloggers, and some of them voiced their concerns. One of those ethical questions is now being addressed by the new FCC regulations requiring bloggers to disclose when they are compensated or given free products, such as were distributed with so much abundance at the conference in exchange for ad placement or endorsements.

That's a significant issue, but I believe there's an even bigger one. Marketers, manufacturers, and advertisers know women make over 80 percent of consumer purchases and recognize the value of putting their products onto the pages of our blogs. They recognize that women trust product reviews and endorsements by fellow bloggers so much that 85 percent of us claimed in a 2009 study conducted for BlogHer and iVillage by Compass Partners that we've made purchasing decisions based on blog feedback.[6]

I didn't mind the commercialism at the conference so much as I was appalled by the lack of conversation about how women who blog could or should use our enormous power, either individually or collectively. Though the sponsors obviously get it, I'm not sure the women do. Actually, based on observable behavior, I'm pretty sure most of the women don't.

With the exception of a tilt toward green products and the opportunity for any swag the conference participants didn't want to take home with them to be recycled at the end of the meeting, we were in full-out "gimme" response mode. It was as though the meeting rooms were poppy fields where over a thousand individuals, intoxicated by the opiate of swag, wandered with dilated pupils, never looking around to ask one another, "How could we organize these 1,600 bloggers to make something happen?"

For example, if we don't like the violent toys our children are clamoring for, 1,600 bloggers could whip up an online protest and get them taken off the market in a nanosecond. If we don't want our daughters to be bombarded with images that reinforce the narrative that a handsome prince will come and rescue them from life's tough choices, we could wield the power of our purse and our pens to change the story. If we'd rather have fresh fruit and healthy whole grain snacks than ice cream and carbonated soft drinks in an effort to stave off obesity-related diseases, then all we have to do is gather the women and tell the marketers so.

Kamy Wicoff, founder of the SheWrites.com social media website for women writers, confided in me later, "I attended sessions where women were wringing their hands about the ethics of blogging about the free vacuum cleaners they had received instead of asking what leverage they could have with those companies to shape the products."

Consumer product marketers know women's precise value; their bottom line depends on it. But how much do we value ourselves as the purchasers? We could be the arbiters of every product that is sold in America if we chose to use our power strategically and consciously to mass our voices and make our demands.

Power unused is power useless.

•   •   •

## Blinking in a Clash of Titans

In a scene that was acted out among many progressive women across the country, Kathleen Turner and I were divided in our presidential candidate pick during the Democratic primary. We'd just spent eighteen months in 2006 and 2007 working together on her memoir, *Send Yourself Roses*. During that time, the field of candidates for the 2008 presidential primaries was beginning to take shape. Inevitably, we talked about politics quite a bit.

I supported Hillary Clinton from the start. While I didn't agree with all her positions on every issue, I was with her on over 80 percent, and I believed she was the one candidate with the political time-in-grade, the necessary ambition, and the fundraising potential to mount a successful race. Plus it was time. On the heels of George W. Bush's presidency, which was by the end of his eight years deemed a disaster by the American people across political persuasions, and with the economy heading into a tailspin, it was, or should have been, women's moment. A woman in the White House, and a reasonably progressive, pro-choice one no less, would be the logical culmination of the women's movement's last generation of work to advance equality.

So it shouldn't come as a surprise that I rolled my eyes when Turner announced to me in the summer of 2007 that she'd decided to support the upstart candidate Barack Obama, who was still early in his first Senate term. She was even going stumping for him in North Carolina's August heat. I thought it a naive choice, but Obama had the good sense to invite her to a meeting with a few prominent women and had asked directly for her support. That's good politics 101, and it paid off.

She'd been impressed with him, as I had been when I first heard him speak at the 2004 Democratic National Convention and later when I had a chance to talk with him soon after his election that fall to the U.S. Senate. Plus, like many others, I was thrilled that the diverse Democratic candidate lineup looked like America, whereas the Republicans were still mired in cookie-cutter white male political hegemony. Nevertheless, it seemed at the time that Hillary Clinton was surging to an unassailable lead for her party's nomination, so I didn't need to press too hard on Turner to join me in supporting her.

The reality shift that Obama and Clinton would be deadlocked for the nomination after the Super Tuesday primaries might not have been predicted in 2007, but we should have known something unpredictable would happen. It always does in politics.

Aldous Huxley wrote, "That men do not learn very much from the lessons of history is the most important of all the lessons of history." I'm here to tell you that this axiom holds true for women, too.

We've already seen that women fought for over seven decades to get the right to vote, if you count from the Seneca Falls convention in 1848, or 144 years if you count from the nation's founding year, when Abigail Adams unsuccessfully implored John to "remember the ladies." We've talked about the pattern that continued after 1920, when the women's right to vote was finally ratified as the nineteenth amendment to the Constitution. Instead of strategically consolidating its gains by developing a unified agenda and using its newfound political power collectively, the women's suffrage movement dissipated, squandering what could have become mass voting power for change and the elevation of women to our just portion of leadership roles much faster than has occurred. And we've discussed how 1992's touted "Year of the Woman," when women surged to the polls and voted in record numbers for Bill Clinton, a change from the Bush/Reagan past, and to send record numbers of women to Congress, was erased just two years later when those same women stayed home and we got the Gingrich Revolution—along with the crushingly sexist ascendancy of the fundamentalist hard right.

Since then, many organizations devoted to recruiting and electing women candidates have arisen, both on the Democratic and on the Republican sides of the aisle, as well as nonpartisan groups such as the Women's Campaign

Forum and the White House Project. They work hard. They've scored some successes, yet at this rate it will be another seventy years before we have gender parity in Congress. And who knows how long before we have a woman president on the heels of Hillary Clinton's loss to Barack Obama?

A Democratic party leader (a woman who asked not to be named but who was fuming about female voters' defections to Obama) told me bitterly, "How many far less than perfect male candidates have I worked for over the years? The first female president will not be perfect in every way either." Not that problematic policy positions or character flaws shouldn't be called out and subjected to public scrutiny, or that every woman should vote for any woman just because they share anatomy. I would not have supported a woman whose political philosophy I disagreed with completely—say a Phyllis Schlafly—nor could I have supported Sarah Palin regardless of her gender for a variety of reasons.

Given that women's needs are not always best represented by women politicians, just how much should we stick together as women to vote other women into higher office? I posed this question to philanthropist and political activist Barbara Lee, principal of the Barbara Lee Family Foundation, which funds nonpartisan research and training to encourage women of all stripes to run for office. Because she is also a leader in getting Democratic women elected to office, I wanted to know her thoughts on whether it is a positive good when, say, an ultraconservative woman like U.S. Representative from Minnesota Michele Bachmann or a Sarah Palin wins election.

Her view, and I hope she's right, is that both parties having a woman on the top of the ticket in 2008 was a game changer. She told me, "This history-making moment normalizes women's leadership in ways that change perceptions. It's a serious, important thing, fundamentally important to changing the power structure in America."

Lee continued, "Saying all that, in my private life, I always support women who are pro-choice and who are committed to ensuring that women retain control over their own lives. It's also important to me to encourage diversity in terms of race and class."

Considering that the United States ranks behind eighty-three other countries in the percentage of women in national office, it's high time we get on with the task of breaking our own gender barrier. But many women don't view that as an urgent problem. Younger women in particular didn't think that it was particularly important or significant to support a woman during the Democratic primaries, when for the most part the candidates had very similar positions on major issues. Many younger women, even self-identified feminists like then twenty-eight-year-old writer Courtney Martin, asked themselves whether they ought to vote for a woman and answered emphatically—perhaps even defiantly, "No!"[7]

But that disconnect between women's voting record and women's interests in seeing glass ceilings shattered is not a new phenomenon. The media loves to foment the notion of female "catfights" about almost everything, and they seemed to conjure a whole herd of cats during the 2008 election season. All the way back to 1994, activist Sherrye Henry wrote a book called *The Deep Divide,* whose title described the discrepancy between the equality women said they wanted and how they voted. Does this divide still exist? Are women our own worst enemy, as those who would like us to be claim?

It's time to ask these hard questions and demand answers from ourselves. Why do so many women shy away from using their power to vote for one of their own when given the chance? And especially when it happened to be a qualified candidate whose positions they largely agreed with? Other groups do this all the time without being negatively judged. Indeed, no one faulted the 96 percent of African American voters of both genders who voted for Obama in the general election. And the approximately 60 percent of white males who voted for the Republican candidate in 2004 and 2008 are more likely to be seen as a problem requiring the Democrats to change their positions than a recognition that the Republicans attract voters who want to maintain their entrenched power hegemony. Is it that women don't yet see ourselves as worthy of the highest office in the land? Is it that we simply don't see that the power is right there in our own hands—if only we choose to use it?[8]

Hillary Clinton's authoritative performance as the first viable woman candidate for president made her not just the possible tipping point, but also the inevitable fulcrum, despite her loss. The fact that she ran a credible candidacy is a huge leap forward toward normalizing women's leadership opportunities. And there's no doubt that if she had won, women would have been catapulted more quickly to that elusive equal playing field.

But if progressive women were determined to oppose Clinton for, say, her stance on the Iraq war (back before the country discovered after the election that Obama's position was pretty much the same as hers in the actual implementation), it would have been smart to form an organized group to go to Obama and make demands beforehand: "We'll throw our support to you if you will guarantee that you will do these things for us once elected." The list of demands could have included placing at the top of his agenda the Paycheck Fairness Act, guaranteeing women equal pay for equal work, and the Freedom of Choice Act, guaranteeing the civil right to make childbearing choices. Or making sure any stimulus package would produce jobs that women are as likely as men to pursue and any health plan would cover abortion as it covers other medical services. Or promising that all his Supreme Court appointments would be liberal, pro-choice women. And then they would have had the clout to hold his feet to the fire afterward to make sure he did fulfill those promises.

Because power was not used in that direct way, despite lip service to some of these issues during the campaign, Obama has not delivered. For example, he jettisoned family planning funding from the first stimulus package at the first hint of controversy. Though the first bill he signed—with much fanfare and surrounded by women members of Congress—was the Lilly Ledbetter Fair Pay Act—a significant bill allowing employees to seek recourse after the fact if they discover gender-based pay inequity—women are still waiting, as of April 2010, for measures like the Paycheck Fairness Act to secure real systemic change to rise to the top of his agenda.[9]

Similarly, though during the campaign he opposed the Hyde Amendment, banning coverage of abortion in government health plans, once elected he proactively sought to incorporate it into his health reform plans via a "compromise" measure called the Capps Amendment. And the end result was even worse: He signed an executive order enshrining the Hyde Amendment restrictions, and his press secretary refused to even acknowledge that the president had previously opposed the coverage restriction.[10]

All of this happened, is happening, because women, yet again, gave power away at the very moment when a push of the fulcrum could have tipped the political world into a completely different perception about women's willingness to use the significant power that we should by now know we possess and by all rights should be willing to wield.

Power ceded. A battle was won when a pro-choice president was elected; but the war for full equality and justice was lost soon afterward. No—given away freely. In exchange for—nothing.

We women who are activists in a thousand worthy social causes might justify in a thousand ways our right to decide as individuals what candidate to choose. And, indeed, it is our right. But is it the sum total of our responsibility? In my mind, no. If we truly want women to be respected by our society so we can lead lives that are not unfairly limited by laws and policies, we must demand significantly greater return for our votes in the future. That would be power used.

## Are Women an "Undervalued Asset Class"?

In September 2009, I was invited to a meeting convened by a venture capital firm to discuss its new women-centered investment fund. The invitation came via email from the Right Honorable Kim Campbell, the first woman prime minister of Canada, and it was written in a chatty, familiar style, though we'd never met.[11] "She most likely found my name among many in the address book of a women's leadership group we both belong to. (I couldn't help thinking of the late Israeli Prime Minister Golda Meir's admonition, "Don't be humble. You're not that good," since I was not in the financial category that would have made me a prospect for becoming an investor.)

The invitation was a soft sales pitch for the women's investment fund. Campbell, who currently teaches a course in gender and power at Harvard, introduced the purpose of the gathering like this: "Based on serious social science research on how gender plays out in various contexts, I have become very interested in recent research that explores the impact of women in management on a company's bottom line. There seems to be a complete disconnect between what the research shows and the willingness to put women in senior management or on boards."

That the disconnect Campbell wrote about exists wasn't big news. Still, my interest was piqued by the promise of hearing about a plan to do something about it. Besides, the speakers sounded stellar. They included Cherie Blair, human rights lawyer, philanthropist, and wife of former British Prime Minister Tony Blair, who was to deliver the keynote address. There would also be a dynamic panel discussion that included Blair, businesswoman Janet Hanson, chronicler of global women leaders Laura Liswood, and Dame Jenny Shipley, former prime minister of New Zealand (and the first woman to hold that position). That's considerable firepower.

As Katie Couric quipped of the 2009 California Woman's Conference, put on by the state's first lady, Maria Shriver, "I love the smell of estrogen in the afternoon."[12] Once there, I had a ball observing an amazing New Girls' Network unfold its interlocking connections before my very eyes as I settled into my cushy teal chair in a Citicorp Manhattan executive conference room to hear their presentations.

The room was buzzing with at least one hundred women and one man, a mid-career master's degree candidate in public administration at Harvard's Kennedy School of Government. I'll call him Michael Brown. Not inconsequentially, he also happened to be the managing director of the venture capital firm. He spoke briefly about the Women's Fund, explaining his idea—now his master's thesis—to secure investment capital from women with the promise to apply pressure on companies to comply with their critical mass goal of at least 30 percent women in top-ranking roles. So far, so good.[13]

Blair gave an engaging speech, sharing the travails of her working-class upbringing and her struggles to advance professionally, recalling a story from college when her professor told her that it was harder for women lawyers to speak before judges because their voices don't carry. Despite many advances, she said, "Women still don't get a fair crack of the whip." Still, she declared that women would not spend the next ten thousand years dominating men as men have spent the last ten thousand years dominating us. She hoped men and women would come together as equals and make it possible for everyone to achieve whatever it is they want to achieve.

How to reach that Utopia? Blair continued: "[I]nvesting in companies that actually do help women harness their potential, not just talking about it but actually making sure that they do have women leaders. . . . And of course, making money for your investors."

She reported that in six hundred companies across Europe, those that were run by females had higher revenues but used less capital than those run by men. "Investing in companies that use the talent, the energy, and the insight of women isn't just the right decision in terms of equity and justice; it's actually a wise decision." All very nice.

After she was done speaking, Blair joined the panel for more discussion, led off by Jenny Shipley. She started the conversation with data showing women make over 80 percent of the world's consumption decisions, a fact that (as we've already seen in the BlogHer example) would support it being a good idea to include women among top organizational decision-makers responsible for choosing what products will be marketed. I eagerly awaited hearing solutions I thought might be forthcoming about how to do this.

Shipley looked perfectly poised, if a bit starchy, and spoke with the forceful voice of someone who knew how to define her terms before anyone else did. She was knighted in 2009, and is a member of the Council of Women World Leaders, which Laura Liswood had incubated at Harvard.[14]

Liswood, who spoke next, literally wrote the book on women world leaders in a trailblazing book of interviews with fifteen women who were sitting or former presidents and prime ministers of nations. A Harvard MBA who later got her JD, she formerly served as managing director of global leadership and diversity for Goldman Sachs, where she remains a senior adviser and was a cofounder of the White House Project and the Council of Women World Leaders, of which she is secretary general.[15]

Liswood talked about what happens when she asks senior male leaders whether their organization advances people based on merit. No matter what the reality of the situation, they always believe the answer is yes. "I've never had a man say, 'I got to this point at the top of my organization because I was advantaged.' They always say that it was a meritocracy and there was a level playing field." The other groups (i.e., women and people of color), historically underrepresented, have a tendency to identify non-meritocratic parts of the system that get into the way, and she told some stories from her own experience to illustrate. Around the room, knowing laughter rippled.

The fourth panelist, Janet Hanson, is a founder and the CEO of 85 Broads, a global networking group of "20,000 trailblazing women who want to leverage their best personal and professional relationships to create greater success for themselves and each other." Started in 1997 by the few women executives at Goldman Sachs, "85 Broads" refers to the Goldman Sachs headquarters address, though it's no longer affiliated with the firm.[16]

The activist in me wanted to cheer when Hanson applauded Michael Brown for "talking about change through investing." But in the end her message disappointed by completely missing the point of why—to what end—such change is a good thing.

She made the analogy that when people began talking about global warming twenty years ago, investors didn't wait for 100 percent proof that the polar ice cap was melting. "Those very astute investors started to invest in clean tech projects and they made a fortune. I think this whole concept of getting early into what has traditionally been an undervalued asset class—and I would argue that that is what women are, if we can talk about investing in women in a way that guys get really excited about—I think that there's a conversation to be had there."

Seriously? Women are an *undervalued asset class that would cause the guys to get really excited?* Shades of dowries and bride prices.

I was reminded of hearing the award-winning Associated Press war correspondent Edie Lederer speak at the 2008 International Women's Media Foundation awards luncheon, where she told the audience that a man had once offered some sheep and cattle to buy her when she was covering a story in Afghanistan. She later learned this was the typical price of a thirteen-year-old virgin. That story was at least greeted with incredulous laughter at the luncheon. Here, in the opulent glass and steel Citicorp headquarters, a symbolic seat of macho monetary muscle, Hanson's categorization seemed to be accepted as merely an interesting insight.

In the end, we were being served warmed-over traditional gender roles in a sparkling new dish. It was the same-old, same-old of women being valued for their market potential. But women weren't going to be the ones initiating the bidding or making the valuation of our skills. Nor, it became clear, were the panel members going to be in charge of any real decision-making for this Women's Fund, even though some of them were serving on its advisory committee. Advisory boards, I learned a long time ago, are not the same as governance boards.

My foreboding was further reinforced after the panel when the first question from the audience was deflected by the panelists. "What do we do about it?" the woman who asked the question almost pleaded, referring to the many gender-based inequities that had been cited with such dismay by the speakers. I was eager to see how they'd sink their teeth into that one. After all, it does little good to rail against the machine unless one is also willing to organize to change the structure that supports the inequity.

Cherie Blair, however, gave a vanilla boilerplate answer about how there's no one answer. Women need mentors, she opined; it's all about choices and capabilities. The New Girls' Network had suddenly gone mute. When none of the panelists came up with anything more substantive, someone else stepped forward, as if bursting to present the solution: Michael Brown.

In lieu of his previously restrained demeanor, Brown popped back up to the podium seeming to have had a rush of testosterone. He explained again, this time more explicitly, that the Women's Fund's strategy would be to leverage the power of the capital raised from women by investing in companies where women already constituted more than 30 percent of senior management and board positions. They should consider investing in companies that had not yet reached the 30 percent mark only when they had the opportunity to use their investments as leverage to get those firms to comply with the critical mass goal.

Now that's power *used*.

Since the women, including myself, weren't using the enormous power that was in their hands, the lone man in the room darn well would—and who could criticize him for doing so? Obviously here was a man who did get excited by the opportunity. The undervalued assets in the room were not taking the hint, and therefore had rendered their considerable potential power flashy but virtually useless. I was speechless at the time, but with twenty-twenty hindsight, I know exactly how I would like to have seen the power in the room used. We must see that we have within ourselves everything we need to change our entire way of approaching and using the power we have effectively, not just to get the doors open, but to go through them, leading other women with us, for good.

## REDREAM: POWER-TO USED

All signs point to a world that wants the qualities women bring to the panorama of life and leadership at this moment. Yet we resist. We leave so much of our power unused, when multitudinous opportunities exist for us to take advantage of for our good and the good of society. How can we not just look but really see, so that we will use what we've got right here in our hands?

Looking back at my own power-unused story that began this chapter, I can honestly pinpoint the moment when I knew that crazy runaway car dream was exactly what I needed to realize I had the power to change my life if I chose to. Women collectively, I believe, need to appropriate the metaphor of a dream and use it to reconstruct our relationship with the incredible power we have at our disposal.

So, let's redream now—not a dream-while-sleeping kind of dream, but rather the kind we have while wide awake. Let's rewind the tape of the venture fund meeting to START, and dream that the story unfolded like this:

The room was buzzing with probably a hundred women and one man, Michael Brown, a mid-career master's degree candidate in public administration at Harvard's Kennedy School of Government and a partner in the women's venture capital firm, formed by Brown and Blair. They spoke briefly about their new Women's Fund, explaining their strategy to secure investment capital from women to invest as a reward and vote of confidence in Fortune 500 companies that have at least 30 percent women in their top executive ranks and on their boards, with the intent to dangle the carrot of greater investment based upon benchmarks met leading to full gender balance in the top decision-making roles. They said they'd consider investing in companies that had not yet reached the 30 percent mark only when they had the opportunity to use their investments as leverage to get those firms to comply with the critical mass goal.

The harmony that Blair and Brown described between women's financial progress and global prosperity was like a golden chord whose resonance increased throughout the day. The women on the stage—a New Girls' Network, as one of the more senior among us had put it—and women in the audience, many of whom had fought long and hard to reach the top levels of their professions, looked around in growing recognition of the collective power we possessed.

When Blair shared her life history, her rise to the top despite all obstacles, the degrading and chauvinist comments that she endured from professors, we didn't just chuckle in sympathy with our own similar life experiences. We got angry. We vowed to do something about it. "We need more than mentors," Blair said. "We need real structural change." And then she highlighted organizations that provide supportive assistance to women seeking to break through the glass ceilings still remaining, and to make sure quality daycare was available for the children.

She reported that in six hundred companies studied across Europe, those that were run by females had higher revenues but used less capital than those run by men. And that in the United States, McKinsey and Company studies had found similar results. "Investing in companies that use the talent, the energy, and the insight of women isn't just the right decision in terms of equity and justice; it's actually a wise decision." The woman next to me whispered that it was quite refreshing to be investors and leaders now that so much progress had been made for women, rather than passive objects of marketing manipulations. To which I quite agreed as I settled in to listen to the rest of the panel as it continued in the same vein.

Jenny Shipley said that if companies do not include women, we are prepared to take our business elsewhere or start our own firms to compete with them. She demonstrated the sophisticated social media website that has been created so women can efficiently mobilize consumer strikes and actions.

Laura Liswood told an amusing story about a boy who asked his mother if it was possible for a man to become president, since his country had elected three consecutive female leaders.

Janet Hanson pointed out that while our contributions have been traditionally undervalued, "Clearly we can show that smart companies do value women and want to have us not just as consumers but also as decision-makers for their own good as well as because it's the right thing to do."

By this time many of the women in the room were standing up to applaud. Several whipped out their checkbooks even before Blair went back to the podium to make the pitch for their investments. These women clearly understood the *potential* power-to accomplish almost anything right there in their hands. They got pretty excited by the prospects.

This is a dream we can make come true. The resources we need to stop resisting power and start using our estimable power-to for good are in our hands. The time for making excuses and rehashing grievances without action plans for change is over.

- Create a group; ask other women in your life to share their power-blocks. Create action plans for unblocking them.

- Look for your power-to keys that are already in your hands. What are they? What helped you to see them?

- What are you going to do to use them now?

Progress without Co-opting

# keli**goff**

Keli Goff has strong opinions about how the political landscape is changing. The old equations that dictate voting patterns and electoral allegiance become more irrelevant with each passing year. "Many of the boundaries that divided previous generations have begun to fall away," Goff says. "Whereas twenty years ago it may have been realistic to assume that black women voters would support Shirley Chisholm's candidacy because of identity, today's black and female voters are more complex than that. In fact most younger voters are."

As a young black woman and a powerful voice in political commentary, thirty-year-old Goff embodies this change at the same time as she diagnoses it. Like many in her multicultural and multiracial generation, she lays claim to an identity and a set of views too complex to fit neatly with the agenda of a single movement. "Black women voters were beaten up in the last election cycle," she recalls. "People kept telling us to 'pick a team.'" The problem, she says, was that they didn't have one.

It was in response to the fierce identity politics of the 2008 Democratic primary that Goff wrote her first piece for the *Huffington Post*. What both "teams" appeared to miss, what Obama and Clinton supporters seemed equally to ignore, she explains, was that "there have been many gender and racial struggles unique to black women, overlooked by both white feminists and black men." She looks back on the experience as a turning point. "It was the first time I had ever exposed myself to such passionate and swift criticism." It was also the first time she had considered her position as a political communicator as one of power.

"Julian Bond, the civil rights legend, sent me a note telling me how much he appreciated my piece and that he had made a point to share it with others," she remembers. "This was particularly significant to me because there was a photo of Bond and the other civil rights heroes from the SNCC on my laptop screen saver as a little extra dose of inspiration for when I got started writing each day." It was a revelation, Goff continues, "to realize that someone I so admire, who had done so much to achieve racial equality, felt I had something important to contribute to the conversation on race and gender."

Bond's note had a special significance for Goff that, as she explained via email, it might not for many in her generation. "Younger blacks and younger women," she says, "have no first-hand experience with the civil rights or women's movements." As one consequence, Goff explains, old-guard black leaders are less popular among younger blacks, who see these figures fighting a battle of the past in large part irrelevant to the here and now. It becomes a tricky business to say what allegiance, if any, younger generations owe to the older movements that empowered them. Even many young people attuned to the struggles of the past don't see group affiliation as an important consideration when choosing a political candidate.

Goff credits her parents with her awareness of the battles fought on her generation's behalf. A "surprise" child and by far the youngest of her siblings, Goff found herself tagging along with her parents to political meetings and volunteering by their side. "They were of a different generation than my friends' parents," Goff explains. Being older, "they remembered segregation far more vividly and that gave them a different perspective." It was a perspective they were able to pass on to their daughter.

I have known and admired Goff for several years, since she worked for Fenton Communications, a public relations firm that at the time managed the SheSource database of women expert spokespersons that was founded by the White House Project. Her strong connection both with the traditional civil rights movement that led marches to desegregate schools, lunch counters, and just about everything else in the 1960s, and with the current crop of black leaders and activists who grew up with doors at least cracked halfway open mirrors in many respects the transitional state of the women's movement. All successful social movements change the social context that shapes the next generation. And all social movements eventually become co-opted—some more, some less, depending on both circumstances and leadership. They win just enough that they have too much to lose by staying on the cutting edge. They become insiders to an extent great enough to result in the kind of political splintering Goff has described. Sometimes they forget whose shoulders they stand on.

Goff has not forgotten. Still, her world is different enough from her parents' generation that she sees and supports a very different political alignment emerging.

At nine years old, Goff was already showing the free-thinking tendency that she would later identify in the character of her generation. "When I was nine," she remembers, "I picked my first presidential candidate. It was Richard Gephardt. I announced this at dinner, and my parents asked why I'd picked him. I said, 'I watched his TV commercials and I like him.'" In her book, *Party Crashing: How the Hip-Hop Generation Declared Political Independence*, Goff explains that the black community is evolving into a broad political spectrum, one that embraces a variety of issues and no longer necessarily votes along race or party lines. (Whether the 2008 presidential race, in which 96 percent of black voters voted for Obama, was an aberration from Goff's theory over the long term or will prove her wrong remains to be seen.)[1]

The trend is apparent in other communities and movements, too. Goff sees a similar dynamic in contemporary feminism, where "older women with more of a connection to the women's movement might think, *Before I die, I want to see a woman president.*" For many younger women, even those who hope to see the same, this might not be a compelling goal in itself or a reason to vote for one candidate over another. "It is a parallel situation," Goff says, "for younger blacks and younger women." The solidarity that once grew out of strong collective goals has waned in the face of legal and social victories.

"The media wants voter blocs," Goff says. "That's how they like to categorize things. But 'hyper-labeling' is increasingly irrelevant. Generic lumpings are going by the wayside." It is a hopeful vision of the future, which, as distinctions fade and identities blur, will demand a much greater tolerance of diversity and difference.

In the meantime this trend cannot help but attenuate the power of movements still working to turn theoretical justice into practical equality. As the country's young come to see themselves as individuals with composite identities, we are bound to revisit the issue of "intersectionality," of how overlapping aspects of identity interact and potentially create smaller, more specific groups of identification.

The questions that begin to emerge go to the heart of what identity means, whether the things we share because of gender or race justify dividing ourselves into groups, or if the uniqueness of individuals is too great for what Goff calls "generic lumpings." In the advice that Goff gives to younger women she hedges her bets. "Embrace what makes you different," she says, "whether it is your gender or your race or your ethnicity, but do not let it define you or limit the expectations you set for yourself." Goff's example is a testament to the fact that, if traditional divisions are on the way out, the distinct perspective built into your identity is a powerful thing to understand, to investigate, to honor, to share—and not to allow to become co-opted.[2]

# be unafraid:
# opt out of being co-opted

*"It's hard to fight an enemy who has outposts in your head."*

**—SALLY KEMPTON,** author[1]

- How does it happen that women can fail to launch rebellion after threatening to bring it on?

- What examples can you cite of times when women have refused to be co-opted?

- How do you get the enemy (*can't, don't, shouldn't, bad, wrong, ugly,* and other negative messages) out of your head when you find they are keeping you from moving forward?

I kept asking myself, as I encountered many examples of women being co-opted during the year I was researching this book: Why did we repeatedly step back and allow other deserving groups, such as African American men seeking the right to vote or returning male soldiers needing jobs, to fulfill their claims for justice and equality rather than moving up together, side by side? Why did Rosie the Riveter accede to the notion that it was perfectly acceptable and even desirable to be pushed out of the workplace and exiled to the kitchen, where she would be complicit in convincing young women of the next generation that once they married (young), their best life would be staying home, keeping house, and tending to their children? Why didn't the suffragists regroup in 1920 after they won the vote and put their organizing power behind a progressive social agenda or at least support the Equal Rights Amendment as suffragist Alice Paul urged them to do in order to keep the momentum going for women's rights?[2]

Why, all those many times in history when we would have had every right to shout out and bite the hands that fed us that crap, did we retreat from activism? To be sure, we have had the various "waves" of feminism because there have been many courageous women through the years and many instances when we have indeed fomented revolution. Otherwise, we wouldn't today be on the verge of the unlimited moment I keep speaking about. Still, we must honestly ask ourselves why today, when women have so many more opportunities, and so much more potential power, do we still placidly allow ourselves to be called an "undervalued asset class" without even raising an eyebrow?

Not one of us—not one of the one hundred or so ostensibly success-ful and worldly women in that Citicorp conference room at Cherie Blair's speech on behalf of the women's venture capital fund, described in chapter 3, challenged the phrase when Janet Hanson characterized women in this way, or her suggestion that the undervaluation of our purchasing power and talents was a good thing because it would "excite" male investors. I myself didn't even realize the significance of what she had said until weeks later, when I was reading the transcript. I was shocked at myself for not having been even mildly alert to its implications.

I can't fault Hanson for thinking in those terms; I know from her leadership of 85 Broads that she is passionately devoted to the organization because its mission is to empower and advance women. Like all of us, she has been socialized within a male-centric, power-over culture where women are as objectified in marketing terms as our physical attributes are objecti-fied in the *Sports Illustrated* swimsuit edition or a Barbie doll's body.

The Sally Kempton quote above is from an influential 1970 feminist manifesto, "Cutting Loose," an essay published in *Esquire* magazine. The "enemy" Kempton warned us about is like an alien that takes up residence in our minds and feeds us negative messages about ourselves and our capa-bilities. It's the voice that tells us that our valuation is below the market standard. Some of those implanted messages seem relatively benign—inertia, math anxiety, sexual passivity, a penchant for pointed-toed shoes with five-inch heels—while others are more blatantly harmful, such as negative self-images based on outdated gender stereotypes, unrealistic ideals about physical appearance or what constitutes happiness, fear of retribution. We have come of age within the primordial soup of a culture that undervalues an entire gender, and sometimes it feels like all we can do is stay afloat. And while men might have shaped the culture, women have bought into it, just as we bought the idea that free goodies at a blogging conference constitute a gift rather than a quasi-bribe to influence our behavior for the profit of the givers—and to buy our voices on the cheap.

We have all been co-opted in so many ways. In sociology, *co-option* describes the process by which an idea or practice from another source gets appropriated by a dominant culture. In this process of assimilation, the specific value, history, and meaning of the original idea or practice is often lost, and it persists as a hollow remnant of what it once was.

Individuals can get co-opted, too. It's not exactly like selling out. At least when you sell out, even though you lose your integrity, you pocket the profit. Selling out implies a conscious transaction, cutting a deal, and driving a bargain.

Co-option, on the other hand, happens silently, a series of small compromises, a chain reaction of resignations, a chipping away here or a minor capitulation there, so that you almost aren't even aware that it's going on. Sometimes it's part of a political compromise, and sometimes it's a change in behavior or language that we take on to get along in an alien environment, to avoid being controversial or rocking the boat. It hardly feels like a betrayal. In fact, it can feel just like ordinary survival, whether to an individual or to an entire social movement. But the results can be—and often are—devastating.

The story of James Chartrand illustrates how being co-opted by a dominant culture can insidiously distort the perceptions of even the strongest and smartest individuals.

# CHANGE YOUR UNDERPANTS, CHANGE YOUR LIFE

I was having a bad night, the kind of night where you're best off turning off your computer and going to bed. But instead I got online and read one last email from earlier that day, and it was the one that got its hooks into me. I opened a link to a December 14, 2009, post on the popular Copyblogger .com website titled "Why James Chartrand Wears Women's Underpants." Who could resist reading that one?

It was a first-person account of influential blogger and entrepreneur James Chartrand, founder of a successful web-based writing company called "Men with Pens." James, it turned out, was a woman.

Here's the story: After leaving a bad relationship, "James" had found herself with two young daughters, living in a "crappy, tiny apartment" in Quebec, where she had lived all her thirty-eight years, as I would later learn when I interviewed her by phone. She found herself flat broke and staring at a welfare application; public assistance increasingly seemed to be the only way to feed her children and pay her rent. She'd once had a nice job in a nice office, but those days were long past. She was highly educated, she had skills, including a talent for writing. But she was struggling.

"I didn't want to be in this situation," she wrote in the blog post in which she publicly confessed her "real" identity. "I'd thought that when you start over, make a clean break, life was supposed to get better, right? But here I was, out of money and out of choices."

She began to look for writing jobs on the Internet, jobs that paid ready cash. At first, she made meager wages—$1.50 an article, for a grand total of about $8 a week, from clients who derided her for working from home. She quickly learned not to mention that she had kids, or that she did her writing at her kitchen table. She worked hard, building her reputation and learning everything she could about writing for the web, and gradually she began to make it—to build a company in her name and hire employees.

"But . . . " Chartrand admitted in the piece, "it still wasn't really working. I was being turned down for gigs I should've gotten, for reasons I couldn't put a finger on."

Other people who did the same thing she did were earning more and more, while her pay rate seemed to have hit a wall. She knew her skills weren't the problem. So she tried to figure out what other writers were doing that brought them more money.

She soon intuited that it wasn't the work she did, her professionalism, or her skills that were causing the disparity. It was simply *who* she was, or rather who her clients perceived she was, and how that affected the value they placed on her work.

And so, one day, frustrated with her stagnating wages and her inability to gain any more ground, she tried something different. "I picked a name that sounded to me like it might convey a good business image. Like it might command respect." She submitted an application as "James Chartrand."

"My life changed that day," she writes. Jobs were easier to get, and clients treated her with significantly more consideration.

"There was no haggling. There were compliments; there was respect. Clients hired me quickly. . . . There were fewer requests for revisions—often none at all." She was earning significantly more than before, with fewer headaches, and more satisfied clients. All because of one simple change. Hardly anything at all, really. All she had to give up was her identity.

How could I not empathize with this fellow writer's story? After all, I had been there. I knew what it was like to be on my own, with kids to support, and nothing but my own wits to rely on. I'd read the studies that show customers rate their satisfaction higher when they have received services from white males than from females or people of color. And I recalled plenty of experiences where a man's words or work were accorded more value than mine, like the many times I contributed an idea to a group discussion and was ignored, yet when a man said exactly the same thing, it became gospel truth. Is there a woman who hasn't had this happen to her?[3]

The temptation to take on the stripes of the (male) people who are getting the respect and the gravy is strong, and it can seem like a blessed way out, maybe the only way. Torn between sympathy for James and anger at the situation that pushed her to change her identity to where the power is in the culture, I tossed and turned after I went to bed and found trying to sleep futile. I got up and emailed a request to info@menwithpens asking to interview her for this book because I felt I had to find out more about her and her motivations.

## IS LIFE TOO SHORT TO BE AN ACTIVIST?

By the time I got up the next morning, my inbox was buzzing with comments about James and her story. It was an object of heated debate on journalists' and women's listserves I subscribe to, as they circulated links to articles about James from numerous media outlets. There in the middle of them was an email reply from James agreeing to talk with me by phone.

As I prepared for our conversation, I mused about her description of her motivations: "I never wanted to be an activist, or to fight the world. I'm not interested in clawing my way up a ladder to a glass ceiling. Life's too short for that. I just want to earn a living and be respected for my skills. I want my kids to be happy and have access to what they need. I want them to go to university and have good opportunities in life."[4]

It's heartbreaking to me that in our half-finished feminist revolution, women still tend to isolate themselves, to think that their problems are individual concerns they must solve alone. We feel our lack of power to make change, because when one person tries to fight the system alone, she is, in fact, relatively powerless. It's when we *just* think of ourselves as individuals rather than reaching out to our sisters and brothers that things are likely to stay the same for the next woman who comes along. More than that, if we fail to recognize how our choices influence the world—either by reinforcing the status quo or challenging it—we're doomed to live lives of diminished possibilities.

How can life be too short to be an activist? Life for most women would be unbearably long had it not been for the many activists, known and nameless, who came before us. Although staying out of the fight may seem like the neutral option, in the battle for basic equality, there is no such thing as neutrality. In the words of Holocaust survivor Elie Wiesel upon accepting the Nobel Peace Prize: "Neutrality helps the oppressor, never the victim. Silence encourages the tormentor, never the tormented."[5] Even if we decide not to take a stand, in any dispute where basic justice is what's at stake, it's naive to pretend that our equivocation is not doing any harm.

In our lengthy phone conversation in mid-December 2009, Chartrand told me that she was opposed to taking a place among those who have been openly fighting for greater equality. "I don't want to be associated with activists or feminists because my personal associations with those words are not positive ones." She insisted she isn't politically apathetic: "I have causes I believe in—Greenpeace, animals, I don't like the military, everybody should have their own religion, they should marry who they want. . . . I have my beliefs and opinions. Going out in some mass riot rebellion to fight for women is not one of them. I don't think that this takes away from my personal values. And I don't think I've betrayed anyone because I never promised to do that either. I never stood there and said I'm going to fight for all womankind." Several times she repeated with clear rancor that she had been criticized for not "taking one for the team," and emphasized her unwillingness to do so.

"No, I'm gonna fight for me and my family first. And that might be very selfish but it's also very smart."

I don't have to tell you those words practically left me speechless.

The *Washington City Paper*'s Amanda Hess and others have noted that what James did went far beyond standing on the sidelines and not fighting for all womankind. She, in fact, not only assumed a male name; she assumed a hypermasculine identity that at times even disparaged women.

After all, she named her company *Men* with Pens! As Hess points out, the design of the Men with Pens website and logo "looks like it was directed by Michael Bay," and James caricatured "Mommybloggers" by alleging that these women try to "shave the balls" of males who comment at their sites and fail to recognize that men have an equal right to comment.

Hess also notes Chartrand *"used a photograph of a man silencing a woman* with his hand as the logo for a 'Men with Pens' role-playing game. When a few commenters pointed out that the photograph failed to create an 'inviting community for women,' Chartrand replied: 'Photography is very subjective. You see a woman being terrorized. I see a man helping a woman stay quiet so he can save her life.'"[6]

In retrospect, this image seems like an allegory for how James Chartrand justified her own big, ballsy posturing. The persona that she had created, she said, was helping a woman stay quiet, so that he could "save her life" by becoming the breadwinner that she never could. But this act of salvation by forced silencing contains the seeds of unsettling violence, even self-annihilation. And it buys right into the narrative of women as helpless creatures in need of masculine saving, a narrative that women have spent decades challenging.

That was just one of the many examples I could give of James overplaying the part, or perhaps she had simply become one with it.

I recalled the words of French existentialist philosopher Simone de Beauvoir, who said, "One is not born a woman; one becomes a woman," and imagined that James seems to have been so thoroughly co-opted by her stereotype of a male "enemy in her head" that she had become the very oppressor she sought to outsmart.[7]

In a blatant example I read on her website, James characterizes her young female employee, Taylor Lindstrom, as "perky" and "adorable," someone who "wowed" them enough for her to be allowed into their "boy's club." For what it's worth, in her conversation with me, James claimed that Taylor had written her own bio, a fact I can only attribute to a younger woman's absorption of the self-co-option modeling by her mentor and a total lack of awareness of her own history as a woman. In any case, there is absolutely no excuse for an older woman to give a younger one leave or perhaps encouragement to stereotype and even to discredit her own gender.

I got the impression that Chartrand truly believed she had no other choice. And I believe her when she says she *thinks* the fight for women's equality was not worth joining.

This bright, thoughtful woman who sounded charming on the phone has been so co-opted that she didn't realize the value of what she was giving up, her true power and voice, as well as the impact that she could have on the world—the real difference that she could make if, instead of taking on her "James" persona as a ruse, she had gone undercover in a controlled study and released the documented results to show how real and prevalent sexist bias is even today. That data could have served as a powerful tool to persuade employers to self-examine their own hiring policies and change them when needed, the way some orchestras now ask musicians to submit their resumes and tapes without names after being presented with similar evidence of gender bias.

So why was Chartrand speaking out now? The vulnerability of her male identity—the position she argued was a form of strength—was evident in the reason for her confession. She was "coming out" as a woman because someone who knew her secret was threatening to expose her identity. But even though her story paints in vivid colors the biased perceptions that hurt many women today, Chartrand remains unwilling to use her reluctant confession to start a protest or to goad people to examine (and change) their attitudes. Instead, she had even convinced herself that James's voice is her "real" voice, that her writing is no different than if she were using her real name—the name that she declined to reveal to me and the voice that had been co-opted so that she had silenced her authentic self. The admonition not to criticize someone until you have walked a mile in her shoes comes to mind. James would tell me that therefore I shouldn't criticize her. But I think it also suggests that once permanently in that other person's shoes, you inevitably see the world differently; therefore James's voice can no longer truly reflect herself as a woman.

Not surprisingly, she suspects someone who does know her real name will out her on that soon as well. And no doubt they will. As a wise friend once told me, you will be found out if you sing a song that is not your own.

Ironically, being an activist, at least in the sense of joining with others of like mind to eradicate the injustices that kept Chartrand's earnings unfairly low, is precisely what could enable her kids—both daughters—to have "good opportunities" in their future lives. Things might not be perfect—despite the generations of women who have fought long and hard for equal opportunities—but without the continued work of women who want to fight for change, and their allies, Chartrand can't expect her daughters to experience anything short of the same kind of discrimination she has faced.

## WOMEN'S WRITING IS ALWAYS CONTROVERSIAL

Writing opens you up to a particularly gut-wrenching kind of vulnerability, Chartrand said. No matter what sort of writing you do, your words are part of the fabric of your selfhood. Yet, even though distancing yourself from your writing may seem like the safer option, the best writing is always animated by the urgency and immediacy of the writer's authentic presence, behind the words.

That's true whether it's today, when some of our best fiction gets too often dismissed as "chick lit," which is always a disparaging designation, or in the past, when we were often vilified for stepping outside the bounds of propriety. But the book *Little Children,* by Tom Perrotta, is as Chick Lit as it gets, though it was written by a man, and quickly became a bestseller and a movie. I think this is a good example of what happens when men co-opt a genre that women are denigrated for—they get celebrated.[8]

This history has repeated itself, from George Sand and George Eliot; the Bronte sisters, who initially published under male pseudonyms; to Alice B. Sheldon, who, under the pseudonym of James Tiptree Jr., published some of the most revelatory science fiction of the twentieth century. (When Sheldon "came out" as a woman, many male readers adamantly refused to believe that she was actually the masterful voice behind the imaginative worlds that she created.) And then there are the more contemporary writers who cloak their gender in the ambiguity of initials—M. F. K. Fisher, P. D. James, J. K. Rowling.

In general, women who write face an uphill battle for recognition and reviews among the mandarins who determine literary fashion, even as women authors are increasingly well-represented in the bestseller lists. In major periodicals that publish literary fiction and serious nonfiction, such as the *New Yorker, Harper's,* and the *New York Review of Books,* there are twice the number of male bylines as there are women's, and the authorship of books that secure coveted reviews in the *New York Times Book Review* is similarly high in testosterone.[9]

## THE VICE PRESIDENT IN CHARGE OF FRIENDLY

Looking at the issues we face as women through a completely individualistic lens presents us with a problem, or maybe it's a just an excuse. I liken it to the so-called choice feminists who say that what the women's movement fought for was solely to give them options, and every option, including opting out of the workforce or total indifference to politics, is equally valid. It's individualism dressed up as feminism.

Without the experience of blatant discrimination, I understand that it's easy to get tricked into believing anything you decide to do has only to do with you and bears no relationship to larger social forces. But when people lose the ability to connect with the big picture, they also lose the ability to organize to make change. Bingo, co-opted, even if you're doing A-OK yourself.

It's like the first woman bank vice president in Odessa, Texas, in the mid-1970s, who was referred to by many—though not to her face—as the "vice president in charge of friendly." I first met her in 1974 because she worked for the bank that donated the office space I worked in to Planned Parenthood. That was about the time when women were breaking through into new roles and the bank knew it needed to appeal to women customers. So they brought in this woman, dressed for success in her navy square-shouldered suit and floppy tie, in charge of—nothing really, except showing that the bank had a woman executive. She just wandered around the bank and smiled, with no real power, no doubt drawing a paycheck significantly higher than the rest of the female bank employees who toiled in low-paying pink-collar jobs. And more importantly, she didn't bring other women along into her elevated status. Women "firsts" like her are often tempted to think they got there on their own, and so have no obligation to help other women. That's how they came to be dubbed "queen bees" by feminist activists. As former Secretary of State Madeleine Albright says, "There's a special place in hell for women who don't help other women."[10]

In a very real sense, co-opting never happens on the individual level alone. Every movement that encounters success is at risk of being co-opted. Because once you've tallied some victories, you suddenly have something to lose. And conversely, you have something of value, some capital to offer others.

As the scrappy outsiders, the underdogs in any society, when they have coalesced into a movement, tend to hold together, their eyes on the same prize. A movement's strength comes from its status as an insurrection. But as I observed and experienced many times in the reproductive rights movement as well as the larger women's movement, as it begins to realize its goal, it often splinters. While the principles behind the movement may not have changed, suddenly everything about it becomes disputable. Its goals, its spokespeople, its methods. Should we have a march; should we not have a march? Should we use the power of our brand and constituency to endorse political candidates who support women's rights, or should we avoid the risk of seeming partisan? Should we fight for abortion coverage, or should we give up on it since we aren't likely to win and might make some enemies in the process?

When you have nothing to lose, you have everything to gain by taking action and being edgy. You are galvanized against a common enemy. There are no spoils to divide. There is no hierarchy to assign. But when a movement gets serious, gets organized, and starts winning, disputes over strategy inevitably surface between the incrementalists who become cautious and risk-averse and those who want to go full bore with the purist version of the movement's mission.

If you have been through the process of movement-building and its aftermath, you are probably nodding your head knowingly. But this kind of internal debate does not need to lead to a frittering away of energies. In fact, internal debate can be the best indication of the health of a movement. In the feminist movement, challenges from women of color, lower-income women, gay women, transwomen, and others who've felt excluded from the mostly white, mostly middle-class ranks of movement leadership have done a great deal to hone feminist principles, change the tenor of the movement, and reveal underutilized alliances with other social justice causes.

But because younger women—women in their twenties, thirties, and even forties—typically have limited experience with what the women's movement was like, they may have a weaker commitment to the idea of a sisterhood, even if they readily accept the spoils that the movement has won them. Media commentator and analyst Keli Goff, profiled before this chapter, has written about this phenomenon among younger African Americans who did not live through the civil rights movement. She told me that younger African Americans "don't have the movement experience" and are less enthusiastic about supporting women politicians or politicians of color.[11] In her book, *Party Crashing: How the Hip-Hop Generation Declared Political Independence,* Goff discusses why there are fewer younger black movement leaders, why increasingly many don't believe leaders need to be confrontational in pursuit of civil rights, and why leaders who are identified first as black leaders are less popular among younger blacks.[12]

Young women and young African Americans, she says, didn't have the firsthand experience of the women's movement or the movement for civil rights to define and structure their experience of the world—they have inherited its advances, but their life experience is of its splintered aftermath.

From the perspective of young people today, the price of joining a movement may seem high, and the rewards underwhelming. So why fight for other people, when it's so hard just to be yourself? My answer is that even if we don't believe we have a direct stake in the matter we are advocating for, our society is at its best for all of us when no one is kicked to the curb and everyone is able to fully exercise her or his talents. Think back to the Vice President in Charge of Friendly in Odessa. Although it's impossible to know what exactly she was thinking—I never took the opportunity to ask back then, though now I wish I had—I can't imagine she was satisfied with the empty husk of authority that she was awarded. Even though the particulars of her scenario may be a thing of the past, how many times have we already documented women remaining in lower-clout positions, or given more limited portfolios, despite our demonstrated abilities? A movement can help change society's expectations, and relegate this wholesale wasting of human talent to the archives.

## "CATFIGHTS" AND FALSE CONSCIOUSNESS

The resistance to "taking one for the team"—a phrase James Chartrand used frequently as an epithet during her conversation with me and others—is reinforced by the stereotypes that surround women's interactions and relationships. Carrying the torch for a purported impossibility of female collaboration are the token female conservative commentators whose complete and utter co-optation enables them to serve as the far right's most effective bullies. Where calculating women in history have often coated poison words with honey, women like Ann Coulter and Michelle Malkin throw their daggers openly; their target is their own gender's power—in essence, they are aiming at themselves in exchange for substantial amounts of male protection money—protection of a sexist status quo. Ann Coulter has even bragged that she believes the United States would be a better place if women had never won the right to vote![13]

As I've said, we're still in the midst of an unfinished revolution. One highly effective way the prevailing culture can co-opt women in order to keep them in their traditional subordinate place, so men can continue wielding their accustomed power, is to belittle women's friendships.

Consider the cultural narrative favored by the *New York Times* and other mainstream media sources—that women can't get along, and that women never support other women. It's worse in the tabloid press, but even the gray lady loves to call out a "catfight." In a recent trend piece, "Backlash: Women Bullying Women at Work," the author—Mickey Meece, another woman with a man's name, go figure—investigates at great length and with various anecdotes (but not many facts) the awful way that women treat each other at work. But the statistic that kicks off the story contradicts its premise: As a matter of buried fact, it turns out that the majority of workplace bullies are men.[14]

Besides, the big overlooked point in this story is that men still determine the workplace culture in most instances, and men hold the majority of top power positions. Bullies will always pick on those with less power. And those who are oppressed tend to oppress others. That is the behavior they have learned.

So what's big or new about the story that women, who are less powerful already than men, are more likely to bully other women who have even less power? Women are overrepresented in the lowest tiers of workplace culture, and those on the bottom are the most likely to be the subjects of bullying. Thus, the subject of the article—women's bullying of other women in the workplace? It's just a statistical artifact.

But if you look at studies of decision-making groups, these investigations are finding that where there are more women, there is better behavior, better decisions, and less corruption. Why isn't that story the headline so that it would become "common knowledge" to replace the catfight myth?[15]

Here's why. Because the social forces of inertia and resistance to change are incredibly strong, any step forward is likely to be presented in the old frameworks: More women gain power, therefore, more women are bullies.

Even worse, the status quo begins to adopt the language that once seemed so revolutionary. Take "choice," for instance. In the pre-Roe days of the abortion rights movement, the notion that it was a woman's decision to make whether she would continue a pregnancy was nothing short of radical. For generations, women's bodies had been pathologized and colonized; the deed of ownership of women's bodies passed from fathers to husbands. Well into my adult life, marital rape was still legal and relatively unquestioned. In this context, insisting on the right and capacity of a woman to make her own choices about her reproductive potential was not only necessary, it could be controversial and shocking.

However, many of us in the reproductive justice movement have known for a while now that the word *choice* has lost a great deal of its potency. Sometimes it seems as though anything at all—plastic surgery, dangerous diets, "opting out" of rewarding careers—can be justified as a woman's choice, and, more important, it seems that this justification puts the choices above comment. How much real women actually use this logical framework to justify compromised decisions is beside the point; it is the favored meme of lifestyle marketers. Indeed, *choice* has lost its power in direct proportion to its rise as a marketing gimmick, a way of pushing product. Claiming that something is a "choice" is no longer an assertion of a right, but a defense against critique. It's been co-opted.

Indeed, the anti-choice movement has recently wholeheartedly and with little sense of its own irony adopted the language of choice. "Choose life" is the message of Sarah Palin and Focus on the Family when they push their restrictive and unwanted agenda on American women. It goes unspoken, and hardly questioned, that their imprecations to "choose life" are in service of a policy platform that would make it no choice at all, but an obligation, enforced upon all women, to carry every pregnancy to term.

When the conceptual frames through which we view and understand the world become co-opted, we lose ourselves. Our language becomes murky. We lose the moral clarity that had previously drawn us together.

Gail Collins, in her history of the second-wave women's movement, *When Everything Changed,* cites an astonishing statistic from the 1960s: "In a survey for the *Saturday Evening Post*—at a time when it was both legal and common to declare some jobs off-limits for women, and to automatically pay them less in others—George Gallup found that only 19 percent of married women and 29 percent of single women said there was sex discrimination in the professions."[16] "The way things are" was the enemy in these *Mad Men*–era women's heads. And for women like this who couldn't see the evidence of their own limitations, feminist consciousness-raising groups were born!

More recently, women had to wage the battle to get contraceptive coverage by insurance plans some thirty-five years after the birth control pill was approved by the FDA, not because the inequity had just then occurred but because it had just then been noticed, after we gathered the data to show most plans failed to cover birth control even if they covered other prescription drugs such as Viagra. Most of us had simply paid for pills without thinking, *This is unfair.* That, too, was "just the way things were" for far too long.

People who have been co-opted can be perfectly sincere and earnest in their beliefs, and miss what is plainly in front of them. Or, more important, misjudge themselves, "undervalue their own assets," and fail to recognize the power that they have.

## SOMETIMES WE SCARE OURSELVES

The late liberal journalist Molly Ivins loved to tell the story about the Texas raconteur and radio host John Henry Faulk, whose mother sent him and his friend Boots, when they were boys, to get rid of a harmless chicken snake that had been lurking in the henhouse on their farm. The boys searched the nests and suddenly found themselves face-to-face with the offending snake, which was lounging nonchalantly on a top shelf in the chickens' residence. This gave them such a fright that they turned and barreled out of the henhouse so quickly that they banged themselves up and took the door off its hinges. When John Henry's exasperated mother reminded them that a chicken snake couldn't hurt them, Boots replied, "Yes ma'am, but there's some things'll scare you so bad you hurt yourself."[17]

There are real, authentic threats in the world—threats to our physical, material, and emotional security. But it's also true that fear is often exploited to maintain the status quo. This is evident at every level of our society, from the macro-level, where the politics of fear is used to perpetuate injustice, down to the micro-level of our personal lives, where fear can keep women within narrow constraints of appropriate and "safe" behavior. The sickening wave of victim blaming that follows any public accusation of rape or sexual assault, or sometimes even murder, sends powerful messages about what women can and cannot do. And the crippling sting of personal rejection that many women feel when they speak out with new ideas and are ignored or shot down keeps some of us from daring to think boldly.

Women who have already been boundary breakers by virtue of being different in some way from what society considers the norm may have an edge against getting co-opted by the dominant culture. E. J. Graff, a journalist and resident scholar at the Brandeis Women's Studies Research Center, told me about delivering her lecture about careers to every younger woman she mentors: "No one will notice you're good if you don't point it out. SAY YES when you are scared you're not good enough for an assignment, and then work your *tuchas* off to *be* that good. Many women do have internal censors that are overactive and need to be overcome. Being a good girl works for you in school but against you in worklife."

She and her ex-girlfriend used to steel one another's nerves before a negotiation by urging, "BE A BOY." She admits, "Of course we were over-simplifying . . . but it worked. We learned to accept rejection and keep pitching, and to do what we wanted and get rewarded for it. It's hard. It's scary. It feels unnatural. It's worth it."

She thinks that breaking boundaries of what is considered "nice" behavior has been easier for lesbians. Why? "We've already had to overcome the 'but that's masculine' problem. So what?! We're already seen that way. Second, we have to learn to make the first move romantically or live alone with a cat (which I can't do, since I'm allergic). That means we have to prac-tice surviving rejection." And finally, she says, "no one is going to support us. We can't even really dream about it. If my ex and I wanted to pay the mortgage, we had to take risks."

Graff is quick to say that she's not implying that every straight woman is waiting for Prince Charming. "In fact, I see a lot of younger straight women now who are courageous about taking calculated (albeit terrifying!) risks and throwing themselves into going for what they want, who are excel-lent at assembling their backup teams, strategizing about where they want to go, and then being as gutsy as they wanna be." She speculates, "Maybe it's Title IX or feminism, but I am wowed by it."[18]

I can remember being a vulnerable pregnant teen who couldn't speak up for myself, then a young woman who felt totally powerless to provide for my children. I was lucky enough to have opportunities to fight for the rights of others; that helped me become more secure in myself. I got stron-ger and less vulnerable in the doing. Coming clean about one's own story, one's truth, is a big part of that. It's also one of the best ways to avoid being co-opted. Remember, co-option happens when women undervalue their own strength, their own selves. When you put yourself out there, signing your name to your beliefs and backing them up with your actions, you are forced to make an honest reckoning of yourself—your skills, your talents, and your strengths, perhaps discovering capabilities you never realized you had before. I truly believe that a woman who knows herself, and who thus knows her true value, can never be frightened into being co-opted.

## SARAH PALIN AND HILLARY CLINTON: TWO SIDES OF THE CO-OPTED COIN

You don't have to wear male drag to be co-opted. In fact, co-option becomes even more dangerous when it masquerades as liberation. Want evidence? Look no further than the 2008 presidential election, when most of us in the Lower 48 got our first introduction to Sarah Palin.

She splashed upon the scene with her aggressively paleoconservative speech at the Republican National Convention, even though her nativist rhetoric sounded so much like homespun wisdom that its extremism was assiduously overlooked by most commentators. Suddenly, we were all a little too familiar with the steep angle of her red peep-toed stilettos, eyes glinting behind those titanium frameless glasses that would become a hot item. And then came the exhausting unspooling of scandals and gaffes: the political missteps and accusations of abuse of power; the rumors about her personal life; the embarrassing interviews; the expensive, brand-new clothing; her profound lack of knowledge about government, foreign affairs, and public policy. None of this mattered to her supporters, however, who were complicit in the lifting up of their idol—she who claimed to be a feminist while not championing a single public policy that would help women advance.

Palin could not have existed without Hillary Clinton. I mean this in the general sense that it would have been nearly impossible for a woman like Sarah Palin to ascend the ranks of political power had it not been for women of Clinton's generation, who broke the ground, changed the laws, and challenged the assumptions. But I also mean it in a very specific way.

Palin would not have been elevated to the role of vice presidential candidate without Clinton's campaign, which demonstrated the enormous potential of galvanized female voters. It's an open secret that Palin was chosen to make a play for those women voters, widely, if wrongly, perceived by the political punditry as up for grabs after their candidate's loss. Palin was meant to lead us over to the red side, Pied Piper–like.

Rosalind Hinton, a professor of religion at DePaul University, pinpointed Palin's designated role in the campaign: "She was a trophy," she told me, comparing her to Cindy McCain, Senator John McCain's "trophy wife." She was what the right wing hoisted as their trophy of how much they had co-opted us, captured our vocabulary, our ambitions, and our ideals.[19]

This is not what they got. Instead they got a woman, who, as the title of her memoir, *Going Rogue,* suggests, had an almost pathological confidence in her own abilities and her own instincts. The women of Hillary Clinton's generation, who had played half-court basketball with "girl's rules," had secured for younger women like Sarah Palin the full-court equality that came with Title IX. "Sarah Barracuda" had honed her competitive edge in high school basketball, and she was bold enough to break from the McCain campaign and seemingly run her own race, going for her own slam dunks even if they did not contribute to her team's score. In her own words, she "did not blink."

There is something admirable in this, I must admit. In a world where women often hold back from speaking out, her bluster was, at times, refreshing. The problem is that Palin didn't use her roguishness, her willingness to break with the pack, for the good of anyone not so fortunate or privileged as she is. Few of the policies that she supported would have improved the lives, opportunities, and position of women in this country. Indeed, many of her policy positions would have made women's lives worse. She remains a creature of pure ambition, someone willing to play the political game not for the difference that she can make in people's lives, but for the points she can score. How like a man!

Clinton, on the other hand, both created and bore the brunt of the flip side of the co-option coin. Many women were reluctant to support Hillary's candidacy. To be sure, some had well-reasoned arguments for why they favored Barack Obama, comparing, for instance, the two candidates' voting records on the war in Iraq. But it seemed as though a fair number of women scared themselves away from supporting Clinton. What if she wasn't good enough? What if she was nominated—and didn't win? What would it say about women like them? Just like John Henry and Boots in the henhouse, there are some things that'll scare you so bad you'll hurt yourself—and your own interests.

Women, and men, applied unprecedented scrutiny to Clinton's candidacy and her fitness for the job. She was pressed mercilessly to bow out when no male candidate of her standing in the race had ever received such treatment. She was mocked: her ankles, her laugh, her pantsuits, the Hillary Nutcracker that was sold by the millions. Would that the average American had subjected George W. Bush to that kind of sustained examination!

There was the "Not Ready for One of Us" argument made by Donna Brazile, Al Gore's presidential campaign manager and now a political consultant, who observed that despite much progress, oppressed groups still tend to assume the rest of society "isn't ready for one of us." That's why more whites than blacks initially said America was ready for a black president and more men than women said America was ready for a woman president.

There were the "I Love Hillary BUT" arguments: But she was carrying too much of Bill's baggage. But she was too polarizing. But she should remain a senator, where she's so effective. And on and on. Many forgot how she overcame the same "buts" in 2000 when she first ran for the Senate. These women worried that if Clinton beat out Obama for the Democratic nomination, she wouldn't be able to hold her own against McCain. They worried that their support for her would ensure a Republican win, and that would ultimately set back their accomplishments for women.

Then there were "Media Fears": The national media tends to trash any leading candidate. Still, women are singled out for criticism if they appear too "feminine" on one hand or too tough on the other. And here's where Clinton co-opted herself by trying to walk such a fine line that she was sure to lose her balance at some point. She would say things like, "I'm proud to be running to be the first woman president, but I'm not running because I'm a woman."[20] She would have lived her authenticity and people would have responded more favorably to her had she taken full-throated pride in the groundbreaking nature of her candidacy and walked directly into the controversy rather than backing away from it. As a previous female presidential candidate, Patricia Schroeder once quipped when asked if she was running as a woman, "What choice do I have?"

I call this gratuitous bashing by the media the "Maureen Dowd effect" after one of its most able practitioners. Dowd wrote that, as first lady, Clinton "showed off a long parade of unflattering outfits and unnervingly changing hairdos," and complained that when Clinton "expressed outrage about Iraq," she "ended up sounding like a mother whose teenage son has not cleaned up his room." In a media that rewards conflict, the kind of incessant and content-free sniping practiced by Dowd is all too typical. It's a variant of "if it bleeds, it leads," but with media critics creating the appearance of bloodshed and controversy to sell copy in a glutted, twenty-four-hour-news marketplace.

Now, Maureen Dowd can't help herself. Snark is her specialty. With Hillary Clinton, Dowd especially loved to use misogynist venom—calling her a "dominatrix" who "flick[s] the whip." But in the same paragraph she let slide Obama's typical male way of diminishing women with his adorable wink that, she opined, would have made warmer-blooded women "melt," but not the "unapproachable" Hillary. Go figure that these things came from someone who would never have her byline featured on the *New York Times* op-ed page were it not for women like Anna Quindlen, who shattered that glass ceiling for her.

Co-option is fertile ground that allowed these reservations about a woman candidate, based I suggest in fear, to sprout into deadly nightshade.

And the weed killer that can extirpate these fears is challenging them head-on by leveraging the controversy, calling attention to the double standards, raising awareness about the hypocrisies, and establishing the true value of women's leadership and individual women leaders. This means also unabashedly calling out the rotten policies of someone like Sarah Palin while simultaneously decrying the sexism that runs through some of the critique against her.

Remember, fear is fuel for controversy, but it can also function solely to shut down discussion. The best way to keep fear at bay is to keep the conversation going, and use the controversy constructively.

## **power**tool number four

CONTROVERSY: embrace controversy. it gives you a platform. it nudges you to clarity. it is a teacher, a source of strength, and your friend, especially if you are trying to make a change.

•   •   •

## CO-OPTING THE HEART

Now let us get to sex. The dark mechanisms of co-option may take firmest root in the most intimate and personal details of our lives—the ways we define our sexual and romantic relationships to others, the models we seek to emulate, and the fantasies in which we indulge. This facet of co-option is where we can witness most clearly its imperative toward self-annihilation, the way it demolishes the kernel of our individual identities. And despite the sexual revolution, and the radically different norms around women's sexuality and desires that have taken shape in the past generation, many women still long to be "swept away" by a powerful male protagonist instead of being the hero (or co-hero) of their own lives; or, regardless of sexual orientation, they feel they are whole persons only when they are in relationships.

In 2008, in bookstores across the country, teenage girls and their mothers, older women unaccompanied by daughters, and the odd boy decked out in gloomy goth togs stood waiting for the stroke of midnight. That time marked the release of the new—and last—volume of the Twilight series, Stephenie Meyer's best-selling stories about a nonpracticing high school vampire named Edward Cullen and his wispy inamorata, Bella Swan.

The Twilight books have sold millions upon millions of copies, and given rise to three blockbuster movies so far. And the intense romantic narrative has exerted an iron-grip on the imaginations of many young (and not so young) women. Although the target demographic for the Twilight books is and remains teenage girls, substantial numbers of older women—dubbed Twilight Moms, by themselves and the eager media—have also fallen under Edward Cullen's thrall.

There is nothing new about the kind of story these books tell. Unlike Buffy in *Buffy the Vampire Slayer*, Joss Whedon's highly enjoyable series about a teenage girl who inherits the duty of ridding the world of vampires, Bella Swan is not the vampire's master, but rather his willing victim. And who wouldn't be? Edward Cullen, as he is depicted by Meyer, is the most perfect man who ever lived. The handsome prince in twenty-first-century attire. He is more than one hundred years old—and has two Harvard degrees!—and yet inhabits the flawless body of a teenager, with the adamantine beauty of a sculpture. His family, ethical "vegetarian" vampires who abstain from drinking human blood, are fabulously wealthy. He drives expensive cars. Bella Swan is the new girl in the town of Forks, Washington, and the one girl whose thoughts the mind-reading Edward cannot penetrate. The first three books of the series—*Twilight, New Moon,* and *Eclipse*—all trace the development of the unconsummated love between these two. Edward holds back from physical demonstrations of his romantic attraction for Bella because if he gives in to one carnal appetite, his sexual desires, he may give in to another, his lust for human blood. Bella, meanwhile, begs him to make her a vampire like him, getting herself into dangerous situations from which she must be saved, a maiden in distress, by the heroic Edward.

As Christine Seifert characterizes it in *Bitch* magazine, this is "abstinence porn" for a new generation of schoolkids raised on abstinence-only education, which objectifies young women just as intensely as real porn, by putting the key to their identity in male hands. It's worth noting that in the fourth book of the series, *Breaking Dawn,* Bella and Edward are married. They consummate their desire, and she quickly becomes pregnant—and spends half the book on bed rest.

Laura Miller, writing in *Salon,* dissects how the Twilight series puts its female protagonist in the subordinate position, and then makes that position seem like it's powerful. The cleverest co-option technique of them all, akin to the adage "the hand that rocks the cradle rules the world" that was used to argue women's suffrage was unnecessary one hundred years ago.

Bella Swan, Miller observes, is a perfect cipher; she is unremarkable, unreadable, with seemingly no interests aside from her adoration of Edward Cullen, and no distinguishing traits aside from her clumsiness. Indeed, when she almost drowns herself in despair after Edward has left her in the second volume of the series, she doesn't see her own life flash before her eyes—she sees his face. But Edward's love for her is what elevates her above the crowd of her peers. Tellingly, she hasn't done anything to distinguish herself from the others—except for being unreadable by the man she loves. (Unfortunately, Miller points out, Meyer hasn't made Bella's mysterious personality anything worth getting to know.)

"The chief point of this story is that the couple aren't equals," writes Miller, who continues: "Some things, it seems, are even harder to kill than vampires. The traditional feminine fantasy of being delivered from obscurity by a dazzling, powerful man, of needing to do no more to prove or find yourself than win his devotion, of being guarded from all life's vicissitudes by his boundless strength and wealth—all this turns out to be a difficult dream to leave behind. Vampires have long served to remind us of the parts of our own psyches that seduce us, sapping our will and autonomy, dragging us back into the past. And they walk among us to this day."[21]

The more troubling elements of the story go quite deep. Blogger Kar3ning compared Edward's behavior to the list of abusive traits found on the National Domestic Violence Hotline, and found that he fit the profile of a classic abusive personality.[22]

As Seifert, writing in *Bitch,* observes, "What's really frightening is Bella and Edward's honeymoon scene. Edward, lost in his own lust, 'makes love' so violently to Bella that she wakes up the next morning covered in bruises, the headboard in ruins from Edward's romp. And guess what? Bella likes it. In fact, she loves it. She even tries to hide her bruises so Edward won't feel bad."[23] There is even a subplot in the last book of the series, where Bella's pregnancy threatens her life, suggesting that she will die to save her and Edward's unborn progeny.

The loss of intention that is exemplified by the Twilight series resonates with the phenomenon of teen pregnancy again as a *choice,* not as accident, the belief that "he'll love me if I have this baby." Young women whose lives feel so out of their own hands, who need external, male validation for their existence so badly, that the only choice they feel they have is to try to become pregnant. That's the only secure identity that they believe might demonstrate their power and influence.

Why would our daughters fall for this, or for the reactionary strains of Twilight? In an era where we'd like to believe that all doors are thrown open to them, that nothing can stand in their way, why would they fall for the utterly nonempowering story of a young woman who is enraptured and enthralled and completely defined by a man who alternately rejects her and threatens to consume her? Why would they identify with the story of another teenager whose identity is more and more based on her sexual "purity"?

There's a thrill to powerlessness, one that girls are trained since early childhood to recognize and even to welcome. How many times do you need to hear the same tale—the storybook princess, rescued from danger by a dauntless prince—for it to form a pattern in your brain, to shape your perceptions and thus your behaviors?

Many incisive writers have taken on the princess culture, including Peggy Orenstein, Dan Cook, and Mary Hoffman.[24] Yet its tentacles insinuate themselves into the stories of girlhood, training us from an early age to deny ourselves power—to try to be the chosen one, not the one who does the choosing.

In the 1990s, the Riot Grrrl movement embodied the "third wave" among young feminist activists. The young women, many of them teens and college students, who formed the dynamic core of the movement recognized that they began ceding power in adolescence, and so they took their inspiration and symbols from a time in their lives when they had felt powerful and omnipotent: girlhood. The movement sought to reclaim that feeling of limitless possibility—of unequivocally feeling like the subject of your own story and the one who called the shots—and to take those traits and carry them further into adult life.[25]

But it's uncertain that such a movement could exist now. Just as adult women have been co-opted, so have our daughters. Perfect little girlish icons—Rainbow Brite, Dora the Explorer—have gone through the makeover cycle, acquiring shapelier bodies, hair that remains suspended as though permanently in an ocean breeze, jewelry, and makeup. Not quite as hyper-sexualized as best-selling Bratz dolls, with their pneumatic lips and their thong underwear accessories, but nonetheless underscoring the message that appearance is paramount, and that the only kind of look you should go for is "come-hither."

There's nothing more co-opting than being told that the only way to define yourself—to stake out what makes you unique—is by relying on the approval of boys and men who may choose you, or pass you by. The occasional escapist fantasy is fine if you are aware of what you're doing. But women always need to be alert to the underlying implications and underlying values of the narratives we consume. Creating controversy where it's deserved—for instance pointing out abusive elements of a beloved character's personality—not only gets people thinking, it can help shape the arc of the stories we hope to live.

## OPT OUT OF BEING CO-OPTED: PLAY YOUR OWN GAME

It is important to address the internal co-option demons because women's self-perception that men are better, smarter, more productive, more logical, and more reasonable is like an infectious disease that spreads the fear that leads us to be co-opted.

In 2008, three researchers at the University of Padua decided to investigate why women were so rare in the upper echelons of competitive chess; fewer than 5 percent of registered tournament players are women, and women compose only 1 percent of grand masters. Chess is a game of intellectual skill and calculation, so it would seem that women, who have shown themselves to be intellectual equals with men when given the chance, should be pulling up alongside men in this capacity. How much of an effect does perception have on performance?

According to their results, when players did not know the gender of their opponents, men and women played equally well. When women were told that they were playing against a male, their performance decreased dramatically. However, when they were (falsely) told that they were competing against another woman, they again played as well as their male opponents.[26]

In every challenge there is an opportunity. In a co-opted world, she who avoids co-option can retain a special kind of power. And even if the external stereotypes and internal barriers that so often accompany gender in the United States seem stubbornly fixed, sometimes being a woman—the exception to the rule, the non-normative case—can give you an unexpected edge, if you stay clear and listen to your own mind.

Writer Lori Valdala Bizzoco is a former PR executive in her late thirties, who happens to be a talented poker player. One evening, after our writing class, where we met, she told me about her thrilling run of success in tournament poker not long ago. She hadn't learned the rules of the game until shortly before she was invited to a game at an "underground" poker circuit in New York City.

This was the first time she had played for money. Lori described taking an elevator up to what looked like a doctor's waiting room; her friend gave the high sign to a woman behind a desk, who buzzed them in to the poker den: She saw seven or eight tables of men playing cards in near-silence. At first, Lori just sat and watched. And talked. The quiet made her uncomfortable.

Eventually, she felt comfortable enough to ante up and wager some of her chips. Unlike many of the "serious" players in the room, she had not studied strategy and had little knowledge of how to calculate the probability of different outcomes. But she had something that the men did not: a natural confidence in her own ability to read people. She trusted her intuition, listened to her gut, and won. Her initial run of good luck reinforced her feelings, and she surprised the men who had initially dismissed her as a chatterbox by beating them repeatedly. And while she could read them, they seemed unable to read her.

"*That's my advantage,*" she recalls thinking. "*This is my opportunity.* Not because I'm a woman—it was not superficial difference. It was about having a different strategy, a different way of thinking, and the men are not going to be able to think the way I think. Doesn't matter how well they may know women, they're not going to be able to think the way I'm thinking when I play. . . . They didn't know how to figure me out."

As she became more interested in the game, she followed the lead of the men she played against and started schooling herself on strategy. She began to play online, where she could not read people's faces. The natural gift she had initially shown began to wear thin. By following the (male) pack, and becoming more of a systematic and typically strategic player, Lori lost her edge. So now she's opting out of being co-opted by going back to relying on her own innate abilities to play the game—with human beings.

## OPT OUT OF BEING CO-OPTED:
## CONFRONT THE ENEMY IN THEIR HEADS

The esteemed editors of *Publisher's Weekly* searched high and low, but were somehow unable to come up with even one book by a woman worthy of inclusion in their picks for the top ten books of 2009. (Of the names on their all-male list, by the way, only one author was not white.) Louisa Ermelino, the *Publisher's Weekly* editor who was designated as sacrificial lamb when this disparity began to draw the ire and ridicule of serious writers and readers, insisted that the list was impartial: "We ignored gender and genre and who had the buzz."

In Katha Pollitt's trenchant characterization: "That makes the editors of *PW* the only people on earth who are not only totally unaffected by the society in which they live, but who have no subconscious."[27] Pollitt mentions the countless studies that have been done demonstrating how gender affects perception of capabilities. It affects the kind of scrutiny we apply to people and their work, and the sorts of conclusions we draw. Moreover, it's hard to dispute that women's fiction is diminished, even ridiculed, by serious critics who find accounts of women's quest for love, family, and balance banal even as they celebrate the same kinds of narratives written by men. But the way to fight back isn't to get sucked into changing one's own identity; it is by being who you are and making the controversy your power tool.

Kamy Wicoff, whose social networking site, SheWrites.com, is a supportive online community of women writers, used the controversy over the *Publisher's Weekly* story masterfully to draw attention to the outrage and to rally more women who write or care about good writing to take on *Publisher's Weekly*. By riding into the storm instead of becoming defensive or backing away from it, she quickly attracted thousands of new members to her fledgling site and generated media attention that raised its profile.

Embracing controversy is a way of challenging the status quo, but it is also a way of maintaining clarity of vision, and clarity of intention, that characterizes revolutions at their most powerful. Embracing controversy draws people to a cause—by encouraging them to examine their principles and come to terms with what they have to lose and gain. Controversy sharpens perceptions; it forces people to take sides and arrive at conclusions that they were perhaps resisting. You have to face the fear that causes you to become co-opted in the first place, and doing that is most gratifying.

## STOP-LOSS ORDER:
## GAINING FREEDOM WITHOUT LOSING OURSELVES

"[L]ogic told me that the loss of my real name was a small concession for the ability to be able to support my family and ensure their financial security for years to come. Truth be told, if just a name and perception of gender creates such different levels of respect and income for a person, it says a lot more about the world than it does about me."[28]

The healthy part of this statement is that James Chartrand realizes the problem is not with her but with others who saw her as less competent when she presented herself as a woman. But does it not break your heart to imagine someone truly believing that sacrificing her authentic identity is a "small concession"?

When we think we can be chameleons in order to save ourselves, we remain emotionally vulnerable; the skin can shed at any time to reveal the secret hidden within. And then what? It is like having massive plastic surgery to comport with social norms of female pulchritude that we consider unjust. And even when the counterfeit identity stays intact, who are we? Where is the integrity?

For James Chartrand, losing her "real name" was a small price to pay for being able to support her family while doing what she was good at. But what if she had refused to pay this price? What if she had stood her ground, and used her growing platform to call out the disparities she witnessed? Or, better yet, what if, after her first string of positive experiences competing for work under a male pseudonym, she had used her experience as a so-called teachable moment? She admits in her confession that at first, she played both hands—applying for the same job under her real name and as James Chartrand. James usually won where she failed. What if, instead of packing up her "real" identity in mothballs, she had doubled down and called the game for what it was: rigged?

Women own nearly half of all businesses in the United States, where James has many of her clients, and between 1997 and 2006, businesses that were majority-owned by women grew at nearly twice the rate of other privately held firms in the United States.[29] Ask yourself this: What if these woman-owned businesses had taken the controversy James created by the horns—checking themselves for stereotyping, making a point to hire women writers themselves while presenting the case for change to male colleagues as well? Or this: James tells a compelling story, and she has vivid proof of the difference a pronoun makes. But what if she had told her tale not to defend her actions, but to create a confrontation that could lead to systemic change?

James points to her success, her ability to feed her children, as justification for her actions. True, she never made any promises to women, after all, and never signed up to be an activist. But my experience in social movements taught me that her success would have been enhanced had she seized the controversy and made a name for herself as someone who had played on both sides of the table, and could therefore testify firsthand to the harm discrimination creates in women's lives. That just might well have given her a deeper, more remunerative, and more gratifying kind of success.

# part**two**

## POWER-TO ESSENTIALS

Reclaiming Her Body—

and Helping Other Women Reclaim Theirs

# michelle**king**robson

When Michelle Robson tells her story today, she glows with confidence, passion, and the air of strong purpose. She radiates these qualities so naturally it is difficult to imagine her as the person she describes. At forty-two, after undergoing a hysterectomy recommended by her doctor, her health went into free fall.

"I got really sick," she says, describing the immediate effects of the operation. "I completely tanked, beyond words." The constellation of debilitating symptoms that Robson faced left her for the most part bedridden, subject to pain, insomnia, memory loss, and loss of libido, among much else. She consulted a dozen doctors and specialists from across the country, who prescribed her no less than nine medications to use simultaneously. None of these measures did anything to improve her condition. "My quality of life was so bad," she confesses, "that I quite frankly did not want to live anymore."

In this state of despondency, Robson made a life-changing decision: a commitment to herself. She would begin advocating on her own behalf, taking a more active role in her treatment, and refusing to suffer silently. Looking back, she sees her stumbling blocks as a problem endemic to women. "White coat syndrome," she calls it. "When women go to the doctor, they advocate for their children, their families. But when it comes to themselves, they leave their antennae at the door." They fail to make themselves heard, she explains, to press doctors for answers to their questions.

Her path to recovery began with the brave, simple step of believing in her own ability to investigate and understand her condition. The skepticism of doctors she'd seen, who saw Michelle

Robson as a beautiful, healthy woman with no diagnosable illness, had led her to doubt herself and what she felt. This, Robson came to see, was another manifestation of white coat syndrome, of deferring to others when she in fact knew better.

Her response was to begin researching her condition, to read any and all books she could find that seemed relevant to what she was going through. Finally, a friend gave her a book, "the thickest I had ever read," she remembers, and doubly difficult "because my memory had become so poor." Even in her clouded state, she realized she had found someone who got it. "The second I started reading," she says, "I knew intuitively that this would be the doctor who would turn my life around." The doctor's name was Elizabeth Vliet, the book *Screaming to Be Heard: Hormonal Connections Women Suspect, and Doctors Still Ignore*. The subhead spoke truth.

There were many lessons to draw from her experience. Dr. Vliet was based in Tucson, Arizona, remarkably for Robson, who had scoured the country for doctors, just a short drive from her home in Phoenix. Dr. Vliet met with her for a few hours, explained what was happening with her body, and adjusted her treatment to a much simpler and more effective regimen. Within days her symptoms began to disappear. She felt reborn.

"Then I got angry," she says. "If it was that easy, why didn't any of the other doctors do this?" At that moment, she made another life-changing decision. "I made the commitment then and there: It was time for me to stand up and represent women in a way they had not been represented before." Robson thought back on the difficulties of finding a doctor who understood her affliction, the simple cure that had eluded so many experts, and the hopeless feeling of being so sick. "I made a promise that no other woman should have to suffer like I did if I could help it."

This promise was the seed that would bloom as EmpowHER, a free online resource devoted to helping women get the health information they need. It had become "crystal clear" to Robson that "we had a problem in our society with the way women were treated in the healthcare system. Women are handicapped for being born women. We are different internally and externally, but there isn't really gender-specific medicine. For so many years, for instance, we've been treated with drugs tested primarily on men." The complications of running trials on women, who are subject to pregnancies and hormonal variations, has meant their frequent exclusion. As a result, women have been treated with drugs and procedures that prove ineffective, or even detrimental, to their conditions.

Robson is now out to further women's health interests on the individual level and group level alike. EmpowHER is set up to connect women to experts, to each other, and to answers. But it is also there to amplify the power of women's collective voice. "When you have a million women signing a petition saying, 'This isn't okay,' that's pretty powerful," she explains. "Channeling that power was one of the goals of EmpowHER. Almost nobody was paying attention to what women needed or wanted." Even with issues that uniquely affected women, these needs and wants were often altogether ignored.

Robson remembers, as one example, a law passed requiring a woman to go home on the same day she had a mastectomy. "It made women crazy. It was sad enough that you had been diagnosed with cancer, that you were going to lose a part of you that was so female. The psychological effects were so great, and then you had to go home while you were still so ill." She thinks legislation of this sort, that negatively and unfairly affects women, is on its way out. Lawmakers are not necessarily malicious, but they are predominantly men and they need to hear from their large female constituencies, whose health and happiness their decisions so directly affect. With the emergence of EmpowHER and other organizations, this voice is being heard.

"There is a rumbling beneath the surface," Michelle Robson declares, "among women who are tired of having their questions and interests ignored. I have started to see momentum build, and I think there is going to be a huge, positive shift regarding women and their health. We're going to demand that those who are representing us truly represent us."

She has seen the power of collective action. When she heard about a "citizen's petition" to the FDA, asking the agency to stop pharmacists from distributing a common menopause treatment known as "compounded" hormones, she worked to uncover a conflict of interest behind the petition. Enlisting the help of a senator, Robson and others discovered a large drug company and the maker of several embattled menopause hormonal medications had spearheaded the petition. Robson acted quickly "to launch a campaign so people could tell the FDA directly that they were against the petition, that they did not want the FDA to prevent compounding pharmacists from providing women with bioidentical hormones."

The result was "the second largest response rate the FDA had ever received." Only the antismoking campaign drew a larger consumer response. "It tells you about the power of women," affirms Robson. As the name suggests, the mission of EmpowHER is to unleash that potential. In a little over a year, the organization has grown into a vital resource and a community of several million. "It's hard for us, as women, to acknowledge the power we have," says Robson. "It's something we grow up with from early childhood on. We were viewed as aggressive or bitchy if we asked for things for ourselves. And that doesn't feel right or good. But we need to own our power or we can't expect to move forward."

The circle Robson has traveled is complete. From the lows of a mystifying illness, a time of such hopelessness that she considered taking her own life, through recovery and the realization of her dream of having "the ability to touch the lives of multiple women," to finally this past Thanksgiving, which she describes as "the real tipping point for me. I realized for the first time in seven years, what I was most thankful for was the fact that I got sick. If I hadn't gotten sick, I wouldn't have done what I am doing today. I started to cry." Michelle Robson would never have believed that she would one day cry tears of thanks for something that had brought her to the point of despair. "Getting sick," she says quietly, "was what led me down this path where I can help so many others."

# CHAPTER FIVE

# unfetter:
# secure £500 and a womb of your own

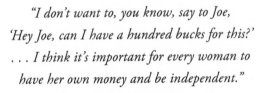

*"I don't want to, you know, say to Joe,
'Hey Joe, can I have a hundred bucks for this?'
. . . I think it's important for every woman to
have her own money and be independent."*

**—JILL BIDEN,**
wife of Vice President Joe Biden and
the first woman in that role to continue
her professional employment[1]

*"No woman can call herself free unless she can
own and control her own body. No woman can
call herself free unless she can decide for herself
whether and when she will become a mother."*

**—MARGARET SANGER,**
founder of the American Birth
Control Movement

What examples can you think of that illustrate the intersection between economic and reproductive self-determination in your life?

Money. Sex. Power. These are the stuff of soap operas to be sure, but that's only because they are the sinew and soul of human existence. And women's relationships with all three are shifting so rapidly today that men and women alike may feel a sense of chaos as a result. No excuses for that. A cultural shift to incorporate women's full equality, after all, affects everyone, and reproductive choice is fundamental to equality.

Money and sex have always been linked. They are symbolic but tangible representations of the two essential precursors to power of any sort: the human right to own and control one's own body and the economic right to earn one's way to independence. And the two, though separate and not always perfectly in tandem, are intensely connected.

When we have these two basic capabilities—economic and reproductive self-determination—we have within our reach the greatest power of all, the one that makes us human and enables us to flourish as human beings: the power of choice, nothing less than the power to chart the course of our own lives.

Economic and reproductive self-determination work together. I think of them like those executive toys, Newton's Cradle, where the movement of one metal ball suspended on a rack with four others creates a kinetic energy that impacts the ball on the other end of the line, even though what makes this so isn't necessarily obvious. The laws of physics are sometimes inscrutable, but they are always there, transmitting the motion even when it's unseen.[2]

My own experience as a teen mother taught me about the enduring relationship between sex and money, and between both of these and power. I often shock people when I tell them that 1957 was the year the United States had its highest teen birthrate since records have been kept. The post–World War II era was remarkable for its enforced ignorance about sexuality and its consequences, but even more so for its lack of career aspirations or even possibilities for girls and women. Not surprisingly, therefore, these were boom years for teen pregnancy. An idealized nuclear family had been constructed with clearly defined gender roles— Mom as the homemaker (privileged white women, it should be pointed out, who looked like June Cleaver, ever cheerfully vacuuming the rugs in freshly ironed, full-skirted dresses and high-heeled pumps), Dad going to the office, and kids growing up adhering to their assigned role models. This is why I genuinely thought I'd be blissfully happy living behind my own freshly painted picket fence.

By the time I was twenty, my husband and I had three young children. I loved them dearly, and I can't imagine life without them. Still, at that point I also knew having one more would put me over the edge. And that picket fence that had once seemed like the buttercream icing on the red velvet cake of my imagined domestic bliss? It was feeling more and more like it was fencing me in rather than keeping trespassers out.

But here's the important point that I like to impress upon younger women tempted to take for granted the power of today's opportunities: Even if I had wanted to change the situation and break the rules of expected behavior, I couldn't have done so because I had no employable skills, which meant few employment opportunities. I also had no reliable way to prevent pregnancies, making it impossible to work steadily even if there had been laws and policies then, as there are now, to keep employers from discriminating against fertile females, let alone women who were pregnant. Even the most stunningly talented women were held back. Future Supreme Court Justice Sandra Day O'Connor, graduating third in her class at Stanford Law School, had a hard time finding a job other than as a secretary. When the late Nobel-winning economist Paul Samuelson quipped that "women are just men with less money," he was speaking from this frame of reference. That succinct, perhaps flippant phrase nailed the patriarchal culture's outlook on the gendered economy perfectly.[3]

Suddenly, in 1960, the world changed for me and so many other women like me when the birth control pill was introduced in the United States. It was like taking a big gulp of fresh air after holding my breath for too long. The pill allowed me to continue my education and eventually finish college, which in turn gave me the ability to earn my own living, contribute to the family income at first, and later to be the full support for myself and my children. The power to control my fertility—to determine when and whether I would have children—preceded and enabled my power to follow my own career and financial path, which in turn enabled me to have greater power in my personal relationships.

It became obvious to me that for a woman to achieve full, meaningful equality, to be able to determine her own destiny in the world, to "call herself free," as Margaret Sanger put it, she must first and foremost be able to determine her own reproductive destiny. She must have moral autonomy over her body and her childbearing decisions. And to be able to have moral autonomy over the rest of her life, she must also have financial resources that she owns and controls.

## BAREFOOT AND PREGNANT = ABUSED

Keeping a woman "barefoot and pregnant" is the epitome of destroying her personal power as an individual. That's why the words "barefoot and pregnant" have so often been intertwined and uttered in the same breath. When a woman is perpetually pregnant, she can't enter the paid workforce, and that leaves her barefoot (i.e., without her own financial means). Conversely, when a woman is prevented from earning money, she can't tell the jerk to go jump in the lake if she lacks the financial means to support herself and the children. She's hobbled as surely as Chinese women of old with bound feet, and for exactly the same reason. She's trapped, controlled, powerless; she can't get away.

Yet the figure of speech drew a roaring laugh in 1963—when the pill was still new—at the then all-male Optimist Club in Little Rock when Arkansas State Senator Paul Van Dalsem railed against uppity members of the American Association of University Women (AAUW), who'd had the temerity to lobby the state legislature for improved educational opportunities for African Americans.

"We don't have any of these university women in Perry County, but I'll tell you what we do up here when one of our women starts poking around in something she doesn't know anything about. We get her an extra cow," fulminated Van Dalsem, who, by the way, also opposed desegregation and voting rights. "If that don't work, we give her a little more garden to tend. And if that's not enough, we get her pregnant and keep her barefoot."[4]

His fighting words did not go unanswered by the women of Perry County, who rightly interpreted them as not just retrograde, but also suggestive of rape. They began to carry signs that said, "We've been pregnant—by choice, not by force."

Their point was good, but it didn't go far enough. Van Dalsem's formula was a denial of the basic right to determine what happens to a woman's body. This threat has such deep resonance because it has profound roots in our culture, where only relatively recently in history have women won the basic components of legal selfhood.

Up through the end of the nineteenth century, coverture marriage was the legal paradigm that defined a woman's relationship to her husband. As described in William Blackstone's legal dictionary, the central text of the time, "By marriage, the husband and wife are one person in law: that is, the very being or legal existence of the woman is suspended during the marriage, or at least is incorporated and consolidated into that of the husband: under whose wing, protection, and cover, she performs every thing."[5]

A woman's identity was subsumed within that of her husband; marriage was the literal, legal erasure of her independent self as an economic and social creature. Coverture essentially meant that women were just tokens in the exchange of economic goods through society, a way of transferring deeds of ownership of real estate and other property from family to family. A married woman's property, including her body and her childbearing capacity, were under the ownership of her husband. She did not have the right to sign contracts. If she worked, she was obliged to turn her wages over to her husband. If she committed certain types of crimes, she was not held responsible, but was instead assumed to have been following the orders of her husband.[6]

By 1963, coverture had long since ceased to be the legal model for marriage contracts. But the lingering effects of this law remained in the way that women's liberties have been considered legally and socially. For instance, for years many state laws did not acknowledge the possibility that a married woman could be raped by her husband. Consenting to marriage essentially meant consenting to sex at any time, in perpetuity, which in turn meant that rape was often a tool of abuse, as was the accompanying threat of pregnancy. The result of taking away this particular form of dominance from men had real consequences. I knew women whose partners flew into rages upon discovering their birth control pills, sometimes even throwing them down the toilet.

This may seem like ancient history, but these laws did not change until recently. The first state to outlaw marital rape was South Dakota, in 1975. North Carolina, the last state to change its law, did not do so until 1993.[7]

I include this information not only because the history still matters—still shapes many people's perceptions of marriage, for one thing—but because of how the laws make cultural change possible.

Those women in Perry County who protested Van Dalsem's slur were at the forefront of a movement to draw attention to a problem that had everything to do with women's power and control over our own lives—freeing themselves from the epidemic of abuse against women by intimate partners and spouses. It was a movement that culminated with the 1994 passage of the Violence Against Women Act (VAWA), which recognized that "violence against women is a crime with far-reaching, harmful consequences for families, children and society."[8] VAWA recognizes the connection between bodily integrity and financial self-sufficiency; Congress, empowered to pass national laws if they involve interstate commerce, passed VAWA because they recognized the "far-reaching" economic effects of violence against women.

Although domestic violence and violence against women are now topics that are openly, if not always accurately, addressed—think of Rihanna and Chris Brown—these issues remain potent. There are recent reports of male partners obsessed with controlling women by controlling their sexuality in two seemingly antithetical ways: First are "coerced pregnancies," in which the man forbids a woman to use birth control so that she is more likely to become pregnant, thus remaining vulnerable; second is the unfortunate truth that once a woman becomes pregnant, she is more at risk of being beaten or even murdered than she would be if she were not pregnant. If she is both barefoot and pregnant, she is, by definition, powerless, and her abuser has considerably more leverage to control her. Not coincidentally, abusers also exercise their power by denying women the ability to work outside the home and earn their own livings.

This relationship between the latent power in women's control of their reproductive and economic capacities plays out in the realm of the political as well as the personal. No wonder the politicians who oppose reproductive justice for women are also the ones most likely to oppose programs that help women and families become or remain financially stable after children are born. States with predominantly anti-choice legislators are less likely to fund services for needy children and their mothers and more likely to prosecute pregnant women who use drugs or alcohol rather than provide treatment for substance abuse or focus on prosecuting the men who batter pregnant women. States with pro-choice legislatures are more likely to support everything that should be "pro-life," from adoption subsidies to healthcare, public education, and financial support for struggling mothers and for their children after they're born.[9]

Not just a little, but a lot has changed since Van Dalsem's 1963 pronouncement, and it has changed with stunning rapidity thanks to the organized and persistent work of those uppity women's advocacy groups that opened door after door of opportunity for women. That's why the front lines for women's equality have shifted, become less clear. Today's issues are more complex and nuanced than simply forcing employers to stop advertising "help wanted male" and "help wanted female" positions.

Many people don't think working for women's equality is an urgent problem anymore because there have been so many firsts. We're accustomed now to seeing women in almost every role in our society—at least one woman. Today a Sandra Day O'Connor would get snapped up by a top law firm, but that doesn't automatically put her into the partner's boardroom. Changing laws isn't easy, but changing the culture and individual behavior is infinitely more difficult. That's the part we have to do for ourselves.

## MEDIA HAS AN AHA MOMENT

The timing is perfect. Circumstances and cumulative choices women have made are converging to give the fulcrum a push toward parity. For the past three decades, more women have finished college than men, and more women get advanced degrees. And we've got the jobs to show for it. The year 2010 will be the first year that women in the workforce outnumber men.

Media plays a big role in both forming and informing us, shaping our thinking as it is reflecting what we do. The significance of women reaching the workplace majority benchmark had been predicted for some time, but when it happened, it caught the media by surprise. A news segment about it on Dylan Ratigan's *Morning Meeting* on MSNBC in September 2009 led with a rhetorical question about whether this could be the breakthrough time for women. *Okay, I've heard that one before,* I thought as I was half-listening. *Next?*

Ratigan asked Karen Finney, a Democratic political strategist, to comment on an article I'd seen the day before about how women legislators perform better than their male counterparts—they pass more legislation, secure more cosponsors, and bring home more bacon to their districts. That women on decision bodies make for better decisions wasn't news to me either—it's become a regular trend story ever since Catalyst, Ernst & Young, the World Bank, and McKinsey all discovered over the past few years that once parliaments and corporate boards reach 30 percent female representation, the quality of decisions improves, the guys behave better, and there is less corruption. (Maybe estrogen is contagious. Now there's an idea!)[10]

Finney opined that women are more collaborative about the legislative process (a real bulletin here: no one said "catfights"), and then cheerily observed that we haven't seen women involved in sex scandals like men have notably been.[11]

Next, Ratigan reported what has now come to pass—that women could soon equal men in the workforce. Pink and blue numbers flashed on the screen to show part of the reason: During the recession, women have accounted for 26 percent of layoffs while men accounted for 74 percent. He lobbed a throwaway "what do you make of that?" question at Finney, who replied, "Let's not kid ourselves. Part of this is that women come cheaper." She pointed out that women tend to hold the lower-paying jobs, and when companies are cutting costs, they lay off the more expensive, higher-paid men. And women consistently earn less than men for doing the same work.

So perhaps we aren't as close to gender equality nirvana as it appeared. The media critic part of me rolled eyes at how superficially this "women's moment" package had been scraped together without one single new piece of information in it.

But then I realized that the real story was one that had not been announced: The mainstream media narrative had finally taken note of this sea change in women's workplace and leadership roles, stories heretofore the purview largely of women's books and blogs and perhaps an occasional newspaper Style section.

The big story of the day wasn't any one of the disparate parts of this MSNBC *Morning Meeting* segment. It was that the overall "women's moment" story line had finally entered the cultural bloodstream. They realize the significance of this moment. Do we?

## WILL WOMEN TAKE THE BRASS RING THIS TIME?

It's critical that women realize this is a game-changing moment—or rather that it can be—if we choose to make it so. The recession is the reason we're witnessing more women than ever in the workforce, so what are we going to do to make sure the story on Dylan Ratigan's morning show isn't just another fleeting blip on the gender power screen? What will be the next step for women?

It's important to ask these questions because somewhere between the classroom and the boardroom and the halls of political influence, many talented and capable women are either disappearing or becoming stranded on the ladder well before they reach the highest rungs of achievement for which they're qualified.

It's no secret that the higher you climb up the ladder of wealth and power, the fewer women you see. Only fifteen companies listed in the Fortune 500 are led by female CEOs. Of the wealthiest four hundred Americans, according to *Forbes*, only forty-two are women—and at least half of these women inherited their wealth from husbands or fathers. Among its list of the sixty-seven most powerful people in the United States, *Forbes* finds room for only three women, two of whom are known by their first names, Hillary and Oprah. And, although for the past two decades approximately the same number of women and men have graduated from law school and entered law firms as first-year associates, a 2009 study by the National Association of Women Lawyers found that women still compose fewer than 16 percent of the equity partners in the two hundred top law firms in the United States. Even women who make partnership are at a disadvantage, earning on average $66,000 a year less than their male counterparts.[12]

Some, perhaps perversely, argue that women opt out because they are just smarter than men—they don't want to work the insane hours with too little family-life flexibility and too much remaining ingrained corporate sexism. Maybe so, but we know that women are still being paid less than men for the same work, despite decades of law and policy meant to combat this. And here's a concrete way to understand the meaning of the disparity: Every year, Equal Pay Day falls sometime in April. It happens in April because that's how many months into the new year it takes for the average woman to start earning a dollar for every dollar the man in the next cubicle over has made since January 1, doing the exact same job with the exact same title. Think of all those freezing days in January, when the darkness falls early. Those miserable gray mornings in February, when the ground is covered in slush and the car refuses to start. Those blustery days in March when spring seems like it's refusing to ever come. Think of working all those days for nothing, zilch, nada. That's what pay disparity means. And for women of color, the differential is even more extreme.

There's no denying that women have drawn closer to even with men in professional and economic matters. So given that most of the legal barriers to women's equal employment have been removed, why does pay discrimination still exist? Why are women still so severely underrepresented in the highest levels of business and finance when the doors are standing open for their advancement?

Dozens of books including Katty Kay and Claire Shipman's *Womenomics* have postulated that it is the "sticky floor" that keeps women in low-level, nonmanagerial, and support roles and prevents them from seeking or gaining promotion or career development. This term may refer to barriers to the advancement of women, such as family commitments, attitudes, stereotyping, and organizational structures, but it has also been used to focus on circumstances where women are promoted but do not receive commensurate wage raises.[13]

Leadership and organizational consultant Rebecca Shambaugh acknowledges that outdated workplace-leave policies still make life particularly difficult for women with children, and strong social messages depicting women as less capable and more likely to drop out of the workplace when they become parents may also shape women's decisions. "But when I see women capable of C-suite leadership mired in middle management, I don't look toward a glass ceiling. Instead, I look toward a sticky floor. In fact, our most useful insights may come from exploring what keeps us stuck: our outmoded, self-defeating and, let's face it, unconscious behaviors. I am not saying this to discount women. Quite the opposite—I say this because I want women to reap the professional and financial rewards they have earned." We have worked hard and amply demonstrated our talents. Yet Shambaugh concludes, "I believe we are stuck because of habits we learned years ago."[14]

But beyond the sticky floor, the intersection between women's economic empowerment and women's sexual and reproductive freedom is seldom acknowledged.

Imagine the consequences of full economic empowerment for women's reproductive freedom. Imagine how true economic equality could allow us to redefine the meaning of consent, and create relationships that are mutually rewarding. It's good for the entire economy, and for men as much as for women, because they would no longer have to bear the full financial burden. Conversely, financial inequality narrows the possibilities we have to define our lives and the way we negotiate relationships, family, and caregiving responsibilities, even basic survival issues such as food and shelter.

And we must recognize that the effects of economic inequality go further than our own individual circumstances, whether we personally draw a fair and equal paycheck or not. The point is that women's work—women's labor—is undervalued across the board, as James Chartrand found out in the previous chapter. She encountered not only pay disparity, but also a difference in the way her clients treated her when she assumed a male name. A large part of what causes the wage gap is this (conscious or unconscious) diminishment of women's work by society at large. Regardless how much we take home each month, it is in all of our best interests to challenge this, to take one for the team, as Chartrand would say.

Today's challenge is to value ourselves and demand that others do, too. I want us to pick our way through the detritus of co-option and isolation, those places where we see ourselves as less powerful than we really are, and find a better way, first to understand and then to focus our own behavior on mopping clean that sticky floor.

### "I NEED NOT FLATTER ANY MAN"

British author Virginia Woolf was a groundbreaking revolutionary in her time, so much so that people thought her nearly daft for taking a then almost-unprecedented point of view that women needed to be able to support themselves financially. In 1928, the same year she and other women in Britain won the right to vote, Woolf's aunt Mary died, leaving her a grand sum of £500 a year to use as she pleased. Woolf, who would go on to write some of the twentieth century's classic works of literary modernism—*To the*

*Lighthouse, Mrs. Dalloway, The Waves*—felt that the financial independence granted to her by her aunt's annuity was of more value than the political power she could now wield at the ballot box. As a middle-class woman, she was excluded from most professions where her intellect could shine; her choices were either to endure the drudgery of an unrewarding job where she would have little hope of advancement, or rely on marriage to give her financial security.

With her aunt's legacy, Woolf felt a new sense of freedom because she "need not flatter any man" in order to have food, clothing, and, as she so memorably put it, a room of her own. She could follow her passion and write her books. Her worldview was transformed. "Therefore not merely do effort and labour cease, but also hatred and bitterness. I need not hate any man; he cannot hurt me. I need not flatter any man; he has nothing to give me. So imperceptibly I found myself adopting a new attitude towards the other half of the human race."[15]

For Woolf, her aunt's legacy provided the security she needed not only to embark upon a career as a writer, but to discover her own voice. That's what is so profoundly important about financial independence; it's not just about consumer power, the ability to pay our own way, and treat ourselves every now and again to some creature comforts. It's about having the ability to define ourselves. To speak our minds. To *be,* in the fullest sense of the word.

But let's be honest. Very few of us are born under a lucky enough star that we can count on the glad tidings of inherited wealth to see us through our days. Instead, we've got something better than luck. We have opportunities that Woolf could only have dreamed of, possibilities for our lives that would have defied even her imagination. We're quickly passing through the era of firsts—first woman astronaut, first woman Supreme Court Justice, first woman CEO of a multibillion-dollar corporation, first woman speaker of the house (though we still have a few more to go). And with all this, where are we getting to, exactly? Somewhere in the neighborhood of equality, but we're not quite there yet.

## LOOKING FOR LEHMAN SISTERS
## AND THE FEMALE BILL GATES

Every time a woman passes a new milestone, the media gives itself the vapors, pontificating, like Dylan Ratigan, about *what it all means*—followed, regular as clockwork, by the editorials proclaiming that if feminism isn't dead, it's at the very least irrelevant. Your work is over, ladies. Time to pack up the banners and go home.

All of the women out there who continue to have to work harder to earn less would beg to differ. As would all of us who work the double shift at the office and at home, or who have seen career opportunities melt away like mascara in a rainstorm after taking time off to raise children. That said, in these difficult times, many of us are just grateful to have a paycheck— even if it only gets us 78 cents to our male coworker's snappy green dollar, at least we have that, and maybe even healthcare benefits. From that lucky £500 that liberated Virginia Woolf to our own hard-earned wages, we know the value of financial independence, even if it's only a little more than just getting by. But we need to go for more.

The broken financial system is ready for people who come with a different set of tools to take a shot at fixing it. After all, who made the mess? It wasn't the women, who are largely absent from that world's decision-making positions.

As *New York Times* columnist Nick Kristof observed in a 2009 op-ed, one question had the oligarchs abuzz at the February 2009 World Economic Forum in Davos, Switzerland: Would investment bank Lehman Brothers have failed so spectacularly, taking a sizable chunk of the global economy down with it, if it had been Lehman *Sisters?* Even this pale male bastion of reactionary bluster seemed finally ready to accept what so many of us have known for so long: Diversity leads to better thinking and smarter decisions. Kristof outlines the increasingly compelling scientific evidence showing that while men surrounded by men—the typical demographic of the trading floor on the stock exchange—tend to escalate the riskiness of their decisions, women tend to keep their cool and more accurately evaluate the consequences.

Couple this commentary with *Half the Sky,* the blockbuster book by Kristof and his wife, Sheryl WuDunn, in which they postulate that the most important imperative of the twenty-first century is to bring women to parity globally through economic development and reproductive health-care, including reducing maternal mortality and family planning services. It's a theme Kristof explores in many of his op-eds, and it's clear that at least on the global scale someone gets the connection between barefoot and pregnant and the need for £500 and a womb of one's own. Somehow, it seems to be much harder to get the same awareness on the domestic front.[16]

This is the time for us not just to demand change but to make change. And not the kind of incremental change that has been narrowing the wage gap by pennies every decade. This is precisely the time to hold hands and take a giant leap toward economic equality. "Where there's confusion in the marketplace, there is opportunity," Bill Gates has observed. So where is the female Bill Gates? This is her moment to step forward.

When more women take their places in the workplace, including in decision-making positions, it is likely to mean a healthier, more resilient economy. And each one of us has to remember that she's bargaining for more than just herself. Financial independence means that women will be able to change the dynamics of relationships on a personal level—just as Woolf's perception of the other half of the world shifted when she was no longer dependent on men. But financial equality will only be achieved when we ourselves change the rules on the collective, societal level. Those changes create some dislocation and chaos, happily for women, for it is a chance to inch forward that fulcrum again and employ chaos advantageously to breathe some new ideas into the system.

# **power**tool number five

CARPE THE CHAOS: change creates chaos. today's changing gender roles and economic turbulence may feel chaotic and confusing. but chaos also means boundaries become more fluid. these are the moments in time when people are open to new ways of thinking. you can accomplish a lot and have access to unprecedented opportunities that you might not otherwise have had.

i say, *carpe* the chaos, for in chaos is opportunity.

"Given women's shifting relationship to money, what are the ways that we can use our financial power-to change the world?" I asked Jacki Zehner, a woman who is doing it.

"Money is a power tool, and women need to learn to use it as one!" says Jacki. And she means it.

Zehner grew up in a middle-class family in a small town in British Columbia, and she entered the workforce in the late 1980s. She graduated college to find ever more doors swinging open. In a decade that started with Lily Tomlin, Jane Fonda, and Dolly Parton outsmarting the male boss in *9 to 5,* and ended with Melanie Griffith outsmarting the female boss in *Working Girl,* women in business were becoming a cultural force to be reckoned with.

In her high school yearbook, Zehner had boldly named her ambition: to make a million dollars before she turned thirty. And she pursued that goal fearlessly. She began working at investment bank Goldman Sachs in 1988; eight years later, at age thirty-two, she became the first female trader—and the youngest woman—to make partner at the firm. She loved her work. She spoke to me with thrill about her first billion-dollar trade, the sense of responsibility and power that she felt, the satisfaction of a job well done.

Though she herself did not personally experience much negative gender bias, she witnessed it for many others and in business in general. "I always deeply resented women who would get up on the podium and say there's no such thing as a glass ceiling," she shared in our interview. "With so few women in leadership positions how could that possibly be true?" She remembers being moved by hearing late Texas Governor Ann Richards tell the women in the firm (who were "divided like the Red Sea" on whether there were still barriers to women advancing) that anyone who thinks there is no glass ceiling is either incredibly self-centered or incredibly stupid.

So when lists of candidates for various positions were presented, she would question if there was a lack of women's names. She also co-created

Goldman's ASCEND Initiative in 2002, an ongoing effort to connect with their top women clients. "I thought that if we could show the male leadership of the firm just how many of our most senior clients were women, it would bring increasing commitment to our internal diversity efforts." Years later Goldman Sachs is one of the most progressive firms in believing that the key to sustainable economic development is investing in women, as evidenced in its "10,000 Women" program to provide 10,000 underserved women around the world with a business and management education.

Though long gone from Goldman Sachs and now deeply immersed in creating social change, Zehner remains deeply grateful for the "financial blessing" that came from being a partner. "Because I was a partner at Goldman I can now give of my time and money to create a more just and equitable world. How cool is that?"

Well-behaved women are not supposed to talk about money, and a similar taboo exists more broadly in corporate culture—often reinforcing entrenched pay disparities that remain hidden from view. Zehner says, "Women need to be so much better about asking for what they deserve in terms of compensation. And sadly, even when you might think you're in the club, you're likely not. Keep fighting for access." She shared how she found out she had been paid significantly less than a man in a similar role who didn't do half the work she did with respect to recruiting and diversity. "I walked in to my boss's office and said, 'You change this or I quit, and I will tell everyone why.'" I asked whether they changed it. She just smiled.

Zehner is now determined to spread her fearlessness about money and how it can be used as a powerful tool for change. "I think a lot of women are afraid of power, and money epitomizes power. If women can get over their fear of money, they will assume greater power. That's my premise." She goes on, "I don't see money as an end, I see money as a means. A means to make for a better world."

Since leaving Goldman in 2002, Zehner has continued to invest in women. She cofounded Circle Financial Group, a private wealth management operation, along with several other women. She is a frequent media commentator and consultant on women's leadership and success in the workplace, and on women and wealth, investing, and social change. She's an investor in women-owned start-up firms through the angel investor group Golden Seeds, and independently. Her latest investment is in a company called Learnvest, which is an online platform to educate and empower women in all financial matters. Her "Purse Pundit" blog shares her knowledge and her enthusiasm for both the business and philanthropic worlds. She says, "I always had that sense of injustice and passion around a woman's leadership and money that lead me into my philanthropic work."

She and her husband, Greg, have a foundation that concentrates its giving on work that empowers women and girls. Asked what she wants for the younger women she mentors and her own daughter, she replied without hesitation "that she has personal financial skills and that she wants personal financial independence." She's adamant that these should be life goals for girls and young women: "Boys are more likely to be brought up that way, but with girls our culture continuously tells them they will be taken care of. Too many women give up their careers for motherhood without thinking through the financial consequences. Yes, be a great mom, but preserve your earning power while doing it. So I think there is a lot about personal activism around this whole idea of being the change you want to see in the world and then actually doing something to make it happen." Emphasizing that this isn't necessarily a gender message, but because we are not yet living in a just and equitable place for women and girls, Zehner believes we all have "an incremental responsibility to try to push for the change, in everything we do."

To that end, Zehner is also a contributor to the Women Moving Millions campaign, a big-vision effort to mobilize the growing numbers of women to use the substantial wealth that they control to give bigger contributions than they have ever made to groups that provide services and advocacy for women.[17]

There are three big lessons all women can learn from Zehner's life and words. First, gender discrimination remains and we have to address it. That doesn't necessarily mean there is a deliberate conspiracy to keep women down. If you don't approach the situation like a victim, but rather as a straightforward assertion of the facts (and your understanding of the rules), you will in many instances effect change more quickly than you think. Second, you do have to track financial information for yourself and ask for what you deserve! Do not expect anyone else to do it for you. Break the taboos that keep you from negotiating about your compensation, too.

And finally, if you have good financial fortunes, pay it forward to help other women. Sharing one's own abundance isn't just an individual kindness. It helps to change the system and raises the floor, sticky or not, for all women.

## WOMEN MOVING MILLIONS

"The king was in the countinghouse counting out his money; the queen was in the parlor eating bread and honey," sang Swanee Hunt, adding a sweet lilt to the old familiar Mother Goose ditty that gave away her Southern roots. I was mesmerized by the story Swanee and her sister Helen LaKelly Hunt told at a press briefing I attended in New York for the public launch of Women Moving Millions. Helen Hunt, author of *Faith and Feminism* and founder of the Sister Fund, talked about how her father brought her husband into his business because, in the 1950s, it never occurred to him to hire his daughters. "The queen was in the parlor . . . "[18]

Swanee Hunt is former ambassador to Austria, the current president of the Hunt Alternatives Fund, and a Harvard Kennedy School professor, and she was singing the lessons about money and gender that she learned on the knee of her Texas oil magnate father. The king not only makes the money, he counts it—and controls the purse strings, she explained for anyone in attendance who might not know the verse, and continued to expand upon the analogy to traditional gender roles in controlling money. The queen in her parlor should be content with what she's given, her honey-sweet reward, and take it gracefully and gratefully, without asking for a penny more.[19]

How Swanee and Helen Hunt went from those traditional beginnings to seed and lead the Women Moving Millions campaign mirrors a journey frequently taken by women of wealth—from financial wherewithal to philanthropy.

Women Moving Millions (WMM) is a new twist on this common theme. "We're not funding charity," declared Chris Grumm, when it was her turn to speak. Grumm is president of the Women's Funding Network, the collaborative that provides the structure to distribute WMM grants. "We're funding change." She said that collaborative networks represent the ways women work, including how they feel most comfortable doing philanthropy.

And their approach works. Women Moving Millions has zoomed past its initial goal of raising $150 million by $30 million, raising more than $180 million for women's funds across the country, all in gifts larger than $1 million. Thinking big did not come easy. Swanee and Helen had to practice saying "a million, a million" in order to get the courage to make the big ask. But once they asked, they were able to get what they wanted.[20]

Grumm pointed out that many of the organizations that receive donations through the women's funds across the country that are the recipients of WMM are advocacy organizations, or have missions that combine service and advocacy. For instance, the Washington Area Women's Foundation, one of the recipients of WMM dollars, helps low-income women and families in the nation's capital increase their financial security by helping them develop skills, find jobs, and purchase housing, but the foundation also successfully lobbied to increase the city's minimum wage.

Helen Hunt added, "We see ourselves transforming gender roles as we're transforming the amount of money going to women and girls. We're funding women's voice in society. Women are the strategic way to fund in the future."

# HOW DO YOU:

- Define money: Is it a means or an end?

- Relate to money: How important is it to you that you have earned it yourself?

- Use money: As power-over, power-to, or to pay the rent?

- View the intersection of money, sex, and power in your life?

- In what ways are women resisting using the financial power-to that the world is trying so hard to give us?

## ANONYMOUS WAS A WOMAN: OVERCOMING RESISTANCE TO FINANCIAL POWER

The vast majority of us will never have enough in the bank to donate a million dollars to advance women's rights, as much as we may want to. Most of us will not even have what Virginia Woolf had—a reliable monthly annuity that we can count on, come rain or come shine. Indeed, many women live from paycheck to paycheck, or struggle to balance the need to save for retirement or for a child's college fund with ever-increasing day-to-day costs like medical care, childcare, paying off student loans, or simply getting enough gas in the car to make it to work.

But just because we may not have the money to engage in the same scale of strategic philanthropy as women like Swanee and Helen Hunt or Jacki Zehner, we are far from powerless. We have a collective power that is only increasing as more of us are in the workforce. But it's a power that we have yet to fully exercise.

The Women Moving Millions story, for example, mirrors a prevalent pattern in the use of financial power: While well-heeled men often go into politics or start businesses, women are more likely to start social movements or give money to charities. And while men seem to give money to charity to advertise their wealth and generosity, women often deploy it for social good—and they tend to keep a low profile. In the past few years, one anonymous female donor has given $100 million to public colleges led by women presidents, earmarked specifically for financial aid for women and people of color.[21] "Anonymous was a woman," said Virginia Woolf in *A Room of One's Own*. Apparently that hasn't changed since 1928.[22]

## "WHERE'S THE CEO'S MATERNITY LEAVE?"

Similarly, in the reproductive justice realm, women are leaving power unused, if not out and out resisting it.

"Where is the CEO maternity leave?" Gina Bianchini asks. "Until we solve that problem, we'll never have equality in leadership of companies." Gina is the founder and former CEO of Ning, a technology platform that allows people to create social networks; more than ninety million people a month use the service. Born in 1972, Gina is a bona fide rising star in Silicon Valley, where women in executive roles are almost as rarely seen as they are on Wall Street. Diminutive and dark-haired, she is unafraid to speak her mind. She's certainly not one of those women who would dare to waver, "I'm not 'a feminist, *but* . . . ' "I'm a feminist period," she asserted to me as we sipped tea at the Plaza Hotel to warm up on a cold day in New York, where she was attending a meeting. "And let me tell you, we have a problem."

A Stanford MBA, Bianchini notes that very few of the women she went to business school with are running businesses. Many have dropped out of the work world after marriage. Her observation applies to more than just her former classmates. A recent study confirms that 50 percent of female MBAs leave the workforce after having children. And although Bianchini had the laser-focus on her company, she empathizes with the choices made by the women she studies alongside: "I want to have children, somehow, but I don't know how I'm going to do that."

How many of us know women in the same or a similar situation? Or talented women who left promising careers once they became wives or mothers? And can any of us blame them? A husband's large paycheck can seem like a welcome respite from the demands of a workplace that too often still belittles women, and, as in the past decade, extracts ever-increasing hours from our day while middle-class incomes flatline. Moreover, with the cost of childcare sometimes exceeding what a woman makes at her job, in some cases staying home to nurture and care for a child can seem like an economically sound decision, as well as an emotionally rewarding one.

But when women retreat from the workforce, it becomes more difficult for the rest of us to rectify the inequities that remain. Gina wants to change the rules, but she can't do it on her own. When all these other smart, educated women with MBAs leave the workforce, rather than using their clout to change the system that makes parenthood and powerful careers incompatible, it leaves women like Bianchini high and dry.

## SEX AND THE POLITICS OF WOMEN'S WORK

Whether we're talking about economic or reproductive issues, we're beyond simply making it possible for women to have these high-paying, high-power jobs or to time their childbearing to when they are ready for children. We have a much more complex set of issues to deal with today as a result of the positive changes that women have won.

The fact is, pay disparity isn't the only thing that affects working women's equality in the office. As Gloria Steinem wrote for the Women's Media Center in October 2009, just after the release of the Shriver report "A Woman's Nation," in an article entitled "It's Not a Man's World or a Woman's Nation":

*Now that women are half of all workers with incomes that are necessary to 80 percent of families—indeed, 40 percent of babies are now born to single mothers—childcare is still nowhere on the list of priorities in Congress, and we have also become the only industrialized country without any requirement of paid family leave. Our skills are valuable, and our contributions to the economy are necessary. Isn't it time that the rules of the economy begin to take notice of our presence, and our needs?[23]*

In the United States, the workplace is organized for a situation that is increasingly rare. Few and far between are the "honey, I'm home!" households, where the man serves as the sole breadwinner and can count on a "homemaker" wife to send the children to school and be at home when they get back at 3:00 PM, vacuum the living room, take the dog for a walk, drive little Suzy to soccer practice and little Johnny to his violin recital, stop by the pharmacy to refill a prescription for Suzy's ear infection, pick up the kids from their various activities, make sure they do their homework, and have dinner on the table when he gets home at 8:30 after a long day at the office and an hour sitting in traffic.

As economist Julie Matthaei, a professor at Wellesley College, explained in a paper presented at the June 2009 International Association for Feminist Economics Conference, this "economic man" emerged in the nineteenth century in the rapidly industrializing United States and Europe. The revolutions of the previous century meant that meritocracy replaced aristocracy—at least for men—and competition, self-reliance, and competency were celebrated as the new ideals; the legal history of U.S. economic institutions and corporations still reflects these original, masculine-centric values.

As Matthaei tells it, the male worker "was able to compete in the economy . . . and had the opportunity to become a self-made man." But this self-made man was incomplete without a woman whom he supported financially, and who tended to his needs. Says Matthaei: "Caring was left to be the purview of homemakers, exercised towards their family members, or

through the volunteer work and social homemaking which eventually transformed into a more or less paternalistic state." But as middle-class women
and men toiled in their increasingly separate spheres, others were left out
of this self-perpetuating cycle. "Race and class hierarchies enforced these
roles—poor whites and most people of color weren't allowed to play these
polarized roles, and hence weren't able to be successful men and women."

*Mad Men* seems like a nostalgic fantasy that gives us the chance to lust
after the amazing clothes and furniture while patting ourselves on the back
for progressing past the blatant discrimination. Yet the rules of the U.S.
workplace are by and large designed for this vanished, possibly imaginary,
world; the white-collar workplace simply functions as though everyone has a
"wife" who stays at home and takes care of all the necessary, nonnegotiable,
and increasingly complex tasks of daily living. Even as women have entered
the workforce in greater numbers, the rules of the workplace continue to be
stubbornly resistant to the reality of women's lives and the need for what we
refer to euphemistically as "family-friendly policies." Once a woman steps
out of the labor force and gets off the upward-bound ladder, the system is
rigged against her stepping back in.

## WHEN YOU HAVE CHOICES, YOU GET TO HAVE A DREAM

Although conservative fundamentalist groups such as Focus on the Family
would likely be apoplectic at the suggestion, the fact is when we're talking
about family, what we're really talking about is sex. Without sex, there is
no family. And when we talk about sex, what we're really talking about is
a complex web of social interactions, all of them defined to a significant
degree by women's personal agency and sexual power.

Michelle Goldberg writes in *The Means of Reproduction,* "There is
one thing that unites cultural conservatives throughout the world, a critique that joins Protestant fundamentalism, Islamists, Hindu Nationalists,

ultra-Orthodox Jews, and ultramontane Catholics. All view women's equality and self-possession as unnatural, a violation of the established order. Yet in one society after another, we can see the absence of women's rights creating existential dangers."[24]

There are strong cultural powers at play resisting women having "a womb of one's own," and it's time to address them head-on. At the women's venture capital fund meeting, I stood up during the question-and-answer time and asked the powerful women on the panel what advice they would give to other women. How did they believe women could or should work, collectively or individually, to turn the potential power they'd been discussing into actual power used?

Old habits die hard, but I had consciously decided not to ask a question in search of a link to reproductive rights for a change. Plus I was honestly intrigued with the theme of this meeting, which was to get women to open their pocketbooks and use their financial power as the fulcrum leveraging more women into corporate leadership. Still, I was surprised but delighted when former New Zealand Prime Minister Jenny Shipley took the microphone and firmly planted her stake in the loamy intersection between women's economic empowerment and women's sexual and reproductive freedom.

"I'm fifty-seven," she started, "and my generation was the first that could control its fertility." She went on to explain that although access to birth control and safe abortion still falls short of need, more than a generation of women has now grown up without ever knowing a world where these possibilities were underground and forbidden—at least in the West. Her answer surprised me because it is so rare for this connection between "barefoot and pregnant" to be publicly acknowledged. That's because to acknowledge it, sex has to be acknowledged, and people tend to avoid that in public conversations. Shipley continued unfazed, though: "We have to recognize that these conversations [about women in corporate leadership] are happening in economies where women do have that choice—who both can and do self-actualize and then make their way. They are, quite frankly, not having the conversations about why they should lead the companies and corporations [in countries where there is not this choice]."

"To come back to your question of power," she observed, "when you have a set of choices, you get to have a dream. We've heard, in many statements, that women who succeeded had parents who were able to encourage them, say they were as good as their brothers."

Giving women the power of choice within their families, communities, and countries, she said, is "critical in both liberating the capability and power of women. I think exercising power and influence and capability will extend to people's experiences—whether you're the shareholder or the owner of the textile mill—and that's going to be a good thing." Well, of course, I would have said the same thing had I been asked, but how affirming it was to hear this explanation coming from the mouth of one of the world's leading woman politicians! As Shipley laid out the facts about women globally, I couldn't help but think how for those of us who count ourselves among the lucky ones, the time for excuses is over; it is time to make sure our good luck becomes just the way things are, for all women.

## THE SOLUTION TO THE PROBLEM
## CHANGES THE PROBLEM

The way we choose to define and structure our sexual relationships—and the families we choose to build—are key here, and it starts with our own perceptions.

UC Berkeley sociologist Kristin Luker has studied American attitudes about sex for decades, from abortion politics, to teenage pregnancy, to the movements for and against comprehensive sex education.

When it comes to heterosexual relationships, Luker's research describes an America that is split down the middle on attitudes toward sexuality, with two completely different worldviews existing side by side. This isn't a demographic divide. Sexual liberals and sexual conservatives are neighbors. They work similar jobs, wave to each other from behind the wheels of similar cars, graduated from the same colleges, bring home roughly equivalent paychecks, and make small talk at the same churches. But despite these superficial similarities, these two groups have strikingly different worldviews. The main object of contention? Nothing less than the proper role of women, and the purpose of women's lives.

Luker conducted extensive interviews for her groundbreaking study, reported in her book *Abortion and the Politics of Motherhood,* and she found that pro-choice women see abortion and family planning as critical to their ability to fulfill their *essential identity* as human beings—to pursue careers and to participate fully in public and civic life. Anti-choice women see motherhood and child rearing as the central, irreducible fact of women's lives, and perceive abortion as a threat to their *distinctive identity* as women. Whereas pro-choice women, and sexual liberals, tend to view sex as pleasurable, natural, and healthy, sexual conservatives see it as a mysterious, overwhelming force, sacred within marriage, destructive outside of it.[25]

Indeed, Audrey Bilger, a professor of literature at Claremont McKenna College, points out in a recent *Huffington Post* editorial that the conservative movement's opposition to same-sex marriage is about more than just restricting marriage to "one man, one woman." It's about enforcing a certain, narrow model of marriage that demands a certain type of man and a certain type of woman—the "traditional" marriage. For conservatives, Bilger asserts, and this is backed up by Luker's research, procreation is the "central or defining purpose" of marriage. She pointed out that the woman who wants to postpone childbearing, or who wants to share childcare responsibilities equally with her partner as they both pursue their careers, or, horror of horrors, families where the father stays home with the children while the woman brings home the bacon, are as "unnatural" to these crusaders as the same-sex marriages that they so tirelessly vilify.

But despite the continued resistance to changing roles of women and changing family structures, many of us know women whose reproductive lives are the mirror image of what I saw when I began working for Planned Parenthood in 1974. Most of the patients then were women who already had three or five or ten children. They simply wanted to know *how to stop*. Today, most of the women haven't had children yet when they first get birth control. They come with the notion that they're going to proactively plan their family, when they are ready. They value and want parenthood, but they value their own lives, too. That is a profound shift. And it changes the entire context and meaning of "family planning."

"The irony," forty-year-old author Sarah Saffian pointed out to me as we were discussing this dichotomy in my living room, "is that biologically, there's no escaping the fact that a woman is most likely to become pregnant in her late teens and early twenties. The pill freed women from the tyranny of biologically determined destiny. But your body can't wait as long as your mind might want to wait for the parenthood siren call. You want to have your life; you want to have your own single identity. That's the new struggle." It made me recall that I'd met two women in their late thirties during the past year who have frozen some of their eggs, just in case they don't meet the man they want to father their children and form a relationship before their biological clocks stop ticking. One of them, Rachel Lehmann-Haupt, even wrote a book about her decision, *In Her Own Sweet Time*, and chronicled it in *Newsweek*.[26]

In 1974, the possibility of an unplanned pregnancy kept many women from pursuing the careers that they wanted. Now that women with stable access to reproductive healthcare are able to plan pregnancies—and we should never forget that for many women, this is still not a reality—it is the rigors of demanding careers that make no allowance for family life that are more likely to keep women from raising the families that they want. Like Gina Bianchini, the former Ning CEO, women are asking: "Realistically where's my maternity leave when I have a company to run or a highly essential position to fill?" These women are in much the same position as men I know—including my own son—who won't take paternity leave even though it is available to them, and even though they yearn to spend time with their newborns. They are afraid to risk the consequences to their careers and possibly even their employment when they're choosing to be out of the workplace for a long period of time.

In part as backlash to these unintended consequences of successful empowerment of women, the defenders of so-called traditional marriage have made headway in recent years. For many young people, the pendulum is swinging backward. Abstinence-only sex education is spreading the same kind of enforced ignorance that I was spoon-fed as a Texas teenager—with dangerous consequences to the health and lives of young people of both genders. Sexism with its power-over intent still puts all responsibility and blame for unintended pregnancy on the women.

Every woman needs economic equality to freely and successfully make her own choices about sex, pregnancy, and childbearing, but the effects play out differently in various economic classes. Low-income women, who are most at risk of being uninsured or underinsured, are correspondingly less likely to have access to birth control or reproductive healthcare. The $30 a month cost of birth control can mean a woman has to choose between paying the bills and buying her pills.

As recent news stories of women selling their eggs and leasing their wombs have poignantly illustrated, a tough economy can stop people from having children they desperately want, or push them to use their reproductive capacities for economic survival. New technologies create new possibilities and a wider array of choices, both positive ones and those fraught with previously unknown dilemmas.

In a *New York Times Magazine* story, Alex Kuczynski wrote about her own heartrending experience with infertility that led her to pursue having a child through surrogacy—something she and her husband could well afford but that is out of reach for most people. The woman in whose uterus Kuczynski's son gestated used the funds she earned as a surrogate to help pay for her college-aged daughter's tuition, though she said she also received personal satisfaction from helping other women experience parenthood. The surrogate's daughter in turn was contributing to her own college tuition costs by selling her eggs.[27] Though in some ways these uses of the body are equivalent to male athletes from poor families getting their bodies bashed on the football field or boxing ring to earn money for their families' keep, rapidly emerging new technologies are bringing a fresh set of variations on the ancient cycle of reproduction, accompanied by new ethical complexities to consider while attempting to ensure that childbearing decisions are really made as a matter of informed choice.

## ASK FOR IT BY NAME

Jacki Zehner believes we have to stop asking permission for our life and career choices. Jen Nedeau, the young social media consultant, thinks we just need to ask for what we want—wherever. But first we have to know what we want, why we deserve it, and then have the courage to ask for it by name.

Nedeau observes that women often don't recognize their own value, especially in the workplace. "I talk women through negotiating salary," she says. "I tell them to aim high. Do your research; talk to a guy who has the same job you want and ask him how much he gets paid." When someone says they didn't get what they wanted, she wonders, *Did they start by asking for it?* She is shocked to find out how many women never do.

Jenna Marie Mellor, the young woman I met when she was commissioned to do my oral history for the Radcliffe University's Schlesinger Library, applies the same principle to sex. When she was a student at Harvard, she taught workshops about sexual violence and assault for her peers. "I realized that people weren't defining consent based on their own terms, because they didn't know what gave *them* pleasure," she explains. "And if you don't know what gives you pleasure, then how can you possibly be empowered in a sexual circumstance? Considering that sexuality is so powerful, women not having access to their own power is a really big problem that I am trying to address."

For Mellor, power is about self-determination and individual autonomy. "It's about being able to navigate what you want in a particular instance and trying to accomplish it, not through force, but through self-understanding and self-actualization." It's about knowing what you want, and asking for it.

The kind of empowered asking-for-it that Nedeau and Mellor both advocate are important components of exercising our power-to create positive change. Economic independence for women amounts to more than just the ability to pay your own way, and enjoy some creature comforts while you're at it. It means restructuring the relationships between money and power, and, in particular, money and sexual power.

Just as I found it hard to advocate for myself until well into my adult life, some women are reluctant to speak up for themselves when it comes to financial empowerment. Part of this is a reasonable fear and recognition of the many barriers that do remain despite all the advances we have made. But we must also ask ourselves why, when the majority of barriers have been visibly dismantled, so many problems remain. We must ultimately look to ourselves to solve the problems of why women continue to be paid less than men for the same job, and to rectify the problem of fewer female CEOs and fewer women in the boardroom.

When women are economically empowered, the power balance changes in all areas of life. On the personal relationship level, look around. Everywhere we see evidence that when women gain more financial and political power, the power relationship between couples changes to one that is more equal and mutually respectful. Indeed, a recent Pew Research Center report found just that: A rising number of women—22 percent, up from just 3 percent in 1970—are out-earning their husbands.[28] Contrary to what one would believe, given the decades of backlash against women's economic advancement, these marriages are more likely than other more "traditional" unions to last.

But it's not easy to make that shift. Right-wing commentators like Laura Ingraham and Rush Limbaugh pounce and try to make women feel bad about our advances. The term *feminazi* comes to mind. It reflects the fear that the old worldviews of women's subordinate place—where we are barefoot and pregnant, where we have neither our £500 nor a womb of our own—is changing. And so it is changing, for the better all around, for men as well as women in my view. It's time for us to pounce back with a positive analysis of the change and the courage to embrace it.

By the way, remember Senator Van Dalsem, who made his men's club laugh with the barefoot and pregnant story? There's a postscript. The "university women" got him voted out of office in the next election. They used the chaos of that era's social ferment and change very strategically, for they saw it was their opportunity to gain political support for the issues they cared about.

As for Van Dalsem, he eventually saw the error of his ways, or perhaps decided he wanted to be reelected so badly that he changed his position. He was reelected to his Senate seat in 1972.

And in 1975, a resolution was introduced urging the Arkansas legislature to pass the Federal Equal Rights Amendment. The cosponsor was Senator Paul Van Dalsem.

Just as the chaos wrought by a changing world can be an opportunity to rewrite the rules, women can use this opportunity to advance our struggle for equality. Once we have secured the two basic precursors to power—£500 and a womb of our own—the other barriers become much easier to dismantle.

Standing in Her Power Means
Never Deferring to the Pie

# mariateresakumar

Maria Teresa Kumar, thirty-six, has seen women claim power against the steepest odds, so it's nothing new to her. Her mother and grandmother, natives of Colombia both, overcame limited education, poverty, and racial tension to raise families. In the area of highland Colombia where they were from, both women were single mothers by the time most young Americans leave college.

Kumar's grandmother was twenty-six and a mother to eight children when her husband abandoned her in a park in Bogotá. At the time, she did not even have a home. "Her tenacity, that despite all these obstacles, she was able to keep the family healthy and together, had a big impact on me," Kumar explains.

Her mother would navigate the challenges of single motherhood with similar resolution, adding to the demands of work and Maria Teresa's care a regimen of night classes to boost her job prospects after the family moved to the United States. "She could negotiate like crazy," Kumar says. She traded housecleaning for rent and took on volunteer work at the parochial school she believed was academically superior to public school in order to reduce the cost of her daughter's education.

Growing up in Sonoma County, California, Kumar remembers family members joking that they really lived "in Colombia, in Sonoma, California." But in spite of her early circumstances, she never considered her life or options in the least constricted. "It wasn't until I went to college that the notion that I had limitations crossed my mind. It was the first time people looked at me as a person of color."

For someone who has made the political engagement of

Latinos in the United States the central issue of her young career, racial awareness may have come to her late in the game. But the biculturalism of her upbringing, the dualities that came with having a white stepfather and traveling often between the United States and Colombia, meant a unique perspective in later life. She remembers Colombia, not the United States, as the first place where she saw "brown people" in business suits. It was not until she traveled to Washington, DC, that she saw racial minorities in the United States similarly clad in those emblems of professional success. "That," Kumar recalls, "was quite a moment."

She also knows there is more to power than professional success. The Latino population in the United States, though growing quickly in size and influence, has a long way to go before it exerts political power equal to its size. Nearly one in six Americans now identifies as Latino, and over the next four decades this figure is predicted to rise to one in three. But unlike other communities, which adopted strong voting habits as they fought for their enfranchisement and civil rights, the Latino community has grown into its political engagement slowly.

This is now changing. The 2008 presidential election saw Latinos claim a substantially greater share of the electorate than even four years before, and Kumar was in no small part responsible for this sea change. As the founding executive director of Voto Latino, she has teamed up with celebrities and tech gurus to encourage young Latinos to vote. The organization boasts actress Rosario Dawson as another of its founders—they started the work in 2004.

During the 2008 presidential election, in each of the five battleground states where Voto Latino focused its energy, voter participation among Latinos surpassed the national average by at least 5 percent.

Kumar began developing the idea as a graduate student at Harvard's Kennedy School, and it was not easy to sell people on at first. "No one quite understood what I was trying to do," she explains, "but I pitched the idea to Laurene Jobs and she got it. She funded Voto Latino's launch. It was a woman who wrote the first check. That was telling, and it was telling that she came from Silicon Valley. No one else believed that the technology would reach Latinos."

Also contrary to certain assumptions, Kumar says, "There are many other issues that Latinos feel are relevant to their lives besides immigration. The truth is that Latinos, more than other young people, were independent and voted on issues in the last election." The emergence of Latino voters as a major force in American politics promises to affect the national agenda, but it does not mean the rise of a one-size-fits-all constituency. Like all Americans, Latinos are diverse in their political views, their needs, and their beliefs.

As she has risen to national prominence, Kumar has worked to alter the perception of Latinos living in the United States. She cites as an example "the vision of a Latina," which for many "is the image of a sex symbol who does the cha-cha-cha in high heels while cleaning and taking care of her husband. It's against that distortion, I think, that Latinas need to assert themselves."

Her firsthand experience with power in formal negotiations from a gender perspective dates back to the mid-nineties and her work as a congressional staffer for Democratic Representative Vic Fazio. "I started working in Congress when I was twenty-three years old," she says, when "the Republicans were really giving it to President Bill Clinton." She remembers representing Fazio in an important meeting. "I was the voice of my boss at the table, but I was significantly junior to everybody there and a Latina. The other people at the table were U.S. Trade Representative Charlene Barshefsky, House Speaker Newt Gingrich, and three or four others from Gingrich's staff, all men. They were not happy that I was representing my congressman."

At a disadvantage for her age, race, and gender, Kumar drew on an inner reserve of strength and self-reliance. The example of the women in her life had taught her "nobody can do it for you; you have to negotiate for yourself." In other areas of life, however, she lacked the role models and teachers who help many get ahead. "I had really long hair at the time," she laughs, thinking back. "The first thing I did when I got the job was cut and straighten it so I looked older but, at the same time, credible and professional. No one had ever walked me through this before."

If there was any secret to Kumar's success, she says, it came from overpreparing. "Know your stuff and don't be intimidated," she advises young women. "My response to the environment in

Congress was not that I had limitations, but that I'd better know my stuff better than anyone else in the room." This would ultimately win her boss's trust and more significant responsibilities, which in turn gave her a greater confidence in her own abilities.

But she has also found that power can be a tricky thing. "When I started working with Voto Latino," she says, "I was naive. The organization is about working to empower the disenfranchised. I thought everyone wanted to empower people. But it turns out that when you empower someone, someone else thinks they are giving up power." The view of power as a zero-sum game (what I call "power-over") has, in Kumar's experience, been a brake on the speed of change.

Kumar is unapologetic. "Show me the pie," she says, referring to the idea of finite power, which she categorically rejects, "and I will defer to the pie." Till then, she continues, with no excuses, to pursue her mission to make the promise of political equality a reality.[1]

# unlimit yourself:
# stand in power, walk with intention

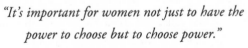

*"It's important for women not just to have the power to choose but to choose power."*

**—KATIE ORENSTEIN**

- What's happening?

- Why is it happening?

- What do you want to have happen?

- How are you going to make it happen?

These four questions were typed on a 3" x 5" note card sitting almost alone atop my utilitarian gray steel desk when I arrived for my post as the chief executive of Permian Basin Planned Parenthood on a steamy August morning in 1974. I was so excited that my previous teaching experience and civil rights work had led me to this opportunity, yet anxious about how to do a good job in my providential new career.

Next to the desk was a cardboard shipping box with a note taped to it instructing me to return the intrauterine devices inside to the manufacturer for a refund. That was about the extent of the directives left behind. That wasn't much to guide a newly minted chief executive with no experience in healthcare administration or managing an organization, let alone clues as to where I'd find the strength, courage, and creativity I'd need to lead a social justice movement during what were to become increasingly challenging times.

The note card with the four provocative questions also turned out to be yet another example of how what you need is always there if you can see it. For in their simplicity the questions served as a relevant framing of intentional leadership and the power-to principles I've employed ever since. I struggle to stay within their framework of conscious intent, standing in the power of my own clear vision of what I want to have happen and walking with intention to accomplish my goals. But the proactive line of inquiry suggested by the questions has stayed with me as I learned on the job about the power to make things happen by defining the terms, setting the agenda, figuring out how to mobilize the necessary resources to make it happen, and never taking my eye off the ball until the job was done.

*Merriam Webster's* says intention is the determination to act in a certain way, suggesting a clear formulation and deliberateness, from the Latin root *intentio,* meaning effort, exertion, attention, and in religious and psychological logic, to signify a mode of being in relation with one's intent: to be self-aware of what is intended, to own it, to claim responsibility for it. It's the power-to in action. Intention, to me, goes a step beyond ambition. Ambition is aspirational—having a goal, hope, or desire. Intention implies assuming you can and have every right to achieve your ambition and that you care enough to make it happen.

This concept is critically important to inculcate in girls from birth, and it's a skill women should practice and hone throughout our lives. Sometimes I wish that along with their Gardasil (the vaccine to ward off HPV) at age eleven, girls could get a shot of intention; maybe that would also ward off the *Reviving Ophelia* moment that so many of them go through at puberty, when their strong selves seem to fade away.

In her 2005 book, *Necessary Dreams: Ambition in Women's Changing Lives,* psychiatrist Anna Fels says, "Women more than men need to actively imagine themselves into their futures because little is mapped out for them at this historical moment. Unlike men, women have few accepted roles mapped out for them in our society—or more accurately they have too many: innovative professional, devoted mother, competent employee, sexually attractive 'babe,' supportive wife, talented homemaker, independent wage earner, to name a few. It falls nearly entirely to the individual woman to carve out a life for herself with adequate meaning and satisfactions."[1]

Boys are socialized from birth to see the world as their oyster, and they have no reticence about claiming their power as a matter of course. Girls are typically raised to attune themselves first to the needs of others, to respond rather than assume their own agency, even though today they are simultaneously told they can do anything they want to do. This duality with which girls are socialized could instill a productive balance if it were extended to boys, too. But it sparks an inherent conflict for girls precisely because it is relegated to one gender; perhaps that's a clue as to why the pink princess trope remains attractive to young girls—it's just so much easier to get swept away than to sort out these conflicting messages and take responsibility for self-definition.

Even though girls and women increasingly understand that our vistas can be unlimited, striking a satisfying balance between aspiration and nurture can put a crimp in anyone's embrace of intention. Whether we're talking about work, politics, or our personal life, those dynamics are the same.

## PLENTY OF AMBITION, BUT DEFICIT OF INTENTION

I'll start with an example from politics to shed light on how intention, or the lack of it, influences women's lives. Goodness knows, the 2008 primary elections brought a mother lode of examples of gender-related ambition, intention, and lack of same to mine for insights.

Hillary Clinton's controversial candidacy for president supercharged public interest in women's political ascent and set off frenzied media attention. At the time, I wrote an article for *Elle* magazine on why women do or don't run for office; that triggered my own inquiry into women's relationship with power. My objective was to showcase the numerous organizations that have sprung up in recent years to recruit, train, and support women candidates. What I thought would be a celebration of the most recent "Year of the Woman" turned out to be a disquieting recognition that I'd have to deal primarily with why women *don't* run.

My research found paradox after paradox, some of which we've touched on in previous chapters: Women today compose the majority of college graduates; four women receive bachelor's degrees to every three men. We believe we can freely choose our own fates, aspire to any profession. We control most of the purchasing power. We even constitute the majority of voters in most elections. But despite all this putative equality, men, by and large, still make the laws that govern just about every aspect of our lives, from public education to war and peace to equal pay policies to reproductive freedom (or its opposite). That's shameful, and America can't have a truly representative democracy when half its citizens are so grossly underrepresented.

True, there's a world of difference from 1905, when President Grover Cleveland declared (without getting impeached!) that "sensible and responsible women don't want to vote," to 2008, when Hillary Clinton very nearly got enough votes to become the first woman to win a major party's nomination for president. Still, it's appalling that ninety-four years after Jeannette Rankin of Montana became the first woman elected to Congress, ninety years after all American women won the right to vote in the Constitution, and thirty-eight years since Title IX gave women equal access to educational institutions, courses of study, and competitive sports, America still ranks an embarrassing eighty-seventh among nations in the proportion of women holding national legislative office.[2] We think we're on the road to eliminating sexism and we have made significant progress; still, we're far behind countries as diverse as Rwanda, Austria, Sweden, and Cuba in regard to which gender is running the political show, and we're losing ground in comparison to other nations. Not only do men occupy 83 percent of congressional seats, they also run city hall in 83 percent of cities with populations larger than thirty thousand. Gender imbalance rules the ticket—up, down, left, right, and center.[3]

"People are floored when they find out how few women we have in elected office at all levels," contends Jennifer Lawless, whom I interviewed for the *Elle* article. A Brown University political science professor at the time, Lawless, then thirty-three, had put her money where her pen was after cowriting with Richard Fox *It Takes a Candidate: Why Women Don't Run for Office* in 2005. She ran for Congress against a male incumbent in 2006. "I didn't win, but I did establish myself as a credible candidate," she told me. "One of these days he will retire, and I'll be in a great position to run for and win that seat." Meanwhile, she founded Real Equality and Progress for Rhode Island (REP/PAC), a political action committee that raises money for women candidates. It's a move that kept her in the center of state politics, building her support base should she decide to run again. Lawless has since moved on to head the American University's Women in Politics Institute in Washington, DC—an opportunity she decided she didn't want to forego—but she plans to stay involved in Rhode Island politics through her PAC, and by doing political commentary for local media.[4]

Timing can delay or detour intention, as Lawless found out, though it need not, should not, derail it. That's why long-term vision and persistence are critical factors.

Another group, Emerge America, is working hard to increase the numbers of Democratic women in office from local to federal government, and has launched an initiative to grow from its current seven to twenty state programs by 2012. And there are a number of such organizations out there—some targeting young women, some all politically motivated women, some pro- or anti-choice women—all devoted to increasing the numbers of women in public office at all levels of government. Many groups are nonpartisan, accepting women regardless of political party, such as the Women's Campaign Forum, the Women Under Forty Political Action Committee (WUFPAC), and the White House Project's Go Run program. Others, like Emerge America and Emily's List on the Democratic side, and WISH List and the Richard G. Lugar Excellence in Public Service Series on the Republican side, recruit on a partisan basis. So if you're a woman with political aspirations, it's easy as pie to find a multitude of support systems whose objective is to lift you into elected office. That makes it even more inexcusable that the dial is still moving so slowly toward parity.

When the Women's Campaign Forum, founded in 1974—and the first group to support pro-choice women candidates with money as well as training—confronted its lackluster success at enlarging the pool of female elected officials, they asked the women in their training programs why they had chosen to run for office. "Because someone asked me," came the almost-universal answer. So WCF started "She Should Run," a virally marketed program to get people to nominate women they believe would be well-qualified candidates. Nominees are then encouraged to take the skills training they need to run an effective campaign. Even so, the majority of women who've been nominated do not translate "She should run" to "I am running."[5]

Similarly, when Lawless updated her 2005 book research for a 2008 paper, "Why Are Women Still Not Running for Office?" she found little had changed. She still dubs women's pervasive reticence to advance themselves in politics an "ambition gap," and calls it the single greatest factor holding women back from equality in political representation.[6]

But I concluded it's not a lack of ambition that holds women back; rather, it's a lack of intention. The fact that many women still wait to be asked to dance doesn't mean they don't want to take a spin on the floor. Women have plenty of ambition. But they don't yet feel they have the agency assigned to men as a birthright. These political programs, therefore, might be barking up the wrong trees when they put their money on helping women overcome external barriers, for the most stubborn barriers remain within. Because the real question is whether women have sufficient *intention* to start from the assumption that they can (and by all rights should) propel themselves to parity in elective office and have the will to stay with it till they do.

Adding to the challenge, just at the time women in these training programs are setting forth to swell their numbers in office, a new hurdle has materialized. As we saw in chapter 4, younger women don't necessarily share older women's feeling of urgency about electing women to office because young women have experienced less overt discrimination themselves. In a good example of the co-opting process described in that chapter, many young feminist Obama supporters assiduously rejected the notion that gender matters in candidate selection and shuddered at the very thought that women should make special efforts to elect women or to build women's political clout per se. Bitter verbal battles erupted about whether women have an obligation to support women candidates, causing third-wave feminist blogger Jessica Valenti to write a cease-and-desist order of sorts in *The Nation* about what she called "The Sisterhood Split." Her message to older feminists was essentially, "We appreciate what you've done to get us here, but bug off now and don't tell us how to vote."[7]

I respect anyone's desire not to be told how to vote in a particular race. Still, in the bigger picture, the need for sisterly solidarity is evident if we want our share of the decision-making power. And that's change we need, because though you can opt out of an area of employment you don't like, you can't opt out of politics, which affects everyone whether they participate or not.

Emerge America's San Francisco–based founder, Andrea Dew Steele, was thirty-four in 2002 when she founded Emerge California, and thirty-seven when the organization launched its national aspirations in 2005. She drove this point home when she told me in an interview, "Men under forty are 40 percent more likely to consider running than women. Young women don't experience as much discrimination starting out. So they don't realize the problem until they get older and have experiences, such as not making partner in their firm because they can't work one hundred hours a week with small kids."[8]

Lawless's research supports the conclusion that the reason many young women don't feel the same "gender conscious" impetus their mothers did to vote for woman candidates is this: They haven't personally encountered the kind of discrimination that leads their elders to fear they won't have another opportunity to vote for a woman for president in their lifetime. Still, if younger women possess a stronger sense of possibility for themselves as individuals in political life than women in previous generations have assumed, I see few signs they're acting on their belief in numbers that can rewrite the narrative anytime soon. There are many excuses.

## "Politics Is a Patriarchal Game."

When she was just twenty and a senior in college, Liz Funk published her first book, *Supergirls Speak Out: Inside the Secret Crisis of Overachieving Girls.* She's had her own political blog and newspaper column. Still, two years later, she says, "I think politics is fascinating, and I feel privileged to have grown up in an era where it's cool for girls to be smart; feminism has succeeded in creating a culture where it's socially acceptable to be feminine and fun, and also to obsess over the primaries and root for our chosen candidate." But any aspirations she may have had to run for office have been diminished by her perception of politics as a "patriarchal, serious, stiff-upper-lipped game." She also reviles "the MySpace culture" in which the most embarrassing parts of one's private life can be made public. "Honestly, I shudder to think what kind of unflattering information could surface from the Internet."[9]

Judging from the male politicians whose sexual peccadilloes make the evening news with astonishing regularity (like former Democratic presidential candidate John Edwards, who fathered a child out of wedlock while his wife was coping with cancer, or Republican Nevada Senator John Ensign, who bought off his staffer with a large financial settlement after an affair with the man's wife—incidents proving sexual misbehavior to be more bipartisan than, say, passing health reform in Congress), it seems they are far less likely to imagine their improprieties will be exposed and far more inclined to have the arrogance of entitlement that leads them to believe they can get away with it. Like babies who believe that if there's a blanket over their own heads, nobody can see them, these male politicians apparently believe the world revolves around them. Meanwhile, women's point of reference is exactly the opposite. We worry too much about what others think of us, we are oversocialized to be "nice," and above all, we fear being rejected.[10]

Funk's comments are dead-on representative of studies conducted by the White House Project, the Women's Campaign Forum, and other groups that have investigated the lack of women candidates in our country. Another hurdle is money: The cost of political campaigns has skyrocketed, and the perceived and real barriers to fundraising that women candidates face keeps them on the sidelines. She or he with the largest list of well-heeled contacts and the longest record of giving to other candidates is most likely to win.

Though women may be as capable as men of asking for money (Emily's List, which raises money for pro-choice Democratic women, is one of the largest, most powerful PACs in the country), women are still less likely to give money to their chosen candidates. Data from the Women's Campaign Forum shows that in the 2008 election cycle, women gave only 31 percent of the total political contributions, and just a third of those were to women candidates. Part of this has to do with the persistent wage disparities that women face; we simply have less money to give. Part of the discrepancy may be that among some married couples, the man directs the political donations. But certainly part of it is that we have yet to consolidate our combined financial power and use it intentionally to demand our due. It's a fact: Money equals influence in elections. And if we are ever to get more women who support women's rights elected, leveraging our collective influence through the power of the purse will be critical.[11]

Thirty-year-old Jamia Wilson was a grassroots mobilizer for progressive organizations before entering NYU to work on a master's degree in humanities and social thought. She has considered running for office because, she says, "It is imperative for underrepresented groups to ensure that our voices are heard. As an African American woman, I was inspired by both of the 2008 Democratic candidates." Her big worry, however, has to do with how much money it would take to mount a strong campaign.[12]

## "A Man Would Never Question
## His Ability to Do the Job."

But what surprised me most was that every single women's political group leader and elected official I spoke with said, in stunningly similar words, that women's resistance to seeking political power has to do with factors beyond family obligations, money, or reluctance to relinquish privacy. Here's a composite of those comments: "A man sees one thing he *can* do in the candidate job description and he'll throw his hat in the ring without being asked. A woman sees one thing she *can't* do and she'll demur. Or she'll go take courses or volunteer to get whatever experience she thinks she needs to qualify, then she'll wait till someone asks her to run. By the time she's sworn in, the man is already in office, and quite likely the committee chair who sets the agenda."

Former Scottsdale, Arizona, Mayor Kathryn (Sam) Campana commented, "A man would never question his ability to do the job; he'd just assume the women in the office would do the parts of it he didn't know." Ellen Malcolm, head of Emily's List, concurred: "Women tend to defer and be asked to run, where men decide they're going to go straight ahead and act on their ambitions." Separate interviews, different levels of government under discussion, different political parties represented, same diagnosis.[13]

But just as we can choose to redefine power to mean the power to accomplish what needs to be done, women can redefine political ambition to fit their intention. They just need to see things from the vantage point of their power-to. As WISH List's Candy Straight pointed out, "Most men run for power and money, while most women run to be public servants."[14]

It's true. When they're ticked off about something that's happening to someone they care about, women run for office—and they do it despite their own fears and reservations about their qualifications. For instance, the late Representative Shirley Chisholm, the first African American woman elected to Congress, beat her opponent in 1968 despite being dismissed as a "little schoolteacher"; she was sick and tired of the way that the people in her Brooklyn neighborhood, many of them low-income and/or people of color, were continually being overlooked in Washington, DC.[15] Senator Patty Murray of Washington State originally got into politics to save an important preschool program from budget cuts; her personal, vocal commitment to improving education led her to victory over a well-financed incumbent in 1992.[16]

Anger can be a positive motivator. Because goodness knows there are plenty of injustices in the world that need fixing. A woman might not be as likely as a man to wake up in the morning and say, "I'm going to run for the Senate" just because she wants the power-over of the position (though there are always exceptions, ahem, Sarah Palin, whom I discussed in a previous chapter). *But,* if a woman sees something upsetting, something unjust, then she is much *more* likely to find the courage of her intention to blast through any barrier, internal or external, to try to use her power-to fix it, and thus becomes more likely to be willing to run for office if that's what it takes to make things right.

Philanthropist and political activist Barbara Lee, who founded the Barbara Lee Family Foundation to find solutions to the underrepresentation of women in government, recounted Washington Senator Patty Murray's story to me. The excitement in Lee's voice as she relayed the details was palpable. When Patty was a young mother, she became riled up because the legislature tried to cut funding to the preschool in her district. "She marched her kids up to the state house one day, one child in her arms, to talk to her state legislator about her concerns and he hardly gave her the time of day. In fact, he dismissed her by telling her she was 'just a mom in tennis shoes.' So Patty put on her running shoes, and she ran."[17]

Murray not only proceeded to get thirteen thousand signatures in support of the preschool to save its funding, she adopted the senator's demeaning epithet, "just a mom in tennis shoes," as her campaign slogan when she ran for the school board as a direct result of the legislator's insult. Later, she ran for the state senate and won. Today, a quarter-century later, that "mom in tennis shoes" is serving her third term as a U.S. senator.[18]

This is a great success story, but it's not typical. Anna Fels cautions, "You won't have women eager to take over men's jobs if they still have two jobs for men's one. For men, having power is perceived as sexy. For women, it's a mixed bag. And the social downside of being seen as aggressive, unpleasant, and unfeminine—think of the rage generated by Hillary's strength as a candidate—is so profound that a lot of women say, 'Forget it.'"[19]

This is a problem we must solve—fast. Women can't afford to say, "Forget it." There's too much at stake. Nor can we partake in our power only at moments when we want it and relinquish it at other times when the going gets too hard (which is exactly what James Chartrand, in chapter 4, has done). This might sound like tough love, but it's really only fair to those who do go out and push the boundaries on behalf of all of us.

Certainly, Clinton's candidacy showed that any woman who threatens the gender power balance as profoundly as she does, by "aiming to break the highest and hardest glass ceiling" as she put it, has to be prepared for the most vicious attacks. She must enter the field understanding it's not about her but rather about the attackers' insecurities. That includes disparagements from political opponents and pundits as well as those from yahoos who don't have a clue—like the creator of the Hillary Nutcracker, who emailed me his assurance that he wasn't being sexist at all by selling a Clinton image whose splayed metal "thighs" have lugs that can crush—nuts. The nutcracker example is all too real, not a *Saturday Night Live* skit, though Tina Fey's "Bitch is the new black" became a classic spoof on the rampant sexism in political media.

## "Add Women, Change Everything."

Hillary Clinton, the woman Stephen Colbert admiringly if indelicately said has "lady balls," demonstrated that women are beyond any doubt tough enough, smart enough, persistent enough, ambitious enough, courageous enough, and can raise money well enough to compete in the political arena at the highest levels, if they choose to do so. She is a role model whose candidacy, even in losing the nomination, delivered the message often chanted at her rallies: "Yes, she can!" to an entire younger generation. Indeed, it might turn out that the most empowering lesson young women learned from Hillary Clinton is that a woman can lose a contentious race and it's okay—she doesn't die, her supporters still love her, and her adversary might even hand her a plum assignment.

And on another positive note, even though Congress seems stuck at that 17 percent to 83 percent female-male ratio, there is a growing cadre of women such as Arizona Representative Gabrielle Giffords, Florida's Debbie Wasserman Schultz, and New York's Senator Kirsten Gillibrand, all of whom ran initially while they were under forty, and are thus young enough to enjoy long careers in Congress—meaning they could become the Ted Kennedys, Patrick Leahys, or Max Baucuses of the future, chairs of the most powerful congressional committees. And that's *huge*. Because most of the women now in Congress didn't run for office until their children were grown. Later-life candidacy doesn't necessarily prevent someone from moving into the leadership, as the first woman speaker of the house, Nancy Pelosi, elected to her first term at age forty-seven, illustrates. Still, it takes years, decades even, to gain the seniority that puts a member in line for committee leadership roles, and, as has been pointed out, she who holds the gavel determines the agenda that everyone else will be voting on.[20]

To help speed up the boundary pushing, we could use a mom in tennis shoes to advocate for daycare for children of elected officials so women aren't faced with that barrier—male politicians whose wives hold employment outside the home would benefit from that, too, and perhaps it could become a model for other organizations and businesses.

Since men—even really progressive ones—have little motivation to change the power structure, women have little choice but to become the change we want to see. Does anyone think Secretary of State Hillary Clinton speaking out against rape in the Congo, or delivering a major State Department policy speech on how reproductive rights are women's human rights, was just random luck? Not a chance.

Jennifer Lawless cites evidence that women in political office, regardless of party affiliation, are more likely to prioritize issues that affect women intimately, such as healthcare, daycare, equal pay, and abortion access. "The Senate Judiciary Committee never again will grill a woman who charges a man with sexual harassment the way they did Anita Hill when she challenged Supreme Court nominee Clarence Thomas because two women—California Senator Dianne Feinstein and Minnesota Senator Amy Klobuchar—now serve on the committee," Lawless avers.[21]

This called to my mind Women's Equality Day in 1998, literally the day I'd seen Clinton speak earlier at the 150th anniversary celebration of the first women's rights convention in Seneca Falls, New York. Back in DC, as I saw on C-SPAN that evening, almost every woman in the House of Representatives stood together on the Capitol steps, a sea of bright-hued skirts and suit jackets, to declare their solidarity across party lines to require that federal employees' health insurance cover birth control. That they prevailed is significant, but that they recognized the injustice of failing to cover contraception while covering other prescription drugs, including Viagra, happened in no small part because of their gender sensibility.

But since power unused is power useless, it's well to remember this victory didn't spring forth organically. Thanks to my early lesson in the value of asking those four important questions if one is in a leadership role, I had instituted a political strategy of advancing our own policy initiatives, both when I was heading up the Arizona affiliate and on the national level after I became president of Planned Parenthood Federation of America in 1996, instead of merely responding to attacks. Had there not been an organized campaign we called Responsible Choices—all credit to some brilliant young women on my staff at the time, who did the research to find out what was happening, called Congress's attention to the fact that insurance didn't typically cover birth control (and why that was wrong), worked with supportive legislators to draft legislation, then organized the power of grassroots support for the measure—it wouldn't have happened. And had there not been a young pharmacist—then twenty-seven-year-old Jennifer Erickson—and a smart lawyer—Roberta Riley—who put a human face on the story by suing Erickson's employer for failing to cover contraception, we might not have been so persuasive.[22]

Though many were afraid to take the risk that proactive legislation brings—you can open up cans of worms you never imagined once legislatures start tinkering with bills—I'm convinced that setting out an agenda is the best way to define political debate on your terms, besides doing some good if it passes.

The White House Project's tagline is "Add women, change everything." You may not like politics, but it affects every aspect of your life whether or not you are personally involved. We have to stand in our political power and walk with intention toward what we want to make happen or we lose all the way around.

Women need to internalize these messages about running for office: Start from the power of your most passionate intention. Let that release your ambition and let your ambition feed your intention. Find the group that best fits your political values—they're ready and eager to help prepare you. But don't wait to be asked. Ask the questions yourself. Look around at what's happening and why. Decide what you want to have happen and go make it so.

" . . . and the day came when the risk it took to remain in the bud was more painful than the risk it took to blossom."—Anaïs Nin

What are you ticked off enough about that you'll get politically involved?

## IN PHILANTHROPY: TWO WOMEN OF INTENTION FEED THE WORLD'S HUNGRY

During a reception before the Women's Forum New York's thirty-fifth anniversary dinner, I struck up a conversation with new member Nicole Sexton. She had moved to New York just that week to become executive director of the Feed Fund Foundation. We had a great talk that started because we'd caught some political happening on the bar's television screen and began fretting over our mutual observation that women have more power than we use.

She told me that the burlap feedbags I'd noticed at the Whole Foods checkout counter were the brainchild of two young women who started the Feed Fund: twenty-five-year-old model Lauren Bush, and twenty-nine-year-old Ellen Gustafson, formerly a public relations officer for the United Nations World Food Programme. Remarkably, in the last two years, these young women had created a multimillion-dollar business with a subsidiary foundation that receives a set donation for every bag sold, equaling about one-third of the sales price. That money is in turn donated to the Food Programme. The Feed Fund Foundation is now its fourth largest private cash donor.

"You should interview them," Nicole suggested. So I made a date to go talk with Bush and Gustafson in their burlap-scented office in an apartment building. Even the doormat follows the beige and brown feedbag theme. These two passionate young women speak the language of intention naturally. Feed Project CEO Bush (yes, from that Bush family; she's George W.'s niece), is well aware she has lived a life of privilege. Projecting a gentle confidence, she's already had her celebrity turn, which is how she became an honorary spokesperson for the Food Programme. But she doesn't care about being a model anymore: "It got me to where I am, but it's not what I want to be." She traveled to Africa as a teenager with her grandmother Barbara, where she saw the plight of women in a Masai village who were married off at thirteen and were accorded little value despite their hard work. She witnessed hungry kids in Chad and realized it was sheer luck that she had been born into a culture where she could aspire to whatever her heart desired. As a result, she decided that she wanted to do something to help. At Princeton, she wrote her senior thesis on women in developing countries. "I think my generation is very mindful [of the global issues] because of the Internet," she said.

Before going to work for the Food Programme, Gustafson, who projects a fierce energy, had studied security policy at Columbia University and worked at the Council on Foreign Relations and at ABC-TV. "I came to food because I started looking at a map of the world and had the sense that, wow, the places where people are terrorists—they're all hungry! And, you know, I'm sort of a terrorist when I'm hungry. I became very passionate about the idea that there are these fundamental problems behind the security issues. Give a kid a free school meal; get them to school; get them educated; get the girls to school; get them nutrients. No-brainer. . . . There's a lot of crossover between what might happen from a security standpoint and what is happening from a humanitarian standpoint."

Bush had already hatched the feedbag idea when she met Gustafson, who became the Feed Project's executive vice president. Both were despairing that the UN bureaucracy would not allow them to implement the feedbag idea, even though they were sure it would generate substantial revenue for the organization's work. Then a moment of opportunity opened up because Gustafson's supervisor left; unsupervised, and no longer reined in by a superior who had quashed the idea, they were now able to develop their plan.

## "It Didn't Seem Easy, but It Seemed Like We Could."

"Lauren and I had a different sense of passion about this issue, and we wanted to make it happen," Gustafson said, with fervent intention. But then came another stumbling block: The UN lawyers decided the bags couldn't be sold under the jurisdiction of the Food Programme. "Maybe because we were young, maybe because we were women, they saw us as people bucking the system. And it was a new idea. For us, it seemed not like an easy thing to do, but certainly something we *could* do."

Bush had contacts from the fashion industry willing to help. They quickly lined up a retailer, Amazon.com, and *Marie Claire* magazine agreed to do a story on them. "We had planned our launch party," Bush relayed. "We had all these elements to really make that first bag a success. We thought we were delivering this perfect package to an organization and all they had to do was fill out the vendor forms for Amazon.com." Still, the lawyers said no.

The two women were left stunned. They both cried. But then they stepped back and took a good look at what was happening, why, what they wanted to have happen, and, most important, what they could do to make it happen.

They concluded, "We have one problem to solve. It seemed very complex theoretically, but actually it wasn't all that complex. If you're able to see the forest through the trees and say, 'Okay, the one thing we need to work on is this,' that's very empowering. A lot of people have done that one thing, which is to set up a company. People set up companies all the time. Here we are, we've been highly educated and have all the resources in the world in New York City. It can't be that hard. To be honest, I think for women especially—maybe for everybody—it's a competence issue. Once you've done that one thing that you think seems so ridiculously impossible, then everything else is probably solvable."

So without a business plan, and with just enough cash and credit to carry them through the first month of production, they launched their first product: the Feed One bag, which provides $20 to feed one child for a year. Now they have almost a dozen different bags and a vision of making Feed a sustainable brand known to and valued by everyone in America, perhaps even globally. Every bag is branded with the number representing the amount of the donation for that item so people can connect the value of their gift to the end result of feeding a child. They created a for-profit business to manufacture and sell the bags. The bulk of the profit then goes to the Feed Foundation, which delivers the contributions directly to the UN Food Programme.

I couldn't resist asking whether they thought that if they'd had a little more testosterone, they would have framed security as more of a war and "let's have more tanks" issue, rather than a nutrition issue.

Gustafson leaned forward and shot back, "I went on an aircraft carrier with the special forces in Fort Lewis. I was just in Annapolis with my former boss, who's now the superintendent of the Naval Academy. I definitely have that side of me that's very interested in power, in hard power. I don't think those [gender] distinctions fit anymore. I don't think it has to do with my gender necessarily that I became very interested in nutrition." Still, she acknowledged, "As a woman, you do tend to have some sort of mother gene in you somewhere, where you look at other human beings and maybe have a somewhat easier time than men saying, 'That could be me, that could be my kid, that could be my mother.' This relatability between human beings that makes you think: *If that's the truth, and I don't do anything, what's my point?*"

I also questioned them about their thoughts around the difference between their generation and previous ones. "For us, demographically speaking, we weren't in any way rare. For us to continue to be successful doesn't seem all that out of the ordinary. I can't remember myself thinking that I was being held back for any reason because of being a girl," Gustafson said. And Bush concurred, adding, "I think it's also exposure. I feel like my world is so much broader than my mom's was at my age." Much of that, she believes, is due to access to information through the Internet and social media.

Gustafson's parents taught her to negotiate the salary offer from her very first job and to value herself, believe in herself, to "go in there and ask for more, tell your story, and prove that you deserve more."

Bush's advice to young women is to have a clear vision of who you are, what you're good at, and what you can do to create change in the world, whether it's through business or nonprofit work. "One thing I've found helpful is thinking back to what I loved to do as a child, before I *had* to do something. For me, it was making things, selling things, creating things. I think women sometimes force themselves into places because they want to prove that they can be there, or they shy away from places because they feel like they're not good enough to be there. So, be clear with yourself first, because then when you face the world you're going to be clearer with others: This is who I am, this is what I'm good at, this is what I deserve. Reflect quietly about what gets you excited and motivated and passionate about doing something, whether it's your career, a hobby, whatever it is. Having that quiet reflection before you go out and try to make your way is important."

Both of these young women had a simple, clear intention—everyone should have a nourishing meal—that they put into action. "If we can just provide the means for these kids and these families to have a nourishing meal once a day, then everything else is going to be a whole lot easier for them."

And did they ever persuade the UN World Food Programme to adopt their project? No, but they say, "Now we have a great relationship with everyone there because they're good at feeding kids and we're good at selling bags."

That is *so* standing in your power and walking with intention.

## IN CAREER CHOICES: EMBRACING FORTUITY WITH INTENTION

Not everyone has the same specificity about their passion as early in their lives as Lauren Bush and Ellen Gustafson did. But when you approach the world with intention, even if you don't have a precise vision of the exact job you'll have at the end of the day, good things are likely to occur. I've generally found that when you make a plan, nine times out of ten you won't achieve all of it, but you'll achieve considerably more than if you hadn't had one. And along the way, because you've staked out a goal and started working toward it, numerous other opportunities will pop up.

There's falling into a good situation (as I did when I took the leap of faith and went to that interview with the Planned Parenthood board in West Texas) and there's actively seeking out a good situation, but either way you have to know it when you see it and be willing to take the risk of going for it. Sometimes it's merely a matter of standing in your own power by having the courage to follow your passion, until your passion surprises you by becoming your vocation.

# **power**tool number six

**WEAR THE SHIRT: declare publicly your gut-level commitment to whatever you decide to do with your one "wild and precious life."[23] what's happening and why? what's your vision of what you think should happen? how can you make it happen? go stand in your power and walk with intention to make it so.**

In 1984, Bonnie Marcus was newly divorced with two young children to raise on her own. She had been teaching kindergarten, but decided that now, as a single mom without a co-parent to relieve some of the pressure, she would have less patience and energy for her own children if she had spent her workday looking after other people's kids. She decided to look for a standard nine-to-five job, the kind where she could leave the day's concerns at the office.

She answered an ad in the local paper for a medical secretary for a cardiac practice. She recalls, "I went in for the interview but they told me I was too qualified (I had a master's degree) and were reluctant to hire me because I would probably leave in a few months. But several days later they called me back and said they were working with a healthcare management company to form a cardiac rehabilitation center with thirty local physicians, and the management company was looking for an administrator for the center. They encouraged me to apply."

Marcus went to the interview with no management experience; in fact, she had no business experience whatsoever. "I didn't talk about my business experience because I had none," she said. "I did talk about my passion for cardiac fitness. I had been teaching aerobics. I talked about how the mission of their company resonated with me because my dad had a heart attack at fifty-seven and my family completely changed our lifestyle at home, becoming more active and eating heart-healthy foods. I showed the cardiac center how their mission and message was my way of life. They hired me! Certainly not because of anything but my passion and energy for the company and their mission."

Marcus learned the business and within a year and a half, was managing eleven cardiac rehab centers for the company. This was the start of a very successful corporate career. She's now a certified executive coach, motivational speaker, and radio show host of Women Mean Business Radio.[24]

## Many Choices,
## but Only Four Strategies for Choosing

Perhaps the younger women are, the less they see standing in power and walking with intention as a surprising thing to do. I hope that's the case, because it would mean we've made significant progress. Asking what they want to make happen and doing it is just the way to be. And some find that daunting. So it's not uncommon to hear young women complaining about all their choices, feeling the pressure of having too many. Let's get real: A choice of options does make life seem more complicated, but would anyone want to relinquish them? For in truth, the increase in options provokes women to walk with intention as an automatic gesture. And having choices, as we have seen, is what makes walking with intention possible.

Writer Courtney Martin has just been jolted by turning thirty, but I'll always think of her as a young-un no matter what. Funny how that happens. We have often appeared together on a panel called the WomenGirlsLadies with two other women. Collectively, we span four decades, me from the World War II "ungeneration," as it has been dubbed, to Gen Y or Millennial (Martin's on the cusp of both, and sometimes we invite a younger student onto the panel). Each of us tells how she came to feminism and what she sees as the unfinished business of the women's movement.[25]

Martin quips that when older feminists like what young women do, we call them "empowered" and when we don't, we call them "entitled." She ponders the dynamic between the younger generations of feminists and those of us who came before them. "Sometimes I feel as if my generation is feminism's Frankensteins. You've created us and now you don't know what to do with us! You've taught us to speak up and advocate for ourselves, and now we sometimes overstep our bounds in the workplace or expect too much responsibility too soon."

Despite the disappointments that may attend the experiences of young women who want it all, Martin believes that this boldness and ambition is a good thing. But in order for the disappointments not to become overwhelming, she thinks younger women should learn that power comes in different forms, and can be used for different purposes. "We have to be mentored to see the distinction between power that is earned and emanates from the inside—the worthwhile kind—and power that is lusted after, grabbed at, gifted from on high—the kind that usually leaves us simply hungry for more 'power.' It took me years to understand that distinction."[26]

Martin, as usual, is right on in spotting the distinction between different kinds of power, and the way that the unseemliness of one kind of power-over can make women reluctant to recognize the potential of other kinds of power-to.

But one of the big questions becomes: Do we change the system from within, or from without? In any struggle, there are only four possible strategies: fight, flee, flank, or change the paradigm.

Fighting—taking on the system, on its own terms—is hard. It can take years, and the rewards are uncertain. Fleeing, opting out—though it may seem like the safe option—can have tremendous hidden risks as well as the obvious loss of earnings, as Leslie Bennetts pointed out in chapter 1. So many women choose to flank, to sidestep the grueling task of scaling the ladder at an organization like Goldman Sachs or male-dominated Silicon Valley startups, and start their own businesses instead. Lauren Bush and Ellen Gustafson exemplify successful flanking; they tried to work within one of the most hierarchical systems in existence, directly with the UN World Food Programme, but soon found that they could only accomplish their objectives outside of the strictures imposed upon them by that organization.

In other cases, women are choosing less powerful pathways within the career area of their choice, and only a very few choose to try to change the paradigm. I once gave a speech to a group called "The Most Influential Women in Radio." While meeting with that fascinating group of women, I found that although women owned only 6 percent of full-power radio stations and composed only 5 percent of the CEOs of commercial stations,[27] women make up an overwhelming majority of the people in marketing and ad sales.[28] Why are the women so common in these two areas? Because they're allowed to maintain a flexible schedule, set their own hours, and thus better balance the rigors and demands of work and family.

Many women leave well-demarcated career paths when the rules of the corporate workplace prove too inflexible to accommodate the demands of family life or other interests, whereas only a minority of men make such accommodations or are expected to. According to the Center for Women's Business Research, 8 percent of the workforce works for businesses where women are the sole or majority owners.[29] There is a tradition in the United States of celebrating the small business and the small business owner, but not as often acknowledged are the hardships and difficulties that many independent entrepreneurs face in getting their ideas off the ground. Nor does it address probably the biggest temptation for striking out on your own—the avoidance of uncompromising policies regarding family responsibilities that fall far short of individual needs, and the pervasive stereotyping that hamstrings professional women with children.

We have a precarious disconnect between workplace policies that affect mainly women, and encouraging our daughters and younger women to pursue remunerative, traditionally male professions. These are the women who have grown up in the era of "Take Your Daughters to Work Day," started in 1993 as the brainchild of Marie Wilson, then president of the Ms. Foundation, and marketing maven Nell Merlino. (Notably, it became so successful that it apparently became threatening and is now a separate organization called "Take Your Daughters and Sons to Work Day.")[30] Leaving the corporate world to become an entrepreneur is not just about turning away from unrealistic work-life policies. It's also caused by women turning away from the use of power that Martin describes—the kind of power that is externally imparted, that does not come from within, and that breeds (at least in the women's minds) not a power-to desire for expansion and change but merely a desire for more power-over people and resources.

In my research for this book, interviewing powerful women, I was surprised by the number of them who have struck out on their own, after high-powered careers, to begin their own consultancies or other businesses. Some women begin working their way up the corporate ladder only to decide that that kind of CEO, in that kind of corner office, is not what they want to be. They don't want to live like that. And they don't like that sort of hierarchical male world. They don't like the power-*over*, basically; they want the power-*to*. The fastest way to get it is not to stay there and fight in the corporate world, but rather to go and start their own businesses.

Obviously, there have been women entrepreneurs for decades—and large numbers of women continue to start their own businesses, even in the midst of a recession.[31] The question, however, is how do we make sure that women aren't only flanking—taking the side route because the main thrust of action is undesirable or impossible—but creating paradigm-shifting strategies, new ways to work? We've seen repeatedly that the workplace and work-life changes that women effect in their own domains are those that should influence the way business is conducted across the field.

Innovation always comes on the margins. One of those women striking out for herself *could* be the next Bill Gates—if she has the intention, the luck, a winning idea, and access to cash. But the key is not just nurturing the next huge star. After all, most women entrepreneurs end up with small-scale operations, with themselves as the only employee. I'm thinking of women who open cleaning businesses, or craft jewelry or handbags, which they sell on the Internet for minimum margins. There is a lot of admirable intention in those small entrepreneurial efforts. However, we should keep our eyes focused both on the fact that women own businesses, full stop, and on how women's businesses can grow to change the workplace for all women.

For one thing, we must change the investment imbalance: According to a Babson College study, the 39 percent of businesses owned by women receive less than 5 percent of the institutional venture capital invested annually. Babson researchers compared three groups of female business owners—those who have not sought equity, those who are seeking but have not received equity, and those who sought and received equity. They found that women owners receiving equity are—not surprisingly—more likely to be in the manufacturing, Internet, and information technology sectors, rather than products that are family- or community-oriented, to have a goal of selling the venture within five years, and their firms were larger in scale to begin with than those that were rejected by investors.[32]

To help expand capital available to women entrepreneurs, Merlino later created Count Me In, which raises money in small amounts to bundle together and give as microloans to women who want to start entrepreneurial businesses. Recently, Count Me In grew up to become Make Mine a Million $ Business to encourage women to think bigger and scale their businesses to seven figures. She sees entrepreneurship as a strategy that allows women to have control over their lives and set their own rules.[33]

Still, we should take a good hard look at what kind of support for women's entrepreneurship has the game-changing effect needed to push the fulcrum to parity in wealth and top leadership roles. Microcredit is often thought of as a popular model for investment globally, especially in the developing world, but it is also a financial empowerment strategy used in the United States: A small amount of money helps a woman invest in a business that enables her to feed her family. Many women who are able to feed their families can take a community out of poverty. More and more microcredit finance institutions are focusing on loans to women because they have found that women are more likely than men to pay back the loans, are more savvy about investing the money they have, and make wiser, more forward-looking decisions. But it doesn't change the system! Indeed, it can reinforce the system.

I'm not criticizing microloans, which have made a tremendous difference in the lives of tens if not hundreds of millions of people around the globe. What I'm saying is that it's not sufficient. We should also be looking at the bigger systemic issues and recognize that it's not enough for male-owned banks, as most microfinance institutions are, to give women $500 loans so that they can start little businesses out of their homes. We still need to change the system, so that anybody has a fair shot at any of the elements of power—and women have an equal chance of calling the shots.

When women compose half of the heads of the financial institutions that are doling out the money and setting fiscal policies for the country, when they constitute half of Fortune 500 company heads and are as likely to be found at the helm of scaled-up entrepreneurial ventures, *then* that's when we'll know we have succeeded in changing the paradigm.

## Paradigms Do Shift, but Only Because of Intention

When Michelle Robson founded the women's health information website, EmpowHER, she used her anger and frustration about her own lack of good health information to fuel her power to walk with intention and create a venture to make sure other women would not suffer as she had. Her use of the Internet and social media technology to shift the paradigm of how women can get reliable health information on their own terms, changing their relationship with their healthcare providers, is the twenty-first-century equivalent of the women's health revolution fomented by the book *Our Bodies, Ourselves* when I was a young woman and continuing in multimedia today by OBOS.[34]

I learned something interesting about paradigm shifts from Marcia Reynolds, now an executive coach, leadership consultant, and author of the 2010 book *Wander Woman: How High-Achieving Women Find Contentment and Direction,* after I met her via Twitter. She told me in subsequent email and phone conversations that because progress is never consistent or universal, women who are today's high achievers as we foremothers wanted them to be have special challenges that must be met if they are to catapult to the next level.

For the past fourteen years Reynolds has been studying and coaching high-achieving women to figure out what makes them tick and, just as importantly, what doesn't. Because women have more advanced degrees than men now, she explains, "It built this expectation, especially for the smart girls, that they would go out and accomplish something amazing. But they didn't clarify what this 'amazing thing' would be."

And, she notes, "There's a difference between a strong woman and a woman of strength and influence." Not understanding that the latter walks in the power of her intention is often what keeps the current surge of high-achieving women out of the boardroom.

Reynolds's initial work as a doctoral student in organizational psychology led her to think, "It wasn't that women had any particular deficiencies holding them back, but they didn't stick around long enough to earn executive positions." The reasons? Disillusionment, restlessness, and trouble communicating productively in the face of the first two.

This research led her to write *Wander Woman,* a book that examines the tendency in successful women to "need constant change so they can keep moving toward 'what's next.' If they don't see a 'what's next,' they say forget it." Their wandering doesn't just get in the way of corporate advancement, Reynolds explains; in the process "they often lose their sense of self and their sense of purpose."

Not that a sense of purpose comes easily. "It was a twenty-year process for me," Reynolds admits, sharing hurdles of a different sort from the health problems Robson encountered, but no less profound. As a young woman growing up, her initial motivations were "anger" and a feeling of "I'll show you!" In her teenage years Reynolds experienced a deep sense of disempowerment. "I was frustrated. I did drugs. I was put in jail." A frightening confrontation with a female inmate ultimately galvanized her into taking control of her life. "I was very, very angry," she says, but it was also "the first time I realized there was a difference between internal and external accomplishments." The personal transformation that grew out of this kick in the pants would convince her that other women could also make internal adjustments toward both greater success and greater fulfillment.

Reynolds's personal experiences continue to inform her understanding that a sense of self—I'd call that standing in power—and purpose—similar to what I call intention—do not always come with success. After she bought her first house with her own money, she says, "I realized for the first time that I was financially independent, and I was so excited. Then one night, as the sun went down and the plaques and pictures on my wall disappeared into the dark, I suddenly wondered who I really was."

High-achieving women may look to their work for a sense of identity and meaning more than men, Reynolds has found. The passion that comes as a result can be a terrific asset. But it also means women are likely to grow frustrated in corporate jobs that don't offer a clear outlet for their energy and ambition. It means they must work to stay in touch with themselves and their sense of purpose and to find creative and empowering ways to channel the energy and ambition that live within them.

"I was very successful in the corporate world, the only woman in my unit," Reynolds recalls, "and as I was driving home one day, something struck me. I asked myself, *What are you doing?* I knew the products my company produced weren't very good, that we were selling people crap. The moment I faced the fact that I was accomplishing nothing of value, I had to resign and find something to do that had some purpose to it." For almost thirty years now, Reynolds has been helping women at the same crossroads find the right balance between commitment and freedom, between their extraordinary successes and the elusive sense of purpose.

Intention is not an either/or construct, but a continuum. Barriers to our ability to walk with intention through our lives range from those totally imposed from external sources to barriers fully embraced by women themselves. There are many points along the continuum, and the places in the middle cause the confusion, approach-avoidance of power, and cognitive dissonance. We could analyze this to death, but in the end, if women "just do it," a new social reality will be constructed and that will change everything. It's up to us to develop a positive relationship with power and embrace both the pain and the gain associated with redefining it as the power-to, having the courage to stand in our own power and to engage the world with the passion of our own intention.

Women need inspiration, aspiration, intention, and affirmation.

But the key is to mass our power. The path to big, systemic change is collective action. That takes Sister Courage.

# barbara**lee**

Philanthropist and political activist Barbara Lee knows you can't get what you don't ask for—and you can't get elected to an office that you don't run for. So, alarmed by the dearth of women in representative government, even in her liberal hometown of Boston, Massachusetts, Lee—inspired by her grandmother who as a girl had watched suffragists march down New York's Fifth Avenue and never missed a chance to vote in her ninety-six years—decided to try a sensible yet groundbreaking solution. She decided to *ask*.

"It all began," Lee explained to me, "when I first started attending political fundraising events. There were next to no women in the room. The old boys' club was visibly in control of politics. When I started talking about a woman president, people thought I was nuts. Even some of my friends thought of me as a flaky blonde."

Hair color aside, Lee had a vision. She wanted to create a "new girls' club," and to do so, she had to increase the number of female candidates. "Women," Lee stresses, "need to be asked. They need to be recruited. We need women telling one another to run. Back when I was in school, women became teachers, nurses, or legal secretaries. Hardly anyone became a doctor or a lawyer, let alone dreamed of becoming president. You can't be what you can't see. My life's goal is to change that, to literally change the face of politics."

Lee says her commitment to seek equality for women through her strategic philanthropy stems from the Jewish value of *tzedakah,* meaning both justice and charity. She has used Sister Courage principles to foster justice for women through "systemic social change," what I call movement building. She's a cofounder of the White House Project, and has funded research on women in state executive positions because she believes that women who have been governors are the most likely future successful candidates for president.

Still, she likes to point to the importance of starting locally to change the face of politics. She's proud of Ayanna Pressley, whom Lee entreated consistently, emphatically, and successfully to run for office—now the first black woman to be elected to the Boston City Council.

"Ayanna worked for ten years as Senator Kerry's constituent services staff person," Lee recounts, "and when I first met her, I thought she'd make a great candidate. I told her as much every time I saw her. Last year, Ayanna and I were at the same event and I told her I wanted to write the first check when she ran for office. I asked the people in the room to stand up if they thought Ayanna should run and the whole room stood up. Then, at Ayanna's inauguration party, her mother told me that Ayanna had called her *every time* I told her she should run."

The take-home message? Lee emphasizes, "We can dramatically increase the number of women candidates at all levels simply by asking." To those who doubt the possibility of change, Lee says, "Be persistent and patient. It took seventy-two years from Seneca Falls to win women the right to vote. Any time people around me are discouraged about the slow pace of progress, I remind them and myself about the history of women's suffrage. It reminds me to be both patient and vigilant about goals."

Even as Lee preaches patience, the face of Massachusetts politics is changing rapidly. Pressley joins a long list of women at the vanguard of a new girls' club that is gaining momentum: Andrea Cabral (Massachusetts's first black female sheriff), Therese Murray (Massachusetts's first female Senate president), Martha Coakley (the state's first female attorney general), Maureen Feeney (the first female Boston City Council president), Sonia Chiang-Diaz (Massachusetts's first Latina state senator), and Niki Tsongas (Massachusetts's first female congressional representative in a quarter of a century).

Like the savvy leader she is, Lee focuses on younger women to ensure that the new generation of leaders considers politics a viable career. Through the Barbara Lee Fellowship, Lee offers promising graduates of her Boston all-female alma mater, Simmons College, the opportunity to work with and find mentors among the women already elected to office.

Amanda Moors, a former Fellow, testifies to the power of being invited into the new girls' club early. "I know it sounds cheesy," Moors says, "but the internship didn't just give me the chance to see politics in action; it gave me the chance to see *myself*. It gave me the tools (and confidence) to make a seamless transition from college to professional politics."

The momentum of women like Pressley and Moors, Lee hopes, will help propel women from local victories to the White House. "Electing the second female president of the United States," she explains, "is the biggest unfinished business of women in politics. The first woman president would be a trailblazer, but the second would be proof we have changed our society."

The United States may not yet boast gender parity, but a snapshot of American leadership no longer looks like the yearbook photo of a Princeton eating club circa 1956. When I asked her about whether Sarah Palin's candidacy had been a good thing for women, she said, "In my personal life I'm a Democrat. I supported Hillary Clinton. But in 2008, for both parties to have a woman on top of the ticket was a game changer. This history-making moment normalizes women's leadership in a way that changes perceptions."

Make no mistake: Change for the sake of change is not what Lee is after. She ardently believes that women in politics change society for the better. Women in Congress, Lee is quick to point out, "introduce more bills, attract more cosponsors, and bring home more money for their districts than the guys do." A landmark study, commissioned by Lee and conducted by the Center for American Women and Politics, found that women in state legislatures, regardless of party, had a strong impact on their male counterparts' willingness to consider the effect of policies on women, ethnic minorities, and the poor.

Want to join the vanguard of change? Pull a Barbara Lee and *ask!* Ask your daring and intelligent friend, your generous and radical sister, your wise and caring neighbor whether she has thought about running for office. Then ask yourself whether you, too, might be a potential candidate. After all, Lee says, "most women enter politics because they want to make a difference and realize that of the routes they have open to them, they can have the biggest impact by running for office."

If you meet any detractors on your way to becoming a card-carrying member of the new girls' club, pull a Barbara Lee once more and remind the skeptics that "people who say it can't be done shouldn't get in the way of the people who are doing it." Without that philosophy, Lee might still be written off as a blonde with a crazy idea. Instead, her doubting friends have changed their tune. "Barbara," they tell her, "I thought you were flaky, you know, but I realize now you were visionary."[1]

CHAPTER SEVEN

# unleash:
# sister
# courage

*"So I am for keeping the thing going
while things are stirring; because if
we wait till it is still, it will take a great
while to get it going again."*

**—SOJOURNER TRUTH**
at Equal Rights Convention, New York, 1867

*"Don't agonize—organize."*

**—COMMUNITY ORGANIZING SLOGAN**

- What makes you angry enough to take action?

- What makes you inspired enough to take action?

- Think about the mentors you have had in your life. How did they influence your career, public service, or personal life choices?

## SPEAKING OF WEARING THE SHIRT

"I love your T-shirt," chuckled Jenny, my twentysomething personal trainer, as she stretched my aching legs. "I never saw that before."

I hadn't noticed which of my many message T-shirts I had thrown on when I rolled out of bed before sunrise. Most of the folks who populate New York's Columbus Circle Equinox gym sport workout clothes that bear designer labels, but seldom do I see any that pack a message punch. I figure my chest is valuable real estate—why not use it to communicate my convictions?

I looked down and saw that I'd grabbed one of my favorites: Well-Behaved Women Rarely Make History. Historian Laurel Thatcher Ulrich's wry observation became one of the guiding principles of the women's movement during the 1970s, and living it seems as natural to me now as balance ball crunches do to my lithe trainer.

Perhaps because of their delicious candor laced with felicity of expression, these words have become a slogan for boundary-breaking women everywhere. But just because it's proudly emblazoned on mugs and bumper stickers and, yes, T-shirts, doesn't mean we should let the message be reduced to merely a personal assertion of gutsiness. The context of Ulrich's observation, the thing that actually makes it true, is both personal and political. Although history is often taught in schoolbooks as a sequence of significant acts by Important Men (and the occasional important woman), what Ulrich recognized is that making history is a communal act, requiring us to break the boundaries of what is considered proper behavior.

And she's certainly not the only one. When Rosa Parks refused to take a seat at the back of the bus, she became a hero—a symbol of the civil rights movement's then-new direct activism—because she refused to be well behaved anymore. It was an individual act, but Parks was also part of a larger movement, one of a burgeoning group of people who were collectively refusing to behave according to rules they considered unjust. People who kept the pot stirring. Her seemingly individual act in turn sparked thousands of other women and men, long discriminated against, to take their rightful seats at the front of the bus, at lunch counters, in classrooms, and in their own minds.

Individual women who break rules may sometimes galvanize those around them to action. But just as often, even when we summon the courage to act alone, we are punished or shamed for our so-called transgressions against propriety or "nature." Shame is a powerful mechanism for controlling people. It can stop you cold, make you question your worth, silence you. It can make you feel like you need to make excuses for yourself just for being, but especially so if you're transgressing some custom, even if you feel certain it should be transgressed because it isn't right or just.

When women come together and collectively decide to stop being well behaved—to shuck the shame and have the courage to stand up for ourselves, with our sisters—then that's a movement. Banding together to speak our truth and effect change allows us to get through the barriers of shame and fear, as well as barriers of law and custom. Together we're a force to reckon with—and people might as well get out of our way.

When you're up against a work-life balance problem that requires changing a long-used process—perhaps you're trying to change a policy like creating flextime, ensuring sick leave, or getting more women onto the executive team—you can, to a limited extent, improve your situation independently of others by negotiating your own terms of employment. But that won't alter the underlying structure that perpetuates the problem. If you want to change the system, you need to function like a movement.

I learned about building a movement on the front lines of a great one—one that's overcome epic challenges to fight for the individual woman's rights and health. From my experience in social movements, I've taken away three simple principles of movement building that can produce wildly successful results for women who want to live an unlimited life. They apply to any aspect of life and leadership, whether in work, politics and civic engagement, or personal life. I call them Sister Courage. Be a sister. Have courage. Put the two together and act with Sister Courage to create a movement.

## WHY DO WE NEED SISTER COURAGE?

I use the word *sister* because individual women who want—deserve—the chance to thrive must act like sisters, like women who support one another. Every other group does this—why shouldn't we? Across different backgrounds, talents, beliefs, and ambitions, we share some experiences, and certainly we share a history of oppression that, as we have documented, we're still on the long road to overcoming. Yet those internal barriers of custom, co-option, and distrust are often much harder to overcome than legal barriers. But you can break through with some simple acts. Reach out to ask for help when you need it, and offer help when someone else needs it. Be a sister.

I use the word *courage* because making change always takes courage. Speaking up takes courage. The Quaker admonition "Speak Truth to Power" that became a byword of progressive social movements describes it best.[1]

When we talk about giving women an equal chance to succeed at work, we're talking about setting seriously big goals and going for them as a group by making the business case for change in a forthright and persistent manner. When we talk about getting more women elected or appointed to public office, we're talking about creating networks to deliver the votes. Sometimes dealing with the tough issues within a relationship takes the most courage of all. Changing the gender power balance in any situation takes extra-special courage. When we talk about giving women an equal chance, we're talking about the most profound power shift toward equal justice in the history of humanity. We're talking revolution. We're talking setting some seriously big goals and going for them. So we must have courage.

By putting the two together—*"Sister Courage"*—we're talking about a concept that allows us to become bigger and stronger than the sum of the parts. We can be a movement. Joining together as a movement in Sister Courage, and with brother partners of like mind (and there are many!) enables us to accomplish great things we could never do as isolated individuals. What we do becomes more than what we do. As anthropologist Margaret Mead said, "Never doubt that a small group of thoughtful, committed citizens can change the world. Indeed, it is the only thing that ever has." And with a big group . . . well, there's no stopping us. We simply must act like a movement if we really want women to make it to parity and stay there. We're at the moment when we can—and that means there are no excuses if we fail to walk with intention and act with *Sister Courage*.

So let's expand upon these three principles and talk about how to become 100 percent successful. Nothing less will do.


## BE A SISTER

It's common to feel isolated when you struggle to solve your problems alone. We're all busy with the realities of daily life. Who has time to make personal travails into group efforts? This mentality is one practical reason why women try to solve big systemic challenges, like achieving work-life balance, or mitigating sexist messages from mainstream media, individually. But we're also more likely than men to burrow in, work hard, and hope that hard work will inherently be recognized; many of us believe in a just meritocracy where competence and skill get rewarded, despite gender, race, ethnicity, class, or orientation. I have a news flash—they mostly don't.

Speaking up and being one's own best public relations pitchwoman is, without question, essential. No one ever assumes you have more power than you assume for yourself. Debra Condren, in her book, *Ambition Is Not a Dirty Word,* suggests ways to get over that internal resistance so many of us are socialized to have even today about seeking power and its symbolic representations, such as money. Speaking of being punished for breaking rules. Condren told me that her publisher had insisted on changing the book's title from *AmBITCHous* to *Ambition Is Not a Dirty Word* when it came out in paperback. Personally, I thought *AmBITCHous* expressed her idea perfectly.

We certainly must practice the fine art of being for ourselves. But if we are for ourselves alone, we're begging for failure in the long run, for all of us. Try giving another woman a public kudo every day—compliment a colleague's report at a staff meeting, post a recommendation on her LinkedIn page, retweet her request, write a positive review for her book on Amazon (hint). And ask your women colleagues to do the same for you.

## Reciprocal Role Modeling

You can also be a sister by being a role model. In fact, you probably already are one whether you know it or not. So why not be proactive about it?

Founder and executive director of the media justice advocacy organization Women in Media and News (WIMN), Jenn Pozner, thirty-five, shared with me via email how important it was to her to have a role model when she was starting her career: "Susan Faludi's *Backlash* was completely formative in my development as a media critic and journalist. Fifteen years later, Faludi signed my original dog-eared copy of *Backlash* while she and I were at lunch to brainstorm women and media issues. She inscribed it, 'For Jenn, thank you so much for your work.' The idea that my role model was now thanking me?!? It was a big moment for me." The impact Faludi had on Pozner speaks to how important it is that each of us realize the impact of being there for others, speaking up, role modeling, mentoring, and being a sister.

But Pozner also recognizes that the sisterhood thing works both ways, and in her own work she makes a practice of reaching out to younger women. "I spend a lot of time teaching students how to deconstruct sexism, racism, class biases, hyperconsumerism, and many other problems within news, entertainment, and advertising content," she explained. She has created multimedia presentations and written a book, *Reality Bites Back,* which both highlight how women are portrayed in reality TV and reveal sexist double standards and inaccuracies in news coverage. "People often tell me, 'A lightbulb just went on for me,' or 'I've always felt uncomfortable when my friends watch *America's Next Top Model* but I couldn't explain why. Now I'll be able to tell them exactly what's wrong.'"

After one presentation Pozner gave to a group of high school students, a senior approached her afterward to tell her how much Pozner's talk had impacted her. The student even showed Pozner a notepad where she had doodled "I hate feminists!!!!" Pozner says, "The girl explained how she thought she 'hated feminists' because she liked boys, lipstick, and skirts, but after the presentation she 'realized that maybe feminism is about, like, not letting people put me down and manipulate me and stuff.' [B]eing the catalyst for this girl's feminist epiphany is one of my proudest moments as a media activist," Pozner told me.[2]

## "I Didn't Have Any Support Network."

When women don't have their networks or sisters to turn to, it's harder to deal with controversy, pressure to conform, and personal attacks.

I met up with Kristal Brent Zook for lunch at a restaurant in our neighborhood, and the very first thing she told me was not to generalize her experience as a black woman to the experiences of white women. People's experiences deserve to be respected as valid without needing to be related to someone else's understanding. "One of the things people do is generalize an experience so that it's relatable to them," she cautioned, "but that dilutes the importance of what has happened." But having heard her story, I feel that all women can learn from what happened to her, even without generalizing it to what has happened to them.

As a young journalist, the first big article Zook ever published in a major national publication caused quite a stir. So much so that she felt slammed to the point that she ran away to Australia where she stayed "in hiding" for six months, rejected a six-figure book contract that came as a result of the article soon after she returned, and then went through a ten-year process of reclaiming her power as a writer on her own terms.

Zook was raised in an all-female working-class Los Angeles household by her African American mother and grandmother, and a female cousin, who's biracial like Zook. Zook's Anglo-American father was never present in her life, and she always saw women earning the family income and making the family's decisions. She got the message early: "Women are stronger, better. We have to be. Independence is vital."[3]

Zook attended UCLA and was the first in her family to graduate from college. Professor Elliot Butler-Evans introduced her to feminism and urged her to go to graduate school, where she earned her PhD. Butler-Evans was a black man who modeled how to challenge authority in a way she had not seen before, and he showed her what having power looks like.

Zook explained in her elegant, soft-spoken, and very self-contained manner, "I was entering writing contests and winning, but instead of congratulating me, he told me, 'What are you doing all that for? You go out there, you can do more.' He was situating my power in a way I would never have thought of. It took a mentor to show me the power out there in the world, and to make me realize that a PhD is more valuable than [winning] a writing contest."

Soon, Zook's powerful writing on women, gender, and cultural issues caught the attention of a *New York Times Magazine* editor, who asked her to write an article on black feminism. It was 1995 and Zook was thirty years old. The piece was pegged to a confluence of current events highlighting what the article called the "Endangered Black Man": the Million Man March; boxer Mike Tyson's release from prison after serving time for sexual assault; and football star O.J. Simpson's acquittal for the murder of his ex-wife Nicole Brown Simpson and her friend Ronald Goldman.[4]

Zook's article, "A Manifesto of Sorts for a Black Feminist Movement," was a brilliantly argued and gut-deep case for respectful and just treatment of black women by the black community and civil rights organizations. She exposed how the centuries-old tension between the priority for women's rights and rights for African American men festers today within both traditional civil rights organizations like the NAACP and women's clubs like the National Association of Colored Women. About the latter, she wrote, "For all the club movement's good works . . . it never abandoned its need to play it safe and be polite." (I'd call this pressure to co-opt by the already co-opted.) She voiced the growing aspirations of a younger cohort of women of color—black, biracial, gay, bisexual, and straight—not so inclined to "be nice." She opened the article by reporting on a classic scene: women meeting to make plans to raise bus fare for low-income teenage boys to attend the Million Man March, but refusing to address the need some of the women present felt to march as well. And while issuing a plea for unity between African American men and women in her piece, Zook made clear she believed the time had come for women to be treated as equal human beings.

Zook was completely unprepared for the aftershock of her article. The enormous reach of the magazine made the ensuing controversy that flared up—the angry letters-to-the-editor, the calls and letters filled with personal attacks—feel extra-threatening. "There was a lot of anger about the airing of black dirty laundry," she said, adding that she was chided about having this conversation outside the circle of black-oriented publications like *Essence* magazine. She was "contributing to the Willie Hortonization of black men," prominent attorney Constance Rice, then counsel to the NAACP Legal Defense and Education Fund's Western region, chided her. But what made the negative reaction particularly hard to take was the fact that she didn't have a network to call upon to cushion the hard knocks or to send a barrage of positive letters-to-the-editor to balance the negative ones. "I didn't have a central community. . . . I tend to go off in a corner and do my stuff on my own. So that's why when I [went] to Australia, I wasn't leaving anything here. *I didn't have any support network—I was in hiding.*"

What Zook lacked was sisters—women to whom she could reach out proactively to support, lift up, or connect with personally and professionally, and who would be there for her when she needed them. This was hard on her from an emotional perspective, but there were other ramifications as well.

By the time she returned from Australia six months later, the controversy was still simmering, and she had a six-figure book offer on the table on the strength of the *New York Times Magazine* article. Within a few months, though, the book contract "evaporated" following disagreements about the central message of the book. Zook felt the editor had an agenda that conflicted with the point of her article, and when Zook refused to change her book accordingly, the offer was pulled. She put her ideas into the drawer in late 1996; it would take a ten-year journey to discover just how important it had been to her development to take a stand and defend her core ideas. Ultimately she found a publisher without an agent and finally got a book deal (with a much smaller advance than the original one) on her terms. *Black Women's Lives* was published in 2006 by Nation Books.

Zook and I met when we both joined the WomenGirlsLadies intergenerational feminist panel, along with Courtney Martin and Deborah Siegel. The panel was Siegel's brainchild after having written *Sisterhood Interrupted,* a book that chronicled the history of second-wave feminism and concluded there was a gap in the conversation across generations of women, a gap we could fill. The four of us have presented the panel on campuses, to women's professional groups, and in public venues across the country. I've learned a lot from the other panelists: Even though I've traversed the stages of life the others are just now going through, being with them helps me keep my thinking fresh. Plus we've provided one another with helpful contacts and advice, as well as meaningful friendships.

"I was never a part of anything like that before," Zook told me. But, she said, our panel and our conversation is invaluable to her now. Before getting involved in the panel, she said, it was just "me, my voice, my words, and however people react, they react." She has always been strong on her own. But now she feels she has community, too. And with it, I hope, no more need to hide.

## Sisters Learn, Teach, and Move the Dial for Women

Being a sister is about more than sharing opportunities and problems. It's about sharing experiences. Women need to learn each other's stories. How did you get to where you are? What barriers did you face? How did you overcome them? We need to let other women know the contours of our experiences, especially younger women who will continue to carry the torch forward. We also need to share stories of when we weren't successful, or didn't overcome what was standing in our way the first time, or the second, or the tenth, but how finally, on the eleventh attempt, we made it. How we forged a different path when our chosen one was impassible. And we need to be forthcoming about sharing stories about the days when we were distraught and depressed and angry and ready to throw in the towel.

Share your stories of your worst moments as well as your best. Let your sisters know their problems are not unique and they are not alone.

And yes, a sister can be a brother, too, as Zook's mentor showed—but since we are setting the world aright, why not let *women* be the stand-in word to represent humanity for a few millennia? I think it's time for that.

Make no mistake, there are plenty of cultural obstacles to sisterhood. Female friendship in the United States is typically derided or dismissed, assigned second-class status behind "real" heterosexual (of course) romantic relationships, which are celebrated on screen and in song. The objectification of women has the disturbing symptom of casting us all as potential romantic rivals. When men disagree, it's an argument. When women disagree, it's a "catfight."

Ellen Gustafson and Lauren Bush, the Feed Fund entrepreneurs, talked about how they had managed to stay in their power and intention as young women in the hierarchical world of the UN. Ellen acknowledged that a large part of their success was due to their own uncompromising belief in themselves and the cause they were working toward, but said that together they were able to work "better, harder, smarter, more effectively than we ever would have worked alone." She dismisses the cookie-cutter notion that there is only one path to success, one ladder to climb—which demands its own rigid sacrifices to gendered norms. "We have to address the fact that the business world and the world of traditional success is really a man's world," she concludes. "Women, as we get more senior, have to remember that the more we can make it easier for all women to do well, the better we will be."

Indeed, Lauren sees this moment not in terms of the challenges it holds for women, but in terms of its opportunity. For years, professional working women felt that the "man's world" of business required us to set our femininity aside, to "dress for success" in male-inspired power suits and play by rules we never had a hand in writing. Lauren perceives women's continued outsider status in business not as a liability, but as a source of strength and opportunity. "I think women, in some ways, are teed up for success in a different sort of way" than men, she told me. "The expectations are a little more random, and thus we can create our path more freely."

It's good to feel special. It's bad to feel so special that you feel isolated and alone. Look around. Be a sister. Reach out to ask for a sister. Never forget whose shoulders you stand on, and that someone else is standing on yours and counting on you to hold steady for her. It does matter that you share your knowledge, your connections, your job openings, your mentorship, and it matters that we boost one another whenever we can.

Every other group helps its own members. Women should, too. Be sisters.

## HAVE COURAGE

Making change, by definition, takes courage. Change is a shifting of the boundaries, creating chaos, and not incidentally, making history in the process. Changing the gender power-balance in the workplace, politics, or relationships takes extra-special courage. Owning responsibility for doing so takes even more courage. When we talk about giving women an equal chance, we're talking about the most profound power shift toward equal justice in the history of humanity. We're talking about daring to set goals that are actually revolutionary in that they transform what we've been told is hardwired into the "natural order" and "how things are." They might be personal goals or goals that involve entire organizations, movements, even nations. Daring to aim for equality isn't just something we do as a matter of course; these things take guts. Large or small, they are courageous acts.

Because so many gender inequalities within the culture still have not been resolved despite women's enormous gains in laws and policies, there remain whole industries where women continue to face very steep hills to climb. Clearly, we can't do it alone, but once that becomes obvious, the next question is how to coalesce with other women to speak our truth-to-power so that we can make beneficial change.

◦　◦　◦

## Bolster Courage with Supporting Data

When I spoke to Mentoring and Inspiring Women in Radio (MIW for short, and the acronym also stands for "Most Influential Women in Radio") in 2007 at the National Association of Broadcasters Radio Show, as I mentioned in the last chapter, I discovered that there aren't nearly enough of those women in radio. My own first paid employment in 1965 happened to be spinning tunes at KFYI-FM in Odessa, Texas, where I never could have imagined a woman owning or having a managerial position in radio, let alone aspiring to run a show herself. But I've come a long way since 1965, so it blew me away to learn that the world of radio hasn't come so far—just 14.9 percent of radio station general managers were women. In 2010, two and a half years after my speech, I checked out the group's website, where women in radio can also find success tips and how to participate in the MIW's formal mentoring program. I found that in their latest survey, taken in 2009, women made up 16.2 percent of general managers, a welcome (though slow enough a participant compared it to watching paint dry) upward trend fomented by this "sister" support group.

Women station managers in the top one hundred markets have increased from 15 percent in 2005 to 17.3 percent in 2009. According to Joan Gerberding, currently executive vice president for the radio and music compliance company Mediaguide and one of the MIW's founders and most devoted supporters, "MIW's mentoring program was initially launched to mentor mid-level female radio managers so that they could achieve their career goals of rising through the ranks of radio. Not an easy task, but all but one of our initial mentees have risen as they wanted to. But," Gerberding acknowledged, "the only real growth has been in sales management positions." As I pointed out in chapter 6, women in radio have fared best in the sales realm, where female marketing directors have exceeded that supposedly magic tipping-point number of 30 percent. The reason given is that women pursue these jobs because marketing positions offer more flexible working hours than on-air or station management; women who have caregiving responsibilities can juggle their time according to their needs.

The MIWs speak their truth to foment evolutionary change, if not immediate revolution and paradigm shift, by tracking these numbers annually, enabling them to measure their own progress and present a solid case for more inclusiveness of women in the upper echelons of the radio business. This is a particularly auspicious time for their data's persuasive value, since broadcast radio, which has a declining listenership, has been losing women listeners at a 20 percent faster clip than men. Talk radio has become the purview almost entirely of angry conservative men like Lars Larson, with whom I tangled in chapter 2. No wonder, since *Talkers* magazine's "Heavy Hundred" 2009 list finds just seventeen female talk show hosts among the top one hundred by audience size, including several who are cohosts with men. In the top ten, only two hosts are women—the ultraconservative outdo-Rush-Limbaugh talk-alikes if not look-alikes, Dr. Laura Schlessinger and Laura Ingraham.[5] Joan Gerberding agrees: "Clearly, we can bring the money in (via marketing), but we are not seen as capable of managing it! Thus the problems in the radio biz today!"

I had told the group back in 2007 that though their efforts have resulted in important progress, and I'd say the same thing today, it's time they kicked it up several notches, and I urged them to set some bold goals, such as reaching 40 percent of the top radio positions across the board in the next five to ten years. Why not? When radio doesn't reflect the vibrant diversity of our country, both the quality of programming and the equality within our democracy suffer.

The men in charge ought to be beating down women's doors and begging them to take over. We've already seen that women make the vast majority of purchases of the goods and services that radio advertisers are selling, for example. Who better to understand what women want than other women? But to transform the radio business, the MIWs will have to muster the courage to speak forcefully and persistently, and to make some demands based on the data they have amassed. It's the kind of situation where women are clearly poised to get ahead individually if they will only reach out to their sisters and have the courage to speak up together to shatter the remaining glass ceilings in their industry—for the good of all.

## The Courage to Speak Is Everyone's Responsibility

When it comes to women speaking up, we have to acknowledge the voices that are being heard and why. For instance, the MIWs have to consider why the Schlessingers and Ingrahams attract such large audiences. Hate sells better than happiness with the status quo, as a 2010 *Vanity Fair* analysis pointed out in a study of how liberal and conservative publications have fared since Barack Obama became president.[6]

What that means is that the courage to speak up when you believe in something positive must be applied vigorously and constantly to prevent sliding backward, and expansively to accomplish forward movement. In my experience, going for positive aspirations requires at least twice the energy of merely whipping up angry resistance. It was always easier and safer for me as a movement leader to get people to react to attacks on family planning services than to create and organize support for new legislative initiatives such as contraceptive coverage by insurance plans. Women seem to need some sort of Pearl Harbor to make us take action.

But being smart and provocative so as to mobilize attention and action needn't be defaulted to the right-wing hate mongers, as talk show hosts like Ed Schultz and Rachel Maddow have proven beyond any doubt. And the rest of us must support those who speak courageously to counteract the negativity or we'll just get more of the same nastiness that has so soured people on the media and on politics in general.

Responsibility to speak out belongs to more than just those whose job it is to lead or those who hold the microphone. My former neighbor—call her Susie—had a habit of getting agitated when she listened to Dr. Laura or some other right-wing host on the radio haranguing against birth control, women's rights, or feminism. (Don't ask me why she listened to them—that's a whole other issue.) She regularly sent me clippings accompanied by trenchant notes expressing her anger. "What can you do about it?" she pleaded, going so far as to send me Dr. Laura's email address.

Why did she send these to me? Unless women like Susie have the courage to speak up or take action themselves as "ordinary citizens" who join together to stand strong and speak out, we aren't going to get very far. It's not just about what people in "official" leadership roles can do; it's about what all of us can do together. Remember that a leader is anyone who gets something done. And yes, I told Susie the same thing and encouraged her to speak for herself. If I were advising her today, I'd also tell her to create a Facebook or Twitter group she could alert to voice their opinions at the same time to amplify the decibel level of their complaints or compliments to media outlets.

## "I Was Concerned the Vocal Minority Would Impose Their System."

Having the courage to speak up in the political realm deserves its own chapter, if not a whole book. Kendra Tollackson, a woman who decided to run for her local school board, is exemplary of the courage it takes to speak one's truth-to-power in a situation where building a large network of sisters and brothers to make your voice heard is the only way to make things happen.

Tollackson's second job after she graduated from Smith College and did a brief stint in hotel management was as a grassroots political organizer at Planned Parenthood in Arizona during the mid-1980s, when I was the CEO there. She came by her activism honestly—her grandmother had been the organization's first executive director during the 1950s. I considered her a mentee and imagined she would end up running Planned Parenthood or some other progressive nonprofit organization. That could still happen, of course; but meanwhile, her passions have taken her in a different direction.

First, she went back to school to get her MBA and became a development officer and fundraising consultant to nonprofit organizations. But once she had children, her interest in the public education system escalated, particularly the Madison school district in central Phoenix, where she lives. This district has always enjoyed an excellent academic reputation, but in the never-ending culture wars, a group of parents began pressuring the superintendent to dismantle successful programs in favor of a more "traditional" rote learning model generally associated with religious and political conservatives. Tollackson's political organizing skills came in handy, especially her willingness and ability to speak out about her ideas and to engage others in the conversation. First, she became involved in trying to influence the school board's actions as a concerned parent, but soon she realized she could have more of an impact if she were in a position to make the policies herself. So, in 2006, when her children were in the third and sixth grades respectively, she ran for the school board and won. A look at her campaign website, kendraforkids.com, reveals that she reached out to and connected with a broad base of supporters across party lines and made the most of their common interests in getting the best possible education for their children.

Tollackson told me, "I ran for [the] school board because I was concerned that a minority of vocal parents would get to impose a very rigid system on the satisfied majority. I had a terrific support base of parents who felt strongly about getting me elected. After I was elected, the superintendent decided not to renew his contract. The board decided to start a small 'traditional school' so those families who wanted to choose this type of environment for their students could do so. It was still quite controversial because starting the school meant squeezing resources from the other schools. However, the curriculum was not imposed on any of the other schools."[7]

What if Tollackson hadn't acted? Perhaps someone else would have stepped up to take on that leadership role, or perhaps the more vocal elements in the district would have prevailed to the detriment of the democratic process, and from her point of view, the children's education. The point is that she spoke her truth to the voters. Though she didn't get everything she wanted once elected, her ideas about what constitutes quality education have prevailed because she had the courage to speak and take action. Now her interest in education has taken yet another turn; she recently completed teacher certification and began teaching seventh- and eighth-grade social studies. Perhaps running for state superintendent of public instruction will be next? Just a thought, Kendra!

If you are reading this and you aspire to be a radio station manager, a community leader, or even president of the United States, then go for it. You get there just the same way, with the same building blocks. I chose to tell Tollackson's story of serving on a school board to make three important points. First, working on issues that are close to home shows you tangible evidence of your impact on people's lives. This kind of activism can be very rewarding, especially when the people are children. Second, what Tollackson did is doable for you, too. It's not expensive to run for these types of smaller offices, and the positions aren't full-time, so members can keep their day jobs. And third, many political careers start in a local position such as school board or city council and then progress to state legislature or higher offices. I'm a sappy enough patriot to think it would be a good idea for everyone to take a chance at this kind of public service at some point in their lives, but the truth is that most people don't even consider the possibility.

That statement across my T-shirt, Well-Behaved Women Rarely Make History, that so amused my trainer, Jenny, is really about having the courage to do what may seem impossible or outside the norm if you want to make progress.

Whatever aspect of life you apply it to, making change takes courage.

•  •  •

## SISTER + COURAGE = A MOVEMENT

When we put together the two principles I've just detailed—be a sister and have courage—then we're a movement. Together we become bigger and stronger than the sum of our parts. We must act like a movement if we really want women to gain equality and justice and keep it for good. Or, actually, if we want to make most anything happen in this world. You have to care enough to make it happen. It's like in *Star Wars* when Yoda, who has no patience for excuses, says, "Do. Or do not. There is no try." I want a T-shirt with that on it![8]

I'm suggesting we take the opposite approach from James Chartrand in chapter 4, who made the choice to perform a pantomime of masculinity rather than use Sister Courage. She'd come out of a situation where she felt isolated and despairing of being able to support her family, so it was understandable that she wanted to try a different approach. At that turning point, she saw her female identity not as a possible source of solidarity and strength, but as a vulnerability that had to be cloaked. Paradoxically, she increased her vulnerability by making herself a target for the kind of "outing" that eventually led her to confess her "real" identity, and reinforced the patterns—both unconscious and conscious—of discrimination that keep us from achieving full equality. When I interviewed her, "James" repeatedly said she wasn't going to "take one for the team," the team being women. I say you don't have to make a martyr of yourself, but the fact is that the only way for individual women to become unlimited in life and leadership is to take one for the team from time to time, because that's what will finally allow us to break through to equality for good. And if we haven't learned that lesson by now, we don't deserve equality.

We all know that those in power, however well-intentioned, don't relinquish their power voluntarily or easily. When changes that need to be made are happening in the context of chaos and rapid social change, the challenge is even greater, the call for courage even more intense. As we have seen, in chaos there is great opportunity, but only if we have the courage to put it on the line.

To speak out, even when it's difficult. To reach out to sisters, even when it's uncomfortable. To be ambitious, and to act with intention. We must think of ourselves as a movement with a purpose larger than any one of us—that's Sister Courage. The purpose is fairness, equity, and justice for women. For you.

# **power**tool number seven

CREATE A MOVEMENT: things don't just happen; people make them happen in a systematic way. "don't agonize, organize!" as labor movement leaders often say. apply the movement building principles of Sister Courage, and you will realize your vision.

## "What If I Could Do This for Other Women?"

We tend to think of movements as being advocacy for social justice, such as suffrage, civil rights, or reproductive justice. But I see a larger definition. Today, now that doors are open for women's advancement, we must constantly find new ways to bring more women through them. Here is an example.

Andrea March acted with Sister Courage before she realized she was doing it. But she saw clearly just how much she could make a difference in another woman's life when she cofounded Women's Leadership Exchange (WLE) with Leslie Grossman in 2001.[9]

"I thought it was just a matter of giving women advice and tools, but it's also seeing that someone else—someone just like you—can do it," she explained to me when I interviewed her for this book. For nearly a decade, the WLE has been committed to providing women entrepreneurs with the skills, information, and networks they need to run and grow successful businesses. As much as anything, however, the organization is about exposing women to what is possible. It has become, in effect, a movement, where women can be sisters, have the courage to take risks, and speak their own truths regardless of what others might say is possible, and to act together with Sister Courage to grow women's individual and collective economic power. As we discussed in chapter 5, "Unfetter: Secure £500 and a Womb of Your Own," economic power is one of the two precursors to women having any kind of meaningful power in this world, and I would not be surprised if the female Bill Gates I'm yearning to see were to emerge from this group.

Andrea remembers her initial conversations with Grossman when they first met but had not founded the WLE. "I was an isolated woman who never left her office, who worked every day, and never knew there was another 'level.' I never spoke to another woman who had a business as large as I had," she explains. "I had no women friends who had big businesses, nor did I know where to go to meet other business owners." The recognition of what she was missing started March thinking. "Leslie approached me to talk about networking. When she said something to me about getting to another level, I didn't know what she was talking about. Until you're exposed to other people doing it, you don't know."

March marveled at how Grossman had built her own business through masterful networking. "I thought, if I didn't know about these skills and they were something that could really help me. . . Wow, what if I could do this for other women and open the doors to something they didn't know about or didn't have the time to learn?"

WLE focuses on women as a rising group of successful entrepreneurs. During the eight years since the WLE was founded, and especially in the current economy, March notes, "We're getting younger women who've had life-changing experiences—children, the loss of a job, a husband's loss of a job—women who've had that Aha! moment and decided to go out on their own. We're getting more women from the professional arena who have turned out to be entrepreneurs."

It's not a choice for everyone, March admits, but it *is* certainly a choice for women as much as men. "There is no sex to being an entrepreneur," says March. It does, however, take a particular skill set. "It's more than leadership. It's being able to take risks, seeing the big picture, seeing how all the parts fit together. When you look at something, do you see the big picture? If not, you're not an entrepreneur."

The central idea of the Women's Leadership Exchange is that women running businesses can help one another, through advice, networking, and the personal examples they set. "You could have a ten-hour conversation with women just telling you what they did and what others did, and basically feeding off each other's strength and experiences," March says. At the same time, she cautions women starting out: "I wouldn't want anyone to discourage you. If you're passionate about starting a business, don't ask anyone if they think you *can* do it. Ask them *how* you do it."

## We Become Stronger in the Doing

Some of the younger women I meet today seem like they were born knowing how to *do*—they have been activists from the cradle, where they must have shaken their rattles in protest or solidarity and run for president of the third grade on a platform of cookies for all at recess. Some, like Courtney Martin, were already respected authors in their early twenties, seemingly fearless women who are undaunted in pursuit of professional advancement; others like Lauren Bush and Ellen Gustafson have started successful business ventures, or like Jen Nedeau secured a seat on an otherwise all-male management team. I say "Hooray for them," and it gratifies me enormously to encourage them and urge them on to greater heights. I have been especially fortunate to be approached by some outstanding young women seeking mentorship and offering to intern with me (which I've gratefully accepted), like Lauren Schreiber, who then went on to Harvard Law School and several years later is launching what I predict will be a highly successful law career—and a great relationship to balance it. But the truth is, there are subcultures and even vast areas of our country where the family support and social encouragement that helped these young women develop their intentions do not exist. Indeed in some instances, women's intentions for careers and egalitarian relationships that allow them to flourish remain actively rejected.

My young trainer, Jenny, represents another group of women who have enjoyed some of the expanded horizons that the women's movement has won, but who haven't been made aware of its tangible impact on their lives. She hails from a small Midwestern town where the values and expectations of the small-town Texas of my youth still reign supreme. In these parts of the country, there are stories about "good girls" and "bad girls," and what good girls should want and the "choices" they are allowed to make. All of this is reinforced by religious fundamentalists' unholy alliance with right-wing politics. Jenny moved to New York to break free from the limited options and preordained roles available to young women. She was determined to pursue her chosen career—to be the protagonist of her own story, and she is now building her own personal training business. Meanwhile, back home, she told me, things seem to be going backward.

Describing a marathon she planned to run with a recently married cousin, she paused and said, "Unless she gets pregnant. They don't believe in birth control, you know." She shook her head, lamenting that a friend of hers is pregnant by a man she wants desperately to marry, a man she plans to follow at the expense of her own job. Jenny feels her friend has made unwise choices, clinging to the fragile hope that having a baby and molding her life around his will secure their relationship. She worries, too, that these young women near and dear to her have not been encouraged to have aspirations for themselves.

Jenny's story seemed a time-warped version of my own upbringing—the values and aspirations, or lack of them, were so comparable that as Jenny explained the circumstances in her hometown, I felt I was having a flash-back. But one striking difference, Jenny and I agreed, is that even girls who don't plan on working for a paycheck when they marry and have children nevertheless more often than not get a college degree. That has to be some indication of feminism's progress, a positive sign of a revolution in a transitional phase. When I asked the ever-insightful Jenny why these educated young women abandon the workplace after marriage, she replied emphatically, "It's so much easier."

If only they were open to hearing how untrue that will inevitably turn out to be from someone who knows from experience. I don't mean to imply that my situation was universally the case, for it most assuredly was not. While all kids worry they're abnormal, I really was: I grew up Jewish in the buckle of the Texas Bible Belt. At times, we were the only Jewish family in town. My immigrant grandparents never lost their Eastern European Yiddish accents (as if a Texas drawl isn't an accent, but never mind . . . ), and my parents never looked quite convincing wearing the Tem-Tex Snaperoo Western shirts Daddy manufactured.

Feeling different makes people feel vulnerable, and conformity to a perceived norm seems like a defense against vulnerability. Vulnerability drains the courage out of you. Every adolescent girl and young woman, regardless of background, knows a variation on this theme, whether or not she is aware of the external cultural pressures that are shaping her, overtaking her internal strength and intention. Many teens do their best to fit in, ducking down and hoping to avoid being the target of "mean girls" or bullies; alternatively, if they are to attract attention, they hope it's the kind they get because they are fulfilling the expectations of others: the pink princess awaiting the kiss of the handsome prince, or yearning for the kind of attention associated with popularity, the very sort of admiration most easily commodified, hypersexualized, or abused.

Hence, my teenage rebellion—like that of so many teens—was to become ever so normal, or what I thought normal was: a wife, homemaker, and mom. My children have been the center of my universe, and I have no regrets about any part of my life with them. Still, if I'd had a strong enough sense of my own identity, I suspect my fifteen-year-old's view of the world and my role in it would have been quite different. Consequently, I'm sure my vision of myself and my future would have been wholly different.

Eventually, the smart girl I'd hidden away reemerged, powered by increased maturity, the pill that put me in charge of my reproductive choices, a cause to believe in, and a career that gave me the financial wherewithal to make other life choices. I began to hear my father's admonition, "You can do anything your pretty little head desires," reverberating ever more persistently in my mind, so that it finally quieted the negative chorus that had warned, "No, you can't, shouldn't, won't be liked if you do."

Jenny also broke free, moving to New York and slipping the shackles of the externally imposed expectations that had bound her to a self that didn't fit her internal aspirations. She exudes the energy and optimism of a woman who is standing in her power and walking with intention. She's creating a website to tell the world about her work and is learning how to blog with the same intensity she gives to her workouts. I'm looking forward to the exercise videos she's developing. Move over, Jane Fonda.

What remains to shift the gender paradigm to equality throughout society is to make sure that all women, not only those who are lucky or privileged enough to have supportive and encouraging families, can develop a strong sense of self while young and maintain it throughout their lives. And, although on its face this is a question of empowering individual women to stand up for themselves and for what they believe in, the mutual support of a movement functions like a mirror of our aspirations, reflecting to us what's possible. And it's a safety net to catch us if we fall while we're leaping to greater heights. The more we practice risking to leap, the more proficient we become, the more our fears melt away, and the more we grow ever stronger in the doing.

## The Fastest Route to Self-Esteem

I've been lucky that mentors have often come to me from unexpected places to help me see the possibilities that were beckoning and to help me test my strength and engage me in the larger women's movement. I began attending community college when I was twenty, when my three children were four, two, and four months old, respectively. I was fortunate to have a civics professor who saw some spark in me, and invited me to a League of Women Voters meeting. I joined, and that's where I learned how the political process works, from party precinct meetings on up, and how a bill becomes a law in the statehouse and in Congress. As my awareness of the political process increased, I became more active in community service.

The futurist Watts Wacker told me many years later that the fastest route to self-esteem is to stand up for what you believe in. This was certainly true for me. In fact, it is still true for me now, and something I have to continue to work on sharpening. For it is always easier not to wear your convictions emblazoned on your shirt for all the world to see.

Just as standing up for the civil rights of other groups who had experienced discrimination and injustice primed me to become aware of the systems of oppression that also held women back, standing up for women's rights enabled me to have the strength to stand up for myself. I discovered there's an upside to being different and feeling vulnerable. My world had malleable boundaries, unlike the worlds of my friends who really were "normal," or at least statistically closer to the norm than I was. I could live in multiple cultures proficiently, if not always comfortably. What began as a weakness became a strength. The experience of being different taught me empathy, and sharpened my ability to detect injustice. It eventually shaped me into a social justice activist—after I realized there was nothing wrong with me for being who I was, but there was a whole lot wrong with people who judged me and others for characteristics that had nothing to do with our characters. It was a process that gradually developed my activist muscles in the same way the football boys developed their physical muscles. (Hey, I'm from Texas; a football analogy is inevitable.)

I also learned from these social justice movements that there are two kinds of energy that motivate people to start or to join up with movements and become activists in them: anger and aspiration.

## Anger Energy Motivates

I was jolted to action by injustices that affected me personally. And I'm not alone in this. Women of my generation were ticked off for a lot of reasons. And all over America, we individually and collectively concluded that we weren't going to take it anymore.

There is power in being ticked off. I don't mean being unnecessarily rude or unkind, or flying into a rage, but rather channeling the anger that comes from a sense of injustice into action for positive change. Turning anger inward makes you bitter and depressed. Righteous indignation for its own sake is a dead end. But being aware of a wrong and using it as a power-to moment to set things right is a redemption. That's what Michelle Robson did when she started the EmpowHER women's health website as a result of her own lack of good, empathetic health information that made her feel like she couldn't make it through another day.

There is even more power in being ticked off together, as a movement.

Why? Because it's through movements that we have the mirror to see that a grievance is more than just personal. While an individual may be able to treat the symptoms of discrimination, movements can address root causes—remake and remodel the structures that maintain persistent inequality. For women in particular, being a part of a movement helps break patterns of self-reproach that can hold us back from getting everything that we deserve. Standing up for what we believe among others who are fighting for the same vision can help us move past the misdiagnosis of our own deficiencies being the source of our problems. It can help us recognize not only the structural causes of inequity, but also our own strengths in rising to the challenges.

I struggled to hide my differences as a girl, and blamed myself for not being "normal," only to realize my differences made me stronger when I joined the civil rights movement. Similarly, as the women's movement gained momentum in the 1960s and '70s, women recognized that they were not to blame for their feelings of dissatisfaction, for the fact that life's richest rewards always seemed to be placed out of their reach. And they had their sisters to multiply their courage to make history.

Because women then lacked the formal power of civic leadership or elected policy makers, they exercised grassroots movement muscle to challenge laws and customs that kept them from having equal opportunities. Women learned to simply shrug it off when we were laughed at, berated, or even attacked for failing to be well-behaved "ladies." We were making history every day, and this was satisfying. But even when we stumbled, simply taking action built our confidence in our ability to make a difference and strengthened those courage muscles—the safety net of sisterhood was there, after all.

I'm not saying it's easy to stay engaged in the movement for social justice. Believe me, sometimes the forces of reaction came at women swift and sure when they weren't well behaved. The nineteenth-century German philosopher Arthur Schopenhauer is said to have written in his notebook that "all truth passes through three stages. First, it is ridiculed. Second, it is violently opposed. Third, it is accepted as being self-evident."[10] Gandhi and others have also been credited with similar observations. I have lived that series of events, as have other women's rights and social justice activists through the centuries. In the 1910–1920 decade just before women's right to vote became enshrined in the Constitution, the suffragists chronicled in the film *Iron Jawed Angels* were beaten and jailed for their advocacy. Margaret Sanger was jailed nine times during that same period for opening a birth control clinic, just at the point she knew public opinion was swinging her way. I myself have dealt with death and bomb threats, anthrax scares, and being ridiculed on my fiftieth birthday as looking "far too young for my age" by a stalker who thought she'd upset me by showing she had personal information about me and showing up where I lived.

Media representations of women can be especially harsh and intimidating, not just to the women who are trashed, but also to other women just trying to better their own lives one step forward at a time. The male media powers—even today under 5 percent of the clout "decider" positions in major national media companies are held by women—saw that it was in their best interest to declare feminism dead, and they began the decades-long process of writing its obituary. The June 29, 1998, cover of *Time* magazine was a classic form of this malevolent undermining. Its deliberately ghoulish black-and-white montage of feminist icons Gloria Steinem, Betty Friedan, and Susan B. Anthony was juxtaposed against the supposedly post-feminist, brittle, and emotionally unstable this-is-what-feminism-has-wrought lawyer Ally McBeal, played by Calista Flockhart. The accompanying article prissily claimed to drive the final nail in feminism's coffin. It's a theme frequently repeated, but don't believe it. Live your life so as to prove them wrong.

Feminism is not only *not* dead, it has become the predominant social norm for both women and men, whether it's recognized or not. Look around you. Feminism is normal; it is, more or less, the status quo. Its victories have changed the entire context of our lives. Women in their

twenties, thirties, forties, and even fifties don't just see a world different from their mothers' experience; they live in a different world. Today
younger men are much more involved in their children's lives than their
fathers were; they also expect their wives to have a fulfilling profession and
join them in bringing home the bacon. Let's celebrate that. But as we have
seen throughout this book, we're a long way from parity, and we have no
valid excuses for failing to keep on moving forward. We have simply to
act like the winners that we are. This can sometimes be hard because we've
been fighting for so long for equality that it can seem like this slog will go
on forever, that we will never be able to declare full-out victory. And on
the other side of the coin, sometimes we let the struggle itself define us, as
though we are locked in an endless Kabuki drama, even when the most
toxic adversary has become not the external opposition but the compla-
cency of our own constituents (see chapter 4: "Be Unafraid: Opt Out of
Being Co-opted" for more on this).

So let's get on with it.

Ask yourself: What ticks you off enough to get involved in efforts to
better the lot of women? What motivates you to action? Or are you too comfortable, too complacent, too well behaved? And what makes you think the
rights and choices you have today will always be here if you don't work to
protect and extend them with the same passion it took to get them? Because
I guarantee you, they won't if you don't carry the fight forward. Get ticked
and get going.

## Aspiration Energy Motivates, and We Need Lots More of It

Anger energy will get you going, but only aspiration energy will get you to
the destination. New issues emerge every day. Political leaders change, and
laws can be rewritten; the shifting composition of the Supreme Court in
the past two decades gives us enough palpitations to confirm how fragile

our grip is, even when it comes to what we would like to consider settled, constitutional rights. With women composing half of the workforce, there is a huge need to reassess the way jobs are structured and the way career trajectories are evaluated.

Younger women's involvement and leadership in advancing women's rights to equality and self-determination are crucial because that's the only way the movement for equality will continue to flourish and grow. I fear for our future unless young women step up to lead a new wave of civic engagement—and indeed, one of my greatest delights is seeing how many young women are doing just that. It's up to them to walk boldly and with intention through the doors that have been opened, or those doors will inevitably slam in their faces. But it's also up to older women to reach out and give a hand up. To show there is something good in it for them by demonstrating the gains we've made, revealing the distance yet to be traveled, listening to what young women think ought to be done now and helping to support those efforts, and opening doors to leadership for young women within established movements working to get us to our final destination: true equality. And to show over and over why it's never enough to fight back; we must always fight forward with a constant barrage of initiatives that move the dial toward justice and parity. We need to light many more torches and together, women of all ages, and men who want to join up, create a blaze that can't be extinguished.

When the UN Women's Commission met March 1–14, 2010, in New York, I participated in a panel on the first day that embodied what I'm suggesting. The panel, "Winning Strategies for Gender Equality," was organized by US Women Connect, a fifty-state network of women's group coalitions that have been keeping alive the flame of aspiration ignited by the UN's 1995 Fourth World Conference on Women in Beijing. Through thick and thin—the rightward shift of U.S. government and George W. Bush's presidency, public apathy, and amnesia about the Beijing agenda—this group has held fast to its goals. But over the years, the leaders became grayer and didn't necessarily reflect the ethnic and racial diversity that is increasingly the face of America's next generation. Not so this panel. Reflective of the group's emerging leadership, it was over two-thirds women of color and diverse in age.

The Honorable Jackie Weatherspoon, a former New Hampshire state representative and UN adviser, currently leads US Women Connect's organizing efforts in the New England states. She revealed that some of the young women in her coalition avowed that the older women "whined too much." So she put them in charge of leading the discussions, and these young women, many of them barely toddlers in 1995, when their grandmothers went to Beijing, have created a multimedia platform that has energized activities around organizing for a Beijing-plus-fifteen meeting and securing U.S. ratification of CEDAW, the Convention on the Elimination of All Forms of Discrimination Against Women, the latter of which we older women have been unsuccessfully striving for for several decades.

To start the ball rolling away from the theoretical to practical application, let me put a small, not even slightly comprehensive, list of my aspirations on the table. Take them, or create your own aspiration energy, but use your Sister Courage to think big and bold.

- See to it that students are taught in history classes about how the women's movement has shaped the contours of the world we live in. Start a movement to incorporate equal time for women's history throughout the school curriculum, and meanwhile set up alternative ways to teach women's history through media and face-to-face programs.

- Start a virtual discussion group to make young women aware of how their choices affect the landscape for other women. It should not be unacceptable criticism to point out that, although everyone has the right to make their own life decisions, choosing to "opt-out" reinforces stereotypes about women's priorities that we have been working for decades to shatter, so just cut it out. Moreover, the "individual choice" women have to become stay-at-home moms becomes precarious when women attempt to return to the workplace and find that their earning power and options have plunged into a seemingly irreversible downward spiral. If we could see child rearing as a necessary task and not an identity, and if we could collectively recognize that facilitating quality child care benefits us all, we would go much further in guaranteeing women's choices than we do when we are expected to uncritically celebrate every individual's decisions.

- While educated women dropping out of the workforce may reinforce the glass ceiling, families regretfully limiting the number of children they have reinforces another lousy pattern—that fathers are still not asked or expected to make the same sacrifices in the home or the workplace that are required of women. Why not work on changing that? (It bears mentioning that a saner approach to domestic life would benefit men as well. A recent survey showed that, as husbands approached parity in taking responsibility for domestic chores, their happiness in the marriage, as well as sexual satisfaction, increased.) And join up with groups like MomsRising to work for workplace policies that are more family friendly all around—while at the same time have been shown to improve worker productivity and loyalty.

- Related to the issue of having children when we want them, organize or join coalitions to pass the federal Freedom of Choice Act. It would create a new civil rights framework for reproductive self-determination, banning discrimination of women on the basis of the childbearing choices they make—whether to have or not to have children.

## Sister Courage and Brother Partners

As powerful as women are, we cannot change the world alone. We need brother partners. There are so many men who are leading the way to a new masculine paradigm: Jimmie Briggs teaching teen boys and young men not to engage in violent or abusive behavior toward women; Michael Kimmel exploding myths about masculinity and working to free young men from the stereotypes that keep them from being whole human beings; and sixteen-year-old Aaron Zelinger, who wrote an impassioned argument for abortion coverage in healthcare and posted it on NotUndertheBus.com during the health reform debate.[11]

Perhaps the next great wave of the feminist movement will be women and men joining together to make sure both can earn a living and be able to deal with the realities of a personal family life at the same time. It's obvious that gender discrimination affects men as well as women, but we usually think of the negative consequences as affecting only women. So let's talk about how stereotypes about what boys and girls "should" do or be keeps both from discovering who they really are, and where their talents lie.

As Cara Lisa Berg Powers, the twenty-six-year-old executive director of By Any Media Necessary, put it in an email conversation we had: "If we're really gonna knockout the glass ceiling . . . we need to knock down the whole building. And if you keep thinking of men as the enemy, instead of potential partners and maybe even, dare I say feminists (I know mine is) then we'll keep having the same dated conversations. And if we don't start including perspectives outside of our own limited experiences in what is considered worthy of feminist discourse, then women of color, working-class women, young women, transgendered women, queer women, and male allies will be more and more disenchanted with a movement that should be about more rights for ALL women and equality for men and women. I like the quote 'feminism is the radical notion that women are people, too.' But I'm kind of tired of listening to women who call themselves feminists but forget that 'too.'"

Every generation has to relearn that banding together into a movement accomplishes transformational change. The folktale is told of a mother who gave each of her five daughters a stick (okay, the original story was about sons, but I'm taking poetic license). She took back a stick from one of her daughters and easily snapped it in two. Then she took back the other daughters' four sticks and bundled them together. She tried to break them but could not due to their combined force. She made her point: Working together, we are much stronger than one person alone. We should make that band as big as possible without diluting the central theme of equality for women this time around.

## CLAIMING SISTER COURAGE FOR THE LONG TERM

Banding together in this historic moment to achieve a new vision of unlimited liberty and justice for women, with no excuses for failing to achieve it, will require immense courage. We'll have to take on powerful reactionary economic and political interests that oppose these advances just as they opposed the Equal Rights Amendment thirty years ago, birth control and women's suffrage ninety years ago, and the Seneca Falls women's rights declaration more than 150 years ago. We won't win every battle, but we can't get discouraged. The ERA hasn't become an amendment to the Constitution yet, despite being first proposed in 1920 by those wise few suffragists who understood the power-to of advancing a new legislative initiative to carry women's rights forward to the next step once the vote had been won. But because a specific piece of legislation was introduced, and it has been reintroduced every year since, it has been a subject of political and public discourse and a rallying strategy. The ERA's principles have become so ingrained in our laws and our culture that women like my trainer, Jenny, and Emily, the eight-year-old soccer player in chapter 1, and many others don't even know that's how they got all the choices they have today.

As philanthropist and political activist Barbara Lee, whose profile precedes this chapter, reminds us, "Be persistent and patient."

In practicing Sister Courage, we might as well recognize we will face frustrations and disappointments—but with sisterhood and courage we can ensure that small setbacks don't become mud slides, that disillusionment will not cause us to throw up our hands and give up hope. Martin Luther King Jr., who spoke eloquently of his spiritual kinship with Margaret Sanger and the women's rights movement and who knew his share of disappointment, many times tasted the bitterness of a hard-fought battle lost. It was in the aftermath of one of those moments, I don't doubt, that he said: "Social change cannot come overnight, but we must act as though it were a possibility the very next morning." Those are words of consolation, but they are also—unmistakably—words of activation, a call to action.

Any movement's success can't be judged by any one short-term goal or event. It can only be judged by what is achieved over time. That kind of success demands consistency. It demands an ability to stay focused on the larger vision. Most important, it demands—even when things look the worst—that we never, ever lose sight of our strengths.

The first woman speaker of the house and the first woman to be a real contender for president didn't just happen. Women earning more than half of all college degrees, and achieving parity in medical school and law school—and even some religious seminaries—didn't just happen. These things happened because women joined together to create a movement that changed the laws and changed the culture.

From my life in a social justice movement, I speak from the depths of my heart when I say: There is enormous power in joining together to work for a common purpose. And I don't mean joining hands just to sing "Kumbaya." I'll repeat: A movement has to move. Constantly. The power and energy that create movement victories come from staying ahead of the curve, from doing what the world needs from you now and tomorrow, not yesterday. We have to keep things stirring. That's how you gather support and set the agenda rather than falling into a pattern of reactivity. The more we move, the stronger we get. We must never become too well-behaved, or we risk losing our opportunity to make history rather than just being carried along by it.

One and one equals more than two in a movement; there's a geometric increase in power when people organize together to make quantifiable change. And the experience of being part of a movement increases our courage as individuals while it multiplies the effectiveness of our individual contributions. Plus, you have a lot of fun.

Rainer Maria Rilke wrote a wonderful poem about how throughout history some special people have acted in bold and audacious ways. It inspires me every time I read it. The last two lines describe what not-so-well-behaved women with Sister Courage can do:

> *The future speaks ruthlessly through them.*
> *They change the world.*

So go change the world. And every time you think, *Oh, I can't do this; oh, I don't want to fight anymore; oh, I'm happy in my job and that's enough; I don't want to take one for the team; I don't want to wear the T-shirt and be seen as badly behaved*—stop!

Think *Sister*.

Think *Courage*.

Think *Sister Courage*.

For the goal is not merely to smash ceilings but to inspire a critical mass of women to seize this moment to realize their highest potential, to pick up their power tools and move beyond both internal and external barriers to equality once and for good.

# julie**gilbert**

Listening to Julie Gilbert, founder and CEO of WOLF Means Business, I almost hear myself talking. She says women don't realize the power they have, and she explains how culturally instilled insecurity causes women to work in isolation unless they're explicitly encouraged to speak in their own authentic voices and learn it's safe, even beneficial, to collaborate with, connect with, network, and support one another. She tells me the same dynamics of gender power apply to the workplace, politics, and personal relationships. Her passion for transformational change for women (and men) through movement building makes my heart sing.

What makes our similarities intriguing is that we've worked in distinctly different fields, we'd never met or spoken before our interview, and we're a generation apart in age. Gilbert, thirty-nine, was expecting her first child when we spoke in early 2010. After a stint as a senior manager at the giant auditing and tax consulting firm Deloitte, where her change-maker proclivities were already evident, in 2000 she joined Best Buy, a $45 billion annual revenue consumer electronics and entertainment company with 140,000 employees.

In 2004, while leading its Magnolia Home Theater initiative designed for the high-end male customer market, she noticed a "sea change" taking place: The overwhelming majority of purchases in Best Buy stores began to be made by women. Even when men purchased products, the women tended to be equally involved in the decision. Said Gilbert of her market research, "When I went to their homes, and I started talking with the man, I would invariably end up talking to his wife. She would have not only a strong point of view about what was wrong, she had solutions in every case that were right on the money." And once the woman was brought into the conversation, the sale was usually closed quickly.

"The intrinsic value that I started to feel emotionally was how connected I felt when I engaged and started listening to the woman's voice," Gilbert said. "And I started to realize how my voice transformed. I became more myself. I could breathe. I had ideas that frankly I used to think about all the time in executive meetings but had never ever said."

This process "unblinded" her to the "subconscious masking of my authentic voice." She realized the phenomenon occurred because the culture of the company, like the culture of the country, had been designed by men for men; women and other groups not traditionally in power roles adapt their voices to fit the voices of men as a matter of survival: "They [the men] can hear you. It's how you get things done."

I've called that process co-option. Becoming aware of it enabled Gilbert to see that the real growth opportunity for Best Buy lay in dramatically changing the way they did business. She set out to bring more women into decision-making ranks within the company and to engage women customers intensively as well.

Best Buy, like most major corporations in America and globally, was naturally attuned to men, Gilbert observed, "because that was their market when they built their companies. Today, that's dramatically shifted. The paradox is that there are very few authentic voices of women in these companies, voices in powerful enough positions to transform the companies." Yet, she asserted, "empowering women changes the conversation and uplifts the community. My passion and unrelenting efforts on this are because the data everywhere validates for the first time in history that women have the dominant consumer spending in almost every industry."

She spouts numbers we've seen repeatedly—over 50 percent of the wealth in the United States is controlled by women, over 80 percent of consumer products are purchased by women—and gives it an added kick that I think is the key to making meaningful change toward gender parity for good. To Gilbert, empowering women and elevating their authentic voices (she uses the word *authentic* a lot) "lifts all boats of opportunity not only for women but also for men, kids." It not only transforms business and fosters innovation that leads to financial growth but also builds leadership skills "to transform societies and make the world a much different place, a much safer and more prosperous place for everyone."

Shortly after she had these realizations, another paradox surfaced. First, a twenty-three-year-old female employee told Gilbert she was a role model for the women in the company's stores where many of the women felt they didn't have a niche. Yet later the same day, a senior male executive told her that though she was highly respected within the company, some of the female executive staff "hated her." Shocked and angry, Gilbert pondered this conflict. And again, the answer came that these women were working in a male culture where they were unable to speak authentically; they perceived the company's power-over model as finite without an expansive portion available to them. As a consequence, they weren't expansive with one another, either. As she described it, "They were completely demobilized by their own fear of putting on this armored suit every day and going to work. When they got out of the car and started walking in, they automatically started to transform themselves and their facts and what came out of their mouths to serve a male culture." There was a lack of mutual support, sometimes even sabotage, and the turnover rate for women was up to 200 percent higher than that of male employees.

Gilbert knew in that moment that she needed to reinvent how the company did business. She was convinced that if they didn't learn to serve women better both internally and externally, they wouldn't succeed over the long run.

Then, after she sold her boss on letting her take her big idea forward within the company, came "the gift of the dream" that catalyzed specifically how she would go about making this transformation. Her dream took her back to her childhood in South Dakota, where she would stay up late at night listening to wolves howl. She saw the commonality between wolves and what was happening at Best Buy.

Wolves are misperceived and misunderstood, she says. Contrary to the stereotypes, wolves are intensely loyal, community-driven animals that collaborate and cooperate. They embrace diversity through taking in stray wolves, and integrating them so fully that they can even become the alpha wolf. They travel in packs that often remain intact social units for generations.

The wolf metaphor became the inspiration for Gilbert's successful work to change the company. She designed "Women's Leadership Forums" with the WOLF acronym. Then she created an innovation architecture that brought female employees and customers together in "WOLF packs" with three outcome goals: growth of female market share, recruitment of women, and retention of female employees. And the three guiding principles were *commitment* to the business, customers, and other members of the pack; *networking* at all levels internally and externally to nurture and support one another; and *giveback* to women and girls in local communities.

Gilbert speaks of this in movement-building language (yes! like Sister Courage!): "We're mobilizing a movement in the company and outside of the company to create these environments, which are teams of women with men to reinvent the company."

"When you cut to the chase," Gilbert believes, "the reason women weren't supporting women is they were immobilized in their own isolated fear. Once you got them in an environment with other women who were passionate about changing the world, passionate about making change happen, passionate about supporting each other . . . the true authentic spirit of the woman started to emerge and turn into support, generosity to help another woman be successful, to create partnership, collaboration, and other things that are naturally innate to women." So the women began to support one another loyally "like wolves do in packs" (and she pointed out, like men have long "been wired to do"). And once they "felt the energy and the warmth and safety, the layers of armor they had built up started to melt away."

The metrics tell the story. WOLF built a network of over thirty thousand women and men (85 percent women) during the four years Gilbert led the effort. The turnover rate for women decreased 5 percent per year. Moreover, the number of women in the company grew by 18 percent, while female district managers increased by a whopping 300 percent. In one test project, women employees and consumers worked together to design a new store; it quickly grew to outperform a traditional store a mile and a half down the road. Company-wide revenue generated by females grew by $4.4 billion during this time, an 11 percent increase and quite enough to vindicate Gilbert's approach and the resources expended on WOLF.

Gilbert told me that when you are isolated and in fear, your natural inclination is not to reach out and help someone else. It's to protect yourself. "I believe that's what has happened to women in business. Which I'll tell you candidly that when I say these things, unless I give examples, many women resist the idea. When I describe what that looks like, every single woman in the audience shakes her head yes."

Gilbert retained the WOLF intellectual property, and formed her own company, WOLF Means Business, in 2009. What's next? Says Gilbert, "This has never happened before in the history of the world. Women are now in a position because of where they have gotten to in terms of education and stature and also indirectly in terms of the family unit—they have a voice and now they have the purse to go with the voice, and they are using the voice. It's no longer the fifteen- to forty-five-year-old male who is the consumer. The customer now is the woman. It's women of all incomes, races, and whatever it might be. So we [businesses] have got to transform."

Gilbert, who has racked up numerous awards for her visionary work including being named to *PINK* magazine's "Top 15 Women in Business in the United States," is optimistic transformation will happen: "I would say, 'You know what, how about we change the world for women and girls?' And not one woman I have ever spoken to has said 'no' to that."[1]

I'll howl for that any time.

# CHAPTER EIGHT

# just do it:
# your
# power tools

*"Just do it."*

**—NIKE SLOGAN**

So what are you going to do about it?

On a snowy January day in Grass Valley, California, 250 women packed the Holiday Inn Express conference room, the only place in the Northern California town of ten thousand large enough to hold such a crowd. A few dozen more who hadn't preregistered stomped the snow off their boots, and explained to the volunteers why they should be allowed in despite the overflow. Even in good weather, it would have seemed remarkable for so many bright-eyed activists from a sprawling rural area to spend a full day in a cramped meeting room discussing what they were "going to do about it."

The "it" was each individual attendee's passion.

I'd been invited to speak about "Sister Courage" at this first Passion into Action conference, organized that winter day in 2010 by Jesse Locks and Elisa Parker, a dynamic duo of young women who created the hub for activism and social change called See Jane Do. But I ended up learning more than I imparted. It was an eye-popping experience. First of all, the attendees were unusually involved and evolved activists for a variety of environmental, health, and women's causes. Second, See Jane Do's unique multimedia platform holds exciting promise as a new model for civic engagement and leadership in today's fast-paced, fragmented world. Its usefulness in rural areas, where women may be less able or inclined to participate in traditional organizations, is especially encouraging.

I wanted to learn more about See Jane Do, so I sat down with Elisa Parker during the afternoon break. When I admired her red cashmere dress,

Parker said she'd bought it for the occasion at a clothing store owned by the woman who'd given the welcome that morning, Lisa Swarthout, who also happens to be the mayor of Grass Valley. Parker is a consummate networker. She's definitely got the "be a sister" principle down.

But See Jane Do isn't about networking for networking's sake, nor is it just a clever social media technique for more chatter with little substance. Parker said she had decided her time for making excuses was over when her five-year-old daughter asked: "Mom, why are we killing the earth?"

The only real way she figured she could answer the question was to do something about it. She began by reconsidering the choices her family was making, the things they bought, the way they lived. But she soon realized that the problem went way beyond the scope of her individual life and her personal choices.

"Where will her voice be in the future for this?" she wondered, thinking of her daughter. "How could I make a positive contribution to the world she would inherit?"[1]

To create a future where her daughter would be able to live and thrive on a green and healthy planet, Parker knew she couldn't allow herself to be daunted just because she was an ordinary mom living in a small town in Northern California.

## "ORDINARY WOMEN DOING EXTRAORDINARY THINGS"

She recognized that, no matter how much she changed her lifestyle, her daughter's future—and the future of the planet—would not be secure unless she reached out and brought others along with her. "Ordinary" women like her, she reflected, watched the same news reports she did about environmental devastation, had the same worries, and were also out there taking action to heal the earth. Why not employ every medium at their disposal to build bridges between women who were working to change the world for the good, create a vibrant and buzzing network of ideas and initiatives, and inspire action and activism?

And so, in early 2009, Parker launched See Jane Do with Jesse Locks, a journalist and entrepreneur. Their mission? "We capture the stories of ordinary women doing extraordinary things," Parker explained. And the media See Jane Do uses is definitely *multi*. With a grant from the Corporation for Public Broadcasting, she produces and cohosts the See Jane Do radio program on KVMR-FM, based in Nevada City, California, in the foothills of the Sierra Nevada mountains and near Grass Valley, where she lives with her family. She interviews women who are doing something about it—taking creative action to help save the planet, improve women's health, and advance a plethora of other social justice initiatives.

By producing the radio program, which is broadcast over the local airwaves and around the world online (and with possible syndication on the horizon), and by creating an online social media network, See Jane Do defines an activist agenda. The Internet allows emerging voices to be heard alongside the voices of anointed media personalities. "You don't have to be somebody special in order to get your voice heard," says one of the organization's supporters in the welcome video on the See Jane Do site. Underlying that principle is the idea that everyone has something worthwhile and important to say and everyone has a contribution to make. The organization's rapid success has been made possible by the tremendous organizing and equalizing potential of the Internet. On the See Jane Do blog, you can subscribe to podcasts, see stories about "Extraordinary Janes," and share your comments. You can also interact with See Jane Do on Facebook and Twitter. Increased use of video is next. With 42 million women already using social media, and with women being 50 to 60 percent of most social media outlet users, See Jane Do is tapping into formidable power.[2]

See Jane Do multiplies the effectiveness of these high-tech methods with the personal touch by organizing off-line events and meet-ups—"Parties with a Purpose"—where people can meet face-to-face to build networks, reinforce connections, inspire women to support each other's work, initiate projects of their own, and have fun while doing it. At the Passion into Action conference, Parker and Locks invited women to nominate their favorite "Extraordinary Janes" with the goal of collecting an additional 1,500 stories, which they will publicize on their website and radio show. They culminated this campaign with an awards event open to the community. Always, their strategy is to give women concrete ways to connect and pursue their passions for social change. Real ways to make things happen.

I mention See Jane Do not because it's an exceptional organization doing incredible work (although it is). I mention it because the power tools they are employing toward creating change are tactics that all of us have at our disposal, allowing each of us to walk in our own intentions.

As Locks explains, it's "not just us putting stuff out in the world, but the world throwing it back to us." See Jane Do celebrates rather than resists this interdependence and mutuality. Moreover, it's a new kind of hybrid entity: It functions like a business—it's even generated venture capital interest—and like a nonprofit that works for the public good, it bridges traditional and new media to enable strong individuals to express themselves within an even stronger collective, Sister Courage–like.

When I asked Parker, thirty-nine, about the age range of their participants, she said that initially the preponderance were longtime activists like seventy-two-year-old self-defined "spiritual activist" Marilyn Nyborg, who founded the feminist group Gather the Women, along with socially conscious Baby Boomers living in the area. But now the group claims younger women like twenty-four-year-old Rachel Barge, fundraiser extraordinaire, who founded Campus InPower to raise streams of money to pay for student-led campus sustainability projects, and Beth Terry, forty-five, who single-handedly organized a successful effort to get Brita water filters to switch from nonrecyclable materials to others that can be recycled.

While See Jane Do is exemplary, it's just one of many women-led networks, businesses, and organizations that are nurturing agents of change, incubating new ideas, and transforming society. The world is sorely in need of transformation, and it needs the kind of change that women's leadership can provide.

# **power**tool number eight

## EMPLOY EVERY MEDIUM: use personal, social, and traditional media every step of the way. use the medium of your own voice. and think of each of the power tools as a medium to be pressed into the service of your power-to.

Fortunately, there are simple, small things that greatly enhance one's capacity to get the job done, just like handheld power tools can save time and labor by leveraging power.

In each chapter of this book, I've talked about one practical power tool that you can use to build your own movement for greater equality, prosperity, and justice. This chapter brings all of them together in one place, and

I'll give some additional details and examples to prepare you to start using some or all of them in your own life.

Below are your nine essential power tools to lead with intention and live unlimited. Take from them what you need to make lasting change where you want it—in work, civic and political life, and personal relationships. This isn't an exhaustive list, and I hope they spur you to create new ones. Check out www.gloriafeldt.com, where I invite you to share your experiences and benefit from the experiences of others. I intend for these power tools and the accompanying tips for using them to be a small taste of the magnificent smorgasbord of opportunities for you to be unlimited in your vision and intention.

## POWER TOOL #1: KNOW YOUR HISTORY AND YOU CAN CREATE THE FUTURE OF YOUR CHOICE

It has often been said that those who don't know history are doomed to repeat it. I'll add that ignorance of history can doom us to forget how history is made, leading us to accept our present circumstances as inevitable and resign ourselves to an unacceptable status quo.

Think how quickly we come to accept and accommodate changes in our lives. Can you imagine now how we survived before cell phones or the Internet? Once a technological hurdle is broached, or a legislative victory attained, or a barrier broken for women in a profession, even those who once opposed the change usually grow accustomed to the new norm quite swiftly.

This is why even though most Americans—there are a few holdouts, to be sure—have accepted the legal justification for women's equality, with our foreshortened sense of history, we tend to forget that these things weren't just inevitable markers of progress, but rather were hard-fought and hard-won. And we saw in chapter 1, "Understand: You've Come a Long Way, Maybe," women in the United States have had a recurrent pattern of making significant leaps forward to the brink of power and then taking steps back of our own volition—albeit abetted by backlash, tradition, and vestiges of discriminatory policy.

But the doors are open now, or at least ready to be opened when we decide we're ready. And *still* women aren't walking through in numbers and with intention sufficient to bring us to equality for good. That is at least in part because of obliviousness to our shared and proud history.

## Do You Celebrate National Toilet Paper Day?

Here's how quickly history can be lost and how one woman's action reclaimed it.

Paula Cullison, a longtime tiller in the fields of women's equality and president of Arizona Women's Partnership, a nonprofit organization that funds grassroots charities assisting vulnerable women and children, went to AOL's greeting cards section looking for a Women's Equality Day card on August 26, 2007—the eighty-seventh anniversary of women's right to vote.[3] She found instead a card honoring National Toilet Paper Day. So she sent this email to her friends with AOL accounts and asked each to send the message along to ten more people in their networks.

"What has happened when one of the most important events in American history, Women's Suffrage Day, is denigrated by American Greetings to Toilet Paper Day! As an American woman who values the right to vote, I am ashamed of this corporate giant who profits from women, who buy the majority of greeting cards."[4]       Cullison's protest quickly went viral. Apologies from American Greetings ensued, and by the next year there were several Women's Equality Day cards to choose from.

Cullison seized AOL and American Greetings' failure as a teachable moment, not only to reprimand two major American companies about their blind spot to women's history, but to raise the visibility of women's history. As William Faulkner once wrote, "The past is not dead. It's not even past."[5]

It's our responsibility to share our history, challenge false revisionist narratives, create a little controversy if necessary (like Cullison did), and teach the history we've lived to younger women. That's a tangible way to pass the torch, or better yet, to light many more torches.

To younger women, emerging into a world where the most obvious barriers have disappeared but where significant obstacles to their achievement still remain, the feminist movement of the 1960s and '70s is a history many are eager to learn. Jenna Marie Mellor, who is in her twenties, said she wants to learn the practical skills necessary to use power for good. Yet she doesn't always feel like she has the connection to the generation of women preceding hers to ask for help. Knowing the history she shares with women who came before her could ease Mellor's feelings of disconnectedness.

Just as it is the responsibility of older women to share our histories to inspire and assist our younger sisters, younger women also need to feel supported to reach out to older women to ask the questions they need answered. Knowing your history, being able to place yourself into the narrative of women's history, can ground you in the world, inspire your activism, and save you the trouble of making the same mistake repeatedly. But most important, knowing your history can give you the tools to shape your future.

## What You Can Do to Know Your History

• GO OUT AND LEARN. Although women in history are now sometimes included in school curricula, and are the occasional subject on cable television and Ken Burns documentaries, women's history is still often presented as an adjunct to "real history," relegated to a few pages at the end of the chapter or "Women's History Month" events. (Not to underestimate the reach of Women's History Month: Google the phrase and you get over forty million citations now that it has been around for thirty years.)[6]

Follow your curiosity: Read, watch, learn. Learn your own family's history. How did your mother, aunts, grandmothers, and great-grandmothers fare in the past? Did they find their own moments of resistance? How can what they lived through serve as an inspiration for you and your life? How can sharing what you know about them inspire others to be bold and seize their power?

• GO OUT AND TEACH. The world is full of teachable moments. By sharing our history, we also share the sense of the possibilities of history, including the ways the world can change and how we can contribute to that change happening. Social media, as we've seen, can be a powerful tool to make this happen. During Women's History Month 2010, Shelby Knox, a feminist activist in her early twenties, used her Facebook status updates as a forum to place short vignettes of notable moments in women's history, which were then shared with her more than 2,500-strong Facebook network. For instance, she posted an update commemorating the day Jeannette Rankin of Montana took office as the first woman elected to the House of Representatives, and the day thousands of suffragists marched on Washington. To explain her motivation, she quoted Gerda Lerner: "Women's History is the primary tool for women's emancipation."

• GO OUT AND RAISE HELL. As I suggested in chapter 7, let's start a movement to get women's representation in history courses to be 50 percent of the content, and/or to include women's history in every school history curriculum. Oh, not enough wars for some people? Too bad. There really are many other important things to learn about and that could serve as better organizing themes for history.

• GO AHEAD AND ASK. Are you a young woman who wonders, like Jenna Mellor, what it was like to be in the midst of the women's movement when it was tilting forward full throttle? Are you an older woman who wonders what it's like now for women in their twenties who have so many choices? Or are you somewhere in between? We tend to lapse into oversimplifying other people into two-dimensional figures. Be curious. Ask questions. Listen. The answers may surprise you, and mutual understanding builds strong bridges. I met Mellor when she recorded my oral history for the Schlesinger Library. Check out the many such repositories where women's stories are housed.

• RECOGNIZE THAT YOU MAKE HISTORY. History isn't only an academic discipline made by other people in other eras. History is constantly unfolding. Every action you and I take moves women forward, takes them back, or maintains the status quo. Do you remember Secretary of Labor Frances Perkins's reason for taking the position in FDR's cabinet, for becoming the first woman to hold a cabinet level position? She felt a "duty to other women to walk in and sit down on the chair that was offered, and so establish the right of others long hence and far distant in geography to sit in the high seats." Knowing your history isn't only about being aware of the accomplishments and challenges of women of the past. It is also about recognizing your own role and responsibility in shaping history for the better. Each of us can play a part, large or small, to push that fulcrum toward justice and true equality. Even a very small pebble thrown into the pool makes a ripple that undulates outward indefinitely.

Only if you are conversant in your own history can you effectively shape the future of your choice.

## POWER TOOL #2: DEFINE YOUR OWN TERMS— *FIRST*, BEFORE ANYONE ELSE DOES

Whoever sets the terms of the debate usually wins it. To shape history and create the future, we must seize the moment and set the agenda. In chapter 2, I made the case for changing the definition of power from *power-over* to *power-to,* to shift from a culture of oppression to a culture of positive intention to make things better for everyone. Power-to is leadership.

At this critical moment when nearly all of the external barriers to women's achievement have been removed, we've proven that we can play by the men's rules and master the game when we need to. But too often, in our pursuit of success, we've failed to question the rules themselves. Instead we accept existing definitions of terms with a shrug, maybe wishing things were different but not working hard enough to do something about it.

It's possible to imagine a hypothetical situation where women reach parity in the major areas of human endeavor—as law partners and CEOs, National Book Award winners, in the halls of Congress, governor's mansions, and in the Oval Office—but nothing changes. If we allow ourselves to continue to be co-opted, gender parity could fail to be transformative.

Imagine, if you will, Liz Cheney as president of the United States. The ultraconservative daughter of former Vice President Dick Cheney might as well *be* her father; her Keep America Safe campaign branded Justice Department lawyers "al-Qaeda" for having served as counsel to individuals accused of terrorist acts—a charge so outrageous that even conservatives like South Carolina Republican Senator Lindsey Graham and former Bush-appointed Attorney General Michael Mukasey accused her of attempting to shred Constitutional protections.[7]

So let's not become so skilled at operating within the traditionally male-dominated *power-over* rules that we forget that we can change those rules if we define power as the expansive *power-to* that makes you feel power*full*.

Nicola Wells is in her twenties, and a community organizer and educator at the Center for Community Change. She worries that some women who seek power don't perceive their responsibility to use that power to improve the world. Simply attaining prominent positions is not enough for her. "I'm *not* glad when there's a woman at the top of a company who's doing things that are hurting people. To me that's not what it means to be a woman at the height of power. To me, so much of being a woman is tied to social change. Because when you understand power as a relationship, you understand that you want everyone to have power."[8]

- What expectations do you have for women's leadership?

- Gandhi famously said, "Be the change you wish to see in the world."[9] Defining power as the power-to—to accomplish good for yourself and for others—how can you become the leader you wish to see?

## How to Become Fluent in the Language of Power

After you define the terms and set the agenda, you still have to communicate it. That requires fluency in the language of power.

Linguist Deborah Tannen has devoted her career to studying the different "communications rituals" that men and women use, the different language cultures and worlds of words that we are socialized into due to gender. She is a very wise woman. I have profusely dog-eared and underlined copies of her groundbreaking first two books about male and female communications patterns—*That's Not What I Meant!* and *You Just Don't Understand.* "Men grow up in a world in which a conversation is often a contest, either to achieve the upper hand or to prevent other people from pushing them around," she explains. "For women, however, talking is often a way to exchange confirmation and support."[10]

Because the meanings we intend, and the nuances we apprehend, are tied to our gendered experiences of language, we've probably all had the experience of male-female conversation seeming bilingual.

When I interviewed her, Tannen gave me the example of a husband and wife in a car driving down the highway. The wife asks her husband,

"Would you like to stop for coffee?" He answers honestly: "No, thank you." Because she had wanted to stop for coffee, she perceives his negative answer as an order she must accept and so she bristles that he didn't take her wishes into account. Later, when he senses or finds out she's annoyed, he is irritated that she did not just come right out and say what she meant, that she wanted to stop for coffee. For him, conversation is exchange of information. For her, it's a path to negotiation.

"She's not playing games," Tannen said. "She's just asking in the way that is the obvious way to her. You start a conversation so he can tell you what he wants and you can say what you want. And then you'll negotiate. He's quite happy to negotiate, but he'd never start the conversation that way."[11]

Because men still control most of the clout positions in this country, we do need to become fluent in different conversational styles—and in asking directly for what we need, or what we desire, rather than hoping that our indirect statements will be interpreted correctly. And at the same time, we must insist that men reciprocate by understanding and becoming fluent in our communication styles, too.

## Don't Cede Ground with Nonverbal Language

I was watching *The Today Show* on the day after a particularly devastating Wall Street drop. Lehman Brothers had just tanked, and Bank of America had bought Merrill Lynch. The economy seemed to be spinning out of control.

To its credit, *Today* had set up an interview with two financial analysts, one male and one female. Matt Lauer was conducting the interview. As the cameras zeroed in on the two supposedly authoritative experts about to be interviewed, I saw classic power tools at work—or, in the case of the female expert, not.

He was wearing a business suit and had neatly trimmed hair. She was wearing a sleeveless dress in a distracting print. Her wavy dark hair was flying loose all over her face—beautiful but less than businesslike. When Matt asked the first question, he looked at the woman but didn't specifically call her by name. Rather than simply answering, she turned to the man as if to ask, "Do you want to take this or shall I?" Well, of course, he jumped right in and dominated the rest of the interview. She attempted to speak several times, but by that time the conversation between the male guest and Matt was off and running, and Miss Polite never had a chance to establish her authority. Her neck seemed to be made of rubber as she whipped her head back and forth from Matt to the male expert rather than training her eyes on the host or the camera. I cringed as she kept bouncing her eyes and nodding her head deferentially at what the man was saying. When she finally had a chance to speak, she hedged her terms, using more words yet less specific language than was called for in a fast-paced television interview about a national crisis.

She might have been the most knowledgeable expert in the world, but she squandered her power to communicate effectively by failing to use a few simple power tools available to all of us.

A counterlesson in how it's done was on air the next day, when *Today* had an all-female panel that included Jean Chatzky, NBC's personal finance editor, real estate mogul Barbara Corcoran, and CNBC's Sharon Epperson. All of them looked directly at Matt or the camera, spoke with strong voices, and wore feminine but strong business suits with jackets. Their attire wouldn't have given them authority had their words not been substantive. But their appearance didn't interfere with their credibility. Each spoke with clarity, and firmly expressed her point of view. Was the dynamic different because there were no men on this panel? I don't know, but having watched these three savvy women define their own terms first on other occasions, I suspected each of them could hold her own anywhere.

The days are long gone, fortunately, when women thought we had to wear severe navy suits, menswear shirts, and those silly bow ties in order to be taken seriously. In a perfect world, we would be judged purely by our merits, and would each feel free to be ourselves in the fullest possible sense of the term—whether shy or bold, piping up in our squeaky voices or intoning our thoughts in a deeper register, dressed in business suits or cute sundresses or cozy jeans. But in order to get there—to be able to define the rules of the game and set the standards under which judgments are made—we have to become fluent in the language of power. The key is to be aware of self-presentation to ensure that we can command the conversation from the outset: to set the agenda, define the terms, and translate the meaning of power from *power-over* to *power-to*.

You have the power to define yourself. Use it.

## Define the Terms and Set the Agenda

• SAY THE FIRST WORD. Almost always, the first word is what sets the tone of the whole conversation. Be poised, prepared, and ready to get the first word in during any debate. Play offense, not defense. Don't hesitate. Don't apologize for having ideas or expectations, and don't end every sentence with an intonation rise as though it were a question. Dive in. No excuses. You are ready. Define yourself. Define the terms of the debate if there is one. Set the agenda. That's your most power*full power-to*.

• SAY THE LAST WORD. If you're in a tough discussion, stick with it until the end. Speak with authority and clarity. Use simple declarative sentences. Don't hedge your words, or append endless qualifications to your arguments. Speak as though you know you will be believed. Remember, you're on the right side of history. I don't mean to hang on to arguments like a dog on a bone; I mean not giving up without speaking your piece to your own satisfaction.

• SPEAK THE LANGUAGE. Understand the conversational rituals that distinguish different styles of communication and deploy them to your advantage. Even if this doesn't come naturally at first, it's a tactic that can be learned and that can become second nature. This isn't about being disingenuous, but about making sure your authentic self emerges and is communicated to the world the way you want yourself to be seen. Being multilingual (and by this I mean being able to communicate with both men and women) expands your world without having to compromise yourself. But in any language, what your mother told you was mostly right. Think about what you're wearing, your posture, the way you enter a room. Make a good first impression. Make eye contact. Smile. Sit up straight.

Your vision, ideas, and plans have the power to shape the future, but not if you keep them to yourself. Set the agenda; don't wait for someone else to set it. Be a thermostat, not a thermometer. Define the terms—first.

## POWER TOOL #3: WHAT YOU NEED IS THERE IF YOU SEE IT AND HAVE THE COURAGE TO USE IT

All of us have had moments when we have felt absolutely powerless. In the contest between drift and mastery, the drift can sometimes seem like an undertow—pulling you relentlessly in a direction you don't want to go. But as every ocean swimmer is told, when you're in the grip of a current, don't waste your strength flailing against it; maintain your presence of mind and swim with it until you're in the clear. It will keep you afloat and safe so you can find the opening when it appears.

In chapter 3, I shared a dream in which I realized the strength and courage I needed to create the next phase of my life was right there in my hands. And over and over I've found that the resources I needed were there once I was perceptive enough to see them. Sometimes that was a big thing, such as using a ballot initiative seeking to ban abortion as an opportunity. By swimming with the wave, we found unforeseen power to educate and motivate supporters of women's reproductive rights who had been either complacent about the looming threats or frozen with fear that we'd lose. This was in conservative

Arizona in 1992. By using what we had—the public's belief, identified by smart polling, as well as the support of the late Senator Barry Goldwater—we defeated Proposition 110 by the largest majority of any ballot initiative to that date in Arizona: 68 percent to 32 percent.[12]

Switching from a political example to a personal one, sometimes the insight you need to make an important life choice is right there if you can see it. Brittany Dillman, a twenty-four-year-old Columbia Law student, recalls the two years after college she spent working as a paralegal at a prominent corporate law firm—at the very bottom of the totem pole. The work wasn't gratifying in the slightest. The hours were long, the work was tedious, and there was little recognition for a job well done. She could have wallowed in her dissatisfaction or moved on. But what she needed to make the job more fulfilling was right there once she saw it. Like many other leading law firms, this one allowed its attorneys to take on some pro bono cases, and they could include their paralegals in the work. Dillman worked on five such cases, and that's where she found the passion that would propel her to go to law school.

"Most of [these clients] were abused immigrant women seeking visas in order to have legal residence here and separate from their batterers," she said. "They had gone through trauma, so they definitely needed to trust me." She found that her presence in the room had unique value. "I think it helped that they could tell their stories to a female," she said. Dillman believes her clients would likely not have felt as comfortable telling their stories of abuse to the male attorneys for whom she worked. She also spoke Spanish, a skill that enabled her to communicate with Spanish-speaking clients and made her more valuable to the attorneys. "I got a little power back for myself in a situation in which I was basically powerless," she said. She knew she would get greater power to control her own work by earning her law degree. But more important, Dillman found that while she relished the authority that specialized knowledge of the law would grant her, she preferred to use this power to advance social justice rather than protect the status quo. That was the insight she needed at that particular stage of her life. And she used it.[13]

## Even the Powerless Have Power
## When They See It and Use It

In *Lysistrata,* Aristophanes's fictional comedy about gender, power, and politics, the women of Greece are sick of the decades-long Peloponnesian Wars, tired of their husbands and sons being gone, or worse, getting killed or maimed. Although the women cannot pass laws and are excluded from the male arena where decisions about war and peace are made, they decide to take action. Lysistrata convenes the women of the thirty Greek city-states in a sort of pan-Hellenic conference to find a way that they can end the conflict. They use the only power they have: sex, or rather, its denial. The women agree to deny sex to their husbands until they cease the violence. And it works. *Lysistrata* was of course considered a hilarious comedy of improbabilities, but there's a serious message. What you need is there if you can see it: You can always figure out a way to accomplish something if you identify where your power is and are willing to use it.

This story of withholding sex for peace was repeated recently in Liberia, but this time it was for real and far from comedy. In a society revealing hideously the worst of what can happen without gender equality and balance, a group of women—Christian and Muslim working together for the first time—rose to demonstrate courage beyond measure.

Scarred by fourteen years of civil war that had terrorized the nation, Liberia was in chaos. The warlord president Charles Taylor had stripped the country of its financial resources and worse, had brutalized its children by conscripting boys as young as seven years old into the military. It would have been a natural human response to withdraw, but women with no official power declared, "Enough. Stop the war. Stop the killing." And the power they found they had was in the power to say no.

As recounted in the compelling documentary *Pray the Devil Back to Hell,* the women, led by Leymah Gbowee, a former trauma counselor who had been working with the boy soldiers after they returned from war, decided they would take action the only way they could—passive resistance in the marketplace. They would gather and sit silently as a reproach to the ruling violence; they also actively denied sex to their boyfriends, partners, and husbands. The men were responsible for the violence, but the women of Liberia saw their path to peace. They recognized the power they had, and used it boldly and fearlessly until they forced Taylor to participate in the 2003 United Nations peace talks that ultimately led to his banishment from Liberia and the election of Africa's first woman head of state, President Ellen Johnson-Sirleaf.[14]

Most of the time when we use the power we have, it's not nearly as dramatic as the Liberian market women bringing down the government, or even defeating a ballot initiative in the United States. It might be recognizing the leverage of your specialized skills to negotiate a raise, or in Brittany's case, to zero in on a longer-term career goal. But the basics are similar in meeting any challenge.

## How to Use What You've Got

• KNOW YOUR VALUE. Honestly assess your talents, skills, experiences, and capacities—how can you best demonstrate your special expertise? Doubt the extent of your powers? Consider the efforts that advertisers and others expend to get you on their side. The swag at BlogHer should be a big clue: Women have clout, clout that we haven't fully leveraged. Find out who values you, who wants you on their side, who needs your skills and talents. And make sure that you're not giving it away for free.

• TOOT YOUR OWN HORN. If you don't, who will? And instead of getting stuck in the weeds of self-reproach, ask yourself: *What did I do right? What experience did I gain that will improve my abilities and chances next time?* As Susanna Opper, business communications expert, noted in her December 2009 newsletter: "While it's always good to recognize accomplishments, it's especially important in tough times." She told the story of a colleague who literally brought horns to a business meeting and passed them out so the participants could toot their own horns about their accomplishments—whether they were meeting sales goals, creating new marketing strategies, or simply making it through a difficult year.

• GIVE YOURSELF A WHACK ON THE HEAD. "'Only the most foolish of mice would hide in a cat's ear,' says designer Scott Love. 'But only the wisest of cats would think to look there.' Don't miss the obvious. What are you overlooking? What resources and solutions are right in front of you?" This fun anecdote can be found on one of Roger von Oech's "Creative Whacks" cards. This particular card is titled "See the Obvious," obviously. I'm a great fan of these types of creativity tools, and of von Oech's accompanying book, *A Whack on the Side of the Head.* His cards are designed to "whack you out of habitual thought patterns and allow you to look at what you're doing in a fresh way." I've often pulled them out in staff meetings when we've had seemingly intractable problems to solve.[15]

Women collectively need this metaphorical whack to get us out of stale thought patterns and help us realize what incredible power we have at this amazing moment when all signs point to a world that wants the qualities we bring to life and leadership.

Use what you've got. What you need is usually there if you can see it and if you have the courage to use it.

## POWER TOOL #4: EMBRACE CONTROVERSY

Although the women of Liberia succeeded in bringing a measure of peace to their country, their methods were surely controversial. They drew fire from entrenched authorities, as well as from some religious leaders. But controversy can clarify your principles, show you where you stand, and help you draw the line—and it can draw others to you. In chapter 4, embracing controversy, rather than ducking it, was shown to be a powerful protection against co-option—and a tremendous way to maintain your integrity even in difficult situations.

I'm not saying to create controversy just to create a dustup, but rather that it is not something to be feared or avoided. Controversy can be a highly potent and strategic power tool in two different kinds of situations: Whether it's the controversy we take because of circumstances that come to us or the controversy we make because it's the best way to shed light on an issue or make the change we want in our lives or in leadership, controversy can be our friend.

To be sure, controversy can be deployed to maintain the status quo as much as it can be used to catalyze a movement for progressive change. Think of the current noisy grumblings of the Tea Party, the group of right-wingers who want the government out of our business—except when it comes to really personal things like reproductive rights and marriage equality. I've never understood why the extreme right is so obsessed with other people's sex lives, but I do know their public disruptions often succeed for two reasons we need to learn from: First, they're passionate and persistent, and second, they know that if they can cause enough discomfort, most people will simply get tired, back away, and leave the field to the reactionaries. Don't let that happen.

## The 7 "C's" of Controversy

Since we can't avoid controversy, we have to learn to love it, embrace it, and not back away from it, but use the energy to advance our goals. Like Rosa Parks and Margaret Sanger did. Or like Kamy Wicoff did to grow She-Writes.com by leaps and bounds on the wave of controversy over *Publisher's Weekly*'s snubbing of women writers. Learning to walk into the wave of controversy and let its energy take us where we want to go rather than backing away from it is the most important communication lesson I learned in my four decades on the leadership front lines. And it applies not just to social movements and politics but to everything we do.

## THE 7 "C'S" OF CONTROVERSY ARE:

**CONTROVERSY** is the

**COURAGE** to risk putting your

**CONVICTIONS** out to the world, because it gets people's attention. It gives you a platform to present your

**CASE.** To teach, engage people, define, persuade. Often this causes

**CONFLICTS**—the clash of uncertainties from which new social realities are constructed—which forces people to

**CLARIFY** their values and beliefs, and that leads to

**CHANGE.**

### How to Embrace Controversy Constructively

• BE UNAFRAID. Withstanding the natural human resistance to controversy begins by using the first power tool, defining your own terms based on what you believe and want to get accomplished in the first place. Breathe deeply; get to a place in your own mind and heart where you feel at one with your own convictions.

Staking out a position you know will attract attention, derision, or objections can be frightening. But if you're secure and confident in your beliefs, if you project strength, not fear, then your actions will compel others to reexamine their beliefs and clarify their values. Your fearlessness will attract more and more supporters. And you'll be better able to resist the urge to become defensive or circle the wagons of defeat. Stay expansive in your thinking. Stay in your *power-to*. What's the worst that can happen, after all? I love what Eleanor Roosevelt said, as it sums up beautifully why we might as well learn to embrace controversy and not fear it: "Do what you feel in your heart to be right—for you'll be criticized anyway."[16]

• MAKE CONTROVERSY. Here's a great example of creating controversy thoughtfully and strategically for a good reason. Beth Terry was recuperating at home in San Francisco from a hysterectomy in 2007 and "feeling pretty sad and powerless." While browsing the Internet, she came across a photo that would change her life: It was the carcass of an albatross chick on Midway Island, thousands of miles from civilization, completely filled with pieces of plastic. Even a toothbrush. "In that moment," she told me, "I realized my personal actions could have an impact on creatures I hadn't even known existed." Someone had to speak up for them, she decided, and that someone was herself. "Perhaps it was the fact that I was wrestling with and grieving the fact that I would never have my own children that I felt so protective of those other babies."

Terry created a website, "Fake Plastic Fish" (http://fakeplasticfish.com), to track her own plastic waste and to research and report on plastic-free alternatives. "Slowly," she said, "I developed a devoted following of readers also trying to change the way they lived." In 2008, she discovered that her plastic Brita water filter cartridge couldn't be recycled. Terry told me: "I decided I would broaden my reach and form a coalition of bloggers and organizations to ask Clorox (the parent company of Brita) to take back and recycle the cartridges." Then she realized a critically important element of making constructive controversy. "I had no idea if I would succeed or fail,"

Terry wrote me in her emailed account of her journey. "What I did know was that if I didn't try, I would never find out."

"The campaign," she said, "was a lesson in stumbling and getting back up, stumbling and getting back up. I had no idea how to write a press release, so I just did the best I could. I had no idea if any organizations would get involved. But I just kept sending out emails. I was beyond thrilled when my local Sierra Club chapter asked me to come and present the campaign, and when they eventually sent an official letter to Clorox asking them to take back and recycle the filters." Although the company recycled filters in Europe, it refused to do so in the United States, claiming that there was not enough demand for the service to make it worth their while. Americans wouldn't be interested in that kind of thing. Terry set out to prove the mega-company wrong.

And what happened next affirmed her strategy. After seven months, sixteen thousand petition signatures, and over six hundred used filters collected from people all over North America, Terry got a call from Brita. Clorox had responded to the pressure. Lo and behold, in that short time, they had created a way to recycle the cartridges. Terry was thrilled. But she didn't stop there. "My blog and efforts are now reaching an international audience, and this cause has become a routine part of my life," she says proudly. Now she's writing a book based on her experiences learning to live with less plastic waste, hoping to inspire others to do the same.

What did she learn? "As women, we have incredible power, if we just learn to use it," Terry asserts, "and if we stop worrying so much about what people think and listen to the voice inside us urging us to speak up for what we believe in."[17]

• TAKE CONTROVERSY. I can't think of a better example of controversy well-taken than then-presidential candidate Barack Obama's thoughtful speech exploring the role of race in American history, delivered in

Philadelphia in the spring of 2008. In response to exploding controversy around his relationship with his pastor and mentor, Reverend Jeremiah Wright, who had made inflammatory (and frankly racist) remarks in his sermons, Obama rode directly into the wave of controversy. He didn't deflect or minimize it, but took the festering issue of race in America head-on, thus defusing criticism, positioning himself as a courageous truth-teller, and building respect and enthusiasm for his candidacy among voters hungry for change.[18] He turned a powder keg of a controversy that could have exploded his presidential campaign into a brilliant platform to teach about a subject so sensitive that it is often avoided in public discourse.

I sincerely doubt Obama or his campaign advisers would have sought out this controversy, but when it came up, they realized they had been handed a priceless moment to demonstrate genuine leadership. I believe this was the turning point that led him to victory, and that if Clinton had treated the equally vicious sexism thrown at her with the same directness and candor that Obama confronted race, the outcome might well have been different.[18]

Embrace controversy. It gives you a platform. It is a teacher, a clarifier, and your friend, especially if you are trying to make change.

## POWER TOOL #5: *CARPE* THE CHAOS

Paradigm shifts don't happen in moments of stability. They occur during periods of upheaval, times when the tectonic plates of our lives shift and make things feel chaotic. Wars, revolutions, famine, drought, earthquakes, economic depressions, diseases like HIV/AIDS, social justice movements— these all cause basic social turbulence. Sometimes "normal" patterns are interrupted because of a technological innovation, such as the wheel, the printing press, the automobile, the television, the pill, the cell phone, the Internet, Twitter. And as we saw in chapter 5, as women gain reproductive and economic equality, the changing gender power balance creates substantial chaos.

- What disruptors have you witnessed when old boundaries were erased, or when familiar rules no longer applied?

- Think about when you've been in a chaotic situation, in work or in your personal life, where expectations became unclear. Did you retreat, or did you step forward and own it, rewriting the rules and setting new parameters?

Fundamental change, in contrast to incremental modification, can tiptoe in barely noticed, or it can crash noisily into the interstices between the old and the new. Those are the tipping-point moments when a fresh idea pushes the fulcrum of change far enough to transform how people think and act. They are the defining moments when ethical leaders must act with courage and intention and when ordinary citizens must keep their wits about them. For these moments of extreme change are also when tyrants like Adolf Hitler or Charles Taylor, the Liberian warlord deposed by current President Ellen Johnson-Sirleaf, can seize power by using chaos to incite voter fears. Today's Tea Partiers use techniques perfected by demagogues through the ages to whip up fears and hatreds in response to the fundamental change in American politics symbolized by an African American president and his change they *don't* believe in. (This would also be true, I imagine, if we had the first female president, who would be an equally potent symbol of a change in the power structure.)

Change itself is agnostic—whether you think it's good or bad depends on where you sit. Gail Collins named her book about the history of second-wave feminism *When Everything Changed* because it perfectly pinpoints the moment when everything started being different as a result of women's efforts—the women's movement to be exact. And it speaks to all women, whether individual readers were part of that movement or not. The Vatican has, not surprisingly, demurred from giving feminism or the pill credit for bettering the lives of women, proposing instead that washing machines liberated us.[19] As for me, I'm proud to be named ten times—more often even than Betty Friedan—in right-wing pundit Kate O'Beirne's 2006 antifeminist screed, *Women Who Make the World Worse.* But then, as I've discussed above, I believe controversy is our friend; part of what makes these fundamental shifts so scary to some people is the controversy that inevitably emerges between those who love the change they're seeing and those who think it's the devil's spawn.[19]

While social change can be frightening, innovation generally has a positive connotation. We all want that washing machine, after all. Since innovation usually comes from the margins, or from people not regarded as the norm—hence the image of a dorky teenaged Bill Gates creating Microsoft software in his garage—we often don't see it coming.[20] Yet it's important to recognize the potential in periods of chaos. The instinct during these moments is to retreat to solid ground, to return to old, familiar values, and to try to achieve stability at any cost. That's a mistake that squanders the incredible potential that disruptive change and its resulting chaos offer to redirect the course of history by creating new channels of opportunity, more incisive vocabularies, and better technologies. But it's up to us to push the fulcrum in the direction we think it should go and not to rely on forces external to ourselves to make positive change happen.

## How to *Carpe* the Chaos

• THINK POSITIVE. Be like Monty Python: Always look at the bright side of life. You might as well, since chaos is inevitable. Because change is inevitable. And whoever is most comfortable with the ambiguity it creates is most likely going to not just survive but thrive. For example, the 2009 recession made the world's male financial leaders "discover" that women might be the solution to better governance and management. But women must see the vast opportunity and take advantage of it. It's coming at us from several directions.

First of all, when there's a mess to clean up, they always bring in the women, right? Second, when those in power can't figure out what to do, they are more open than usual to new solutions, to opening the table to previously untapped individuals who offer new ideas for the solutions they are desperately seeking. And finally, as the public and investors lose confidence in the men who've been in charge for so long, pure pragmatism says that if a woman can offer a solution and it works, they'll no longer care whether you have higher-pitched voices and breasts and don't follow football scores.

Women can move—and we have—into leadership positions that have never before been open to them. Then, suddenly, guess what? Women in powerful leadership roles becomes normalized; considering ability before gender becomes standard operating procedure. So think positive and you'll be able to take advantage of a chaotic moment and transform it for good for yourself and other women. Personally, I can't wait to see what happens in the next decade!

• TAKE THE LEAD. Remember that a leader is anyone who gets something done, large or small. When I was leaving my first CEO position, a board member asked me what I thought the chief qualification for the job was. I blurted out "raw courage." And I still think courage is at the core of leadership thirty-plus years later. The courage to act even in the midst of chaos, to own responsibility even when you don't have total authority, to make decisions even when you know none of the options is perfect.

We're fascinated with leaders and leadership because we never really know exactly what the outcome of an act or a decision will be. This is a skill and an art, but not a science. But I came to believe that chaos presents opportunity, and that has given me the courage I've needed to act many times when I was actually quaking in my boots.

Society tends toward stability. The moment of chaos our country is facing in 2010—with the deep structures of our economic and social order up for revision—will almost certainly be temporary. The time to seize the advantage is now, and the need for leadership is now, while borders are hazy and the world is open to new solutions where women are central. Don't make excuses. This is our time.

• SEE THROUGH OTHER EYES. Sarah Palin understands the potential of chaos extremely well. Learn from her and others whose views might differ from yours by trying to see through their eyes. Consider how she seized chaos for her own purposes. During McCain's 2008 presidential race, when her selection as his running mate was a Hail Mary pass to try to rescue his tanking campaign, she took the opportunity offered. And after the election, Palin saw the crisis of leadership in the Republican party, sensed that the aggrieved, noisy base of the party was eager for her brand of rhetoric, and seized it for her own advantage. She's since emerged as a leading voice via her postings on Facebook and Twitter, as a commentator on Fox News, at Tea Party gatherings, and raising the all-powerful money for ultraconservative candidates. All this even after resigning from the governorship of Alaska with the weakest of rationales. She took the platform unapologetically and without hesitation. As loathsome as I find most of her political positions, her strategy for staying in the public eye has been bold and it has paid dividends. Would that progressive women in the political and media eye were as sure of themselves and as willing to wear the shirt of their convictions. That alone could change the world for good.

In chaos is opportunity. Change creates chaos. Chaos means boundaries are fluid so you can accomplish things you might not have been able to do otherwise. *Carpe* the chaos.

## POWER TOOL #6: WEAR THE SHIRT

Next to defining your own terms, wearing the shirt is perhaps the next most effective power tool. Sound crazy? I don't mean just any shirt, of course. I mean either literally or figuratively sharing your intention with others. I'm referring to standing up for what you believe, what the source of your passion is.

I got this metaphor when I was chatting with Planned Parenthood clinic staff in rural Arizona. At work, they wore shirts with the organization's logo. One of the women told me that every day before she left the office to go home, she had to decide whether to wear the Planned Parenthood shirt or change clothes: "I ask myself, *Do I want to discuss my beliefs with the grocery store checker? Do I want to risk being challenged by the man who pumps my gas?*" I saw other heads nodding, and I understood her feeling of vulnerability. After all, I put my face on television—you can't get much more public than that.

But after I thought about it, I replied, "That's exactly when it's important to wear the shirt. Other people more often than not support what you do, but they need to see that you're proud of your work. And when you stand up for what you believe, they respect you more, and often this gives them the courage to stand up for their beliefs, too." Ever since that day, I've held the symbol of wearing the shirt to declare my intention, as I illustrated in chapter 7 when I wore my Well-Behaved Women Rarely Make History T-shirt to the gym and had a conversation with my trainer about its meaning.

Elisa Parker, of See Jane Do, believes passion is the essential basis of any endeavor. Fueled by concern for the world her daughter would grow up to inherit, her "shirt" is the environment. Michelle Robson's passion is women's health. After her hysterectomy, she became incapacitated—and was further diminished by doctors who couldn't give her a valid diagnosis, and who essentially told her that her problems were all in her head. She now sees the suffering she went through as a blessing in disguise, giving shape to her desire to help other women, and to change the medical system so that no one has to repeat her experience. She wears the shirt by putting her story and her money into EmpowHER, the women's health website she founded.

Ellen Gustafson and Lauren Bush were passionate about bringing an end to world hunger in the twenty-first century. Despite being young and relatively inexperienced, and despite being told that they would not be able to make a difference in the massive problem of world hunger by selling their feedbags, their passion fueled their momentum toward success.

For all these women, their passion was sparked by an intensely personal experience, but the energy flowed outward—and it's connected them with the rest of the world. Whether expressed as anger at injustice and inaction, or as aspiration toward a creative, professional, or personal goal, passion fuels the internal combustion engine that gets things done. More than that, passion fuses the personal with the political.

## How to Wear the Shirt

• SAY IT OUT LOUD. The first step to wearing the shirt is to make a public commitment about it. Declare your intention by telling a friend, or like Sophfronia Scott, whom I met at a gathering of self-proclaimed "Women on Fire," post your intention on your blog. Scott's passion helped her manage the self-limiting fear that hinders so many women from achieving to full potential. And saying it out loud made her accountable to do what she said she wanted to do.

Scott, a best-selling author and entrepreneur who helps others get their own books written and published, proclaimed on her New Year's Day blog that 2010 would be her "year of living fearlessly." Scott wrote: "I can give you a short but highly relevant list of things I've held back from getting or pursuing or doing for a variety of reasons: I don't have the money, time, ability, reason, support, energy, ideas, skills, strength, you name it . . . to do X, Y, or Z. I've allowed myself to be talked out of things: 'Oh, you don't really need to do that. Why would you put yourself through that? Why don't you just do this, it's easier.' The reasons," she continued, "are all plausible and even true in their own ways. However, at the heart of each reason—and I am scared to even say this out loud—is fear. There's this little girl voice in the back of my head and many, many times a day she is saying, *Oooh! You're gonna get in trouble!* And I believe her. And I stop short. Because that's what a 'good girl' does."

Once Scott declared her fears, and how tired she was of letting them stop her, she was able to pledge: *"I'm stepping out onto the high wire.* There may be a net down there or there may not be. I don't know, I'm too high up to see. This year, 2010, will be for me the Year of Living Fearlessly. I'm going to explore every dark corner of my soul and shine the light in there and ask, 'What do I REALLY want?' A lot of this, I know, will challenge me on what I really want to *write,* how I want to be with my family, how I want my business to be run."

She invited her readers to join the conversation through forums she has created to banish their own fears and to help her keep to her promise to live fearlessly, write fearlessly, and expand her business fearlessly. "What does living fearlessly mean to you?" It's a great question that we can all benefit from answering out loud.[21]

• DO THE IMPOSSIBLE. The amorphous, underdetermined future that looms ahead of us is ready to be shaped. But as Jennifer Buffett learned and shared in chapter 2, we must stand in our power before we can shape the future with intention. We must let ourselves be large, think outrageously big thoughts, and challenge ourselves to take on ambitions worthy of our capabilities.

When I insisted that Planned Parenthood create a twenty-five-year vision for its future back in 2000, I chose that quarter-century horizon so people could break out of their daily worries and shed the obdurate resistance to change that we all have. I wanted them to think in break-through ways about what they wanted to have accomplished when they looked back twenty-five years hence.

The goals set seemed impossible to many and perhaps some of them will prove to be. Nevertheless, I strongly believe you can't increment your way to success and that setting goals allows you to accomplish vastly more than you will if you don't set those bold goals. I knew we had to shift a number of paradigms to have even a chance at continuing the bold progress toward universal access to reproductive healthcare and rights that founders like Margaret Sanger began. But without that kind of passionate intention, why bother? And what value is power if it isn't used to reach a worthy intention, even if doing so seems impossible?

I'm not saying it's easy. Once they had imagined their bold idea to raise $100 million for Women Moving Millions to fund women's charities and advocacy, Swanee and Helen Hunt had to practice asking for million-dollar gifts before they could summon the guts to ask for that much from real live donors. Many people were incredulous about the plan, but they have exceeded their original fundraising goals by over $30 million so far, and they aren't stopping yet.

Remember that the fastest route to self-esteem is standing up for what you believe. Your gut-level commitment to whatever you decide to do with your one "wild and beautiful life" is one of the most potent power tools you have. Wear the shirt and you'll stand comfortably in your power and walk with intention wherever your passion compels you to go.

## POWER TOOL #7: CREATE A MOVEMENT

When the Liberian market women stood together, or more accurately, sat down together, refused to sell their wares in the market, and denied sex to their partners until the wars stopped, their united front gave them power that changed the course of history. In chapter 7, I laid out the three simple principles of movement building that, as the Liberian women discovered, apply to each and every endeavor that you want to undertake: Be a sister, have courage, and act together with Sister Courage. I also discussed how you can gather the steam you need to embark upon a movement by mobilizing either anger energy or aspiration energy.

When a movement grows by leaps and bounds, it can feel electric—as networks light up, more and more people are inspired to act and partnerships develop both across great distances and within close communities. Individuals begin to consolidate around what needs to get done; inertia and stalled efforts dissipate as the path clarifies. Opponents may get louder, their words may become sharper, but those who are doing the work in turn become more resilient, more creative, more intentional, and ever stronger in the doing. In a world where positive change can sometimes seem stubbornly difficult to achieve (think of the one-hundred-year struggle to pass health reform and the seventy-two-year battle for women's suffrage!) finding like-minded individuals who can stand with you, support you, and amplify your voice is indispensable. And you in turn will do the same for them.

## How to Create a Movement

• TAKE IT PERSONALLY. Carole Carson has had a varied career as a business leader, consultant, and public relations professional, but her extraordinary story starts with a personal experience at age sixty that became her passionate intention—and which led to her bringing thousands of others along. Here's her story as she told it to me:

"I stepped naked on the bathroom scale on an ordinary morning. The numbers flew to 183 pounds and then the scale broke. At five-one, I was not just pudgy or sturdy; I was fat. My system of denial broke along with the bathroom scale. In that moment, I decided I would get fit (not diet but eat differently and exercise routinely) and that I would make these changes for the rest of my life. I also decided I would make the experience fun and appropriate for my body, and that I would get help. (My acronym was F: Fun; I: Individualized; T: Together.)"

She offered to write a local newspaper article around the idea that it is never too late to get fit; the editor turned it into a weekly series that included photographs, measurements, progress, and setbacks: "Initially I was embarrassed, but the support from others was so wonderful that I overcame my embarrassment and was happy to share the experience."

She lost sixty-two pounds. What happened next took her personal experience into a new and unexpected career turn after she offered to lead a community weight-loss event. Enthused Carson, "Over a thousand neighbors and friends showed up for the Nevada County Meltdown. Over the following eight weeks, we grew in size as we shrank on the scale. In the end, over two hundred teams lost four tons. Our efforts received national and international attention."

This movement began to pick up heft while Carson and her local colleagues lost theirs, and Carson realized other communities might benefit from their example. A book followed, *From Fat to Fit: Turn Yourself into a Weapon of Mass Reduction*. But she couldn't find a publisher because she wasn't a doctor with a specific diet. Not to be deterred, Carson created a publishing company, Hound Press. That was a worthwhile risk; the *Wall Street Journal* reviewed the book and called her "an apostle for fitness." As a result, AARP, with 43 million members, used the book as the basis for an online community, the Fat 2 Fit Community Weight-Loss Challenge. She's now coaching over four thousand members online and working with communities throughout the United States to create their own weight-loss campaigns. Canada's version of AARP (CARP) has also adopted the Fat 2 Fit program.

Carson sums it up: "What my experience shows is that when one person changes, everything around them changes as well. Who would have guessed that one profoundly embarrassing moment stepping on the scale and having it break would lead to this outcome?"[22]

• TAKE IT POLITICALLY. We've seen repeatedly that though change might be helped along by serendipitous events, it doesn't happen passively. It takes intention, and an effort to overcome resistance. It takes acting as a movement. During President Obama's Health Reform Summit, held on February 25, 2010, Representative Louise Slaughter, a Democrat from upstate New York (and one of only four women invited!), testified to how a concerted effort by a group of women had changed women's health and lives as she urged the president and the members of Congress assembled to pass a comprehensive bill.

"I believe that all Americans should be treated the same," she began. Then she reminded those assembled that there are eight states where domestic violence is considered a preexisting condition and thus insurance plans need not cover medical attention needed in its aftermath. "Believe you me, that is really discriminatory," she declared.

Then Slaughter pointed out another example of when a similar injustice had been identified and rectified, only because women had been at the table and had taken action on their own behalf: "In 1991, women were not included in any of the trials at the NIH because we had hormones. It wasn't until we had a critical mass of women here [Congress] that we said, 'This will not do for more than half the population of the United States who pay taxes.' That we made certain that diseases like osteoporosis, mainly a women's disease; cervical cancer, only a women's disease; uterine cancer; and others were really looked at. Up to that point, 1991, all research at the Institutes of Health were done on white males. Now think about that for a minute if you will. We couldn't [change] that because we just said, 'Now, kindly stop doing that.' It took legislation [to make the difference]."[23]

• BE PERSISTENT. So here's the secret sauce for successful movement building: Never stop, never give up, and persist until the goal is reached. That's simple but not easy. If you don't think you've been heard the first time, say it again, and again, and again, until your message gets across. If the key in your hand doesn't open the door the first time, then try it again. Try another door. Get another key. Call the locksmith if necessary. Or go in through the window.

"When you put your hand to the plow, you can't put it down until you get to the end of the row," advised Alice Paul, the indomitable suffragist leader and drafter of the Equal Rights Amendment. There will be pebbles in the road to trip you up, but get up and keep going. The movement has to move. It must continue to build power and energy by going into new spaces and remaining relevant and optimistic. Try new strategies if the first ones don't work, but don't stop trying. Care enough to make it happen, and it will.

Things don't just happen; people make things happen in a deliberate way. Create a movement and apply the three principles of Sister Courage to whatever you want to accomplish, large or small, in your work and professional life, civic and political endeavors, or personal relationships.

## POWER TOOL #8: EMPLOY EVERY MEDIUM

We live in a totally mediated society today. How we learn about people, trends, and issues gets filtered through a media lens that still objectifies women and shoehorns complex issues into linear, bifurcated extremes. This is the opposite of how women tend to see and think about things. Our job, if we are to lead with intention and live unlimited, is to cut through the media's false balance and one-size-fits-all framing of issues to deliver our messages clearly and fully and to get information we need from sources we trust. That's why the power tool for this chapter is to use every medium at our disposal.

America has advanced to the point where we see many diverse faces reading the news and delivering the programming, yet in mainstream media, women hold under 5 percent of top decision-making positions with real power to determine what constitutes news and what the story lines will be. The percentage of women on boards and in key executive positions overall in Fortune 500 communications companies hovers at the seemingly ossified 15 percent. All this despite the fact that women earn over 50 percent of journalism degrees.[24]

To the positive, media itself has become so diverse and diffused that breaking through communications barriers is eminently possible. That's what makes See Jane Do such an exciting new model for activism, and why Kamy Wicoff of SheWrites.com was able to push back instantly, via the power of her social media website, on behalf of women writers against *Publisher's Weekly*.

- How do you consume media? Where do you get your information?

- What percent of your media time is spent with traditional media versus social media and newer digital modes of media delivery?

## How to Employ Every Medium

• BE THE MEDIA. Think of media work not as added on, but as integral to everything your organization does and everything you want to accomplish personally. When planning the work, include a media component, even if it's "just" internal communications within a company.

You can't be heard if you don't speak, and you can't be published if you don't submit pieces. As Katie Orenstein of the OpEd Project pointed out, women can't whine about not having parity on the op-ed pages if we don't pitch at least 50 percent of the op-eds to the editors of those pages. It's up to us to change that ratio to 50-50, or better yet, aim for 60-40 just to have a margin that will ensure editors have no excuses for failing to fill half of their pages with women's opinions.

Fortunately, it isn't difficult to find women with opinions and the ability to write them compellingly. What we need is more courage to pitch and more persistence to keep pitching. And if they still don't respond, well, do what Carole Carson did and start your own publishing house, or like Tina Brown did with *The Daily Beast* and come up with a whole new paradigm for delivering the aggregated top news of the day.

The chaos in the media world these days definitely presents the opportunity to become the media, and women are taking advantage of this by populating the Internet in equal numbers to men, composing over half of bloggers and up to 60 percent of social media users. But what are we doing there? Are we naming, claiming, and defining the terms? Are we choosing the story lines that frame the social narratives that get into the cultural bloodstream and shape how we think about substantive issues? Or are we getting co-opted along the way? That's the next big question we must confront without excuses.[25]

• AMPLIFY YOUR MEDIA VOICE. At the Fourth World Conference on Women in Beijing in 1995, a story that captivated my imagination was told by an African woman who had created a unique way to combat domestic violence. If the perpetrator didn't mend his ways and local law enforcement wouldn't arrest him, as was often the case, she mobilized the women of the village to bring their pots and pans and gather outside his house. Then they would bang the pots loudly until he agreed to stop. And he knew that if he broke his promise, these women would return to telegraph his bad behavior to the entire village with their kitchen cacophony.

The rise of social media offers women a great opportunity to bang the pots—to amplify our diverse, individual voices and collectively demand resolution for inequities that are revealed as all too common. We will be heard. Facebook, Twitter, LinkedIn, texting, Ning sites, and many other platforms allow us to learn from each other's experiences, and to connect with people professionally, politically, and personally whom we otherwise may never have had a chance to interact with. Although younger, white, middle-class individuals in urban and suburban areas are still more likely to avail themselves of Internet technologies, the disparities are steadily and surely breaking down. Make deliberate efforts to speed up this process by building networks of diverse women, young and old, white women and women of color, straight and queer, mothers and the childfree, women with PhDs and women studying for their GEDs.

As blogger and social media maven Jen Nedeau put it, "In the past year and a half, I've climbed my way through the blogosphere simply by being someone who speaks her mind and has smart things to say from time to time. I've been able to basically collapse the hierarchy that I saw and meet people, talk to people, and keep encouraging the development of my own power because I am not afraid to reach out. I'm not afraid to talk to people." Jen, who is in her midtwenties, is pretty fearless in face-to-face life as well. But blogging allows her to amplify her voice, and build her power.

There are many reasons to keep blogs or maintain websites. To advance our professional lives by displaying portfolios of our work; the thrill of the open confessional; documenting a hobby, talent, or obsession; or simply as a place to document our daily lives. Just as my T-shirt is valuable real estate to proclaim my convictions, so is your online platform—you can wear the cybershirt. You can tell your story uncensored and find a community of people who share your problems and your passions.

In the sometimes lawless frontiers of the Internet, it can seem as though you're facing attacks alone when negative commenters flood your site objecting to something you've written, or to your very right to express your thoughts. So leave a comment offering praise or agreement for others, especially if it seems like the author is under fire. Credit other women's work, and link to other women's sites and profiles. Post your praise on a friend's LinkedIn site, take action on friends' campaigns, and promote other women's work. Online communities thrive as networks. Do your part to be a good sister-citizen.

And finally, support women-centric media. Journalism sites like

Women's eNews are critically important venues for telling women's stories that never make it onto network television news. Public radio and television programs like Maria Hinojosa's *NOW* and Rose Aguilar's *Your Call* deserve attention and support. The Women's Media Center publishes original reported stories and commentaries as well as being an advocate for women in the media. BlogHer and special interest sites like Political Voices of Women aggregate women's blogs so you can easily find what you're looking for. If you're a journalist, frequent the SheSource database and the Progressive Women's Voices database—both findable through the Women's Media Center website—to locate female experts in any topic you need to source. And you might be interested in applying for membership in the WAM feminist journalist listserv for a great network of colleagues. These resources can help us reach parity in the media at all levels.

• BE A MEDIA MOVEMENT. The media responds to constituents much like elected officials do. That's how the right wing amassed so much media power and control and how they have frightened many mainstream outlets by hurling "liberal media" at them like an epithet. So if your letter to the editor or op-ed is to be published, or if you have an article or blog post that you anticipate will be controversial, organize your own grassroots to follow up even before you're published. Line up five friends, for example, to submit supportive letters immediately upon publication, as well as blogging and posting it on social media. Offer to do the same for them. Create your own media activist network just as you have a grassroots political activist network for the policy agenda you support.

One simple, time-efficient tool for influencing media is to keep email addresses of your ten top media sources handy on your desk or computer desktop. Once a day, send two emails: one to compliment a media outlet that told a woman's story well, and one to complain to a media outlet that didn't. Think of this technique as a shovel to move bad stuff out and good stuff into the media. And to stay ahead of the bull.

In short, employ every medium. Use personal, social, and traditional media proactively. And always, the most effective medium is yourself and the power you communicate by your intention and your story.

## POWER TOOL #9: TELL YOUR STORY

It would be hard to surpass in eloquence or precision what Bioneers founder Nina Simons says in her speeches, as quoted more fully in her profile on page 91, about the nature and purpose of stories: "Stories are medicine for our false isolation. A way to forge connection and community and help shift our course . . . the seed forms of culture we carry around within us."

Indeed, the stories we tell ourselves about ourselves and about others define us, shape us, limit us if we don't watch out, and help us be unlimited if we do it right. Simons discovered her own hidden stories had limited her by defining her as the woman behind the man. Once she had that awareness, she was able to create and believe in a new story about herself as a leader. And that allowed her to discover, as I had, that she held the key to her liberation in her very own hand.

Julie Gilbert's profile, preceding this chapter, tells her story of remembering the howling wolves at night when she was growing up in rural North Dakota; the metaphor of those loyal, mutually supportive animals gave her the insights she needed to persuade her male-centric employer, Best Buy, to listen to their women customers and create a new, inclusive business model. After all, the women, unlike in decades past, were now making the majority of purchases in the store and held the potential to Best Buy's future profitability. And the resulting $4.4 billion in increased sales to women proves she was right. In the process she also developed an entirely new leadership model for the company and its female employees in particular. The story of the wolves and the metaphor of WOLF Packs to carry out the new strategy within the company engages the imagination more effectively than dry management theory ever could.

- What stories do you tell yourself about yourself? How do they enhance or limit you?

- How have personal stories moved you to take action at work, in politics, or in your personal life?

Stories have immense power. My friend, the master storyteller and storytelling teacher Laura Simms, sees stories as a path to healing oneself and the world. Harriet Beecher Stowe's 1852 novel, *Uncle Tom's Cabin,* told a story that changed how Americans thought about slavery and intensified support for the Civil War. It became the second best-selling book of the nineteenth century, behind only the Bible, itself a collection of stories.

In fact, throughout this book, I've told the stories of women—and men—who have inspired me, moved me, mentored me, and taught me in the hopes that their stories do the same for you. I would literally not be the me that I am without their stories.

I've told my own life story so often I am sometimes bored with it, but it is always what people are most interested in, no matter what other substantive content I might think I prefer to impart.

So telling stories is a power tool for self-help—and for helping others. We can use stories to communicate in ways that heal them, deepen our connection with them, and move them both personally and politically. Like Tiffany Campbell did in telling her story that was emotionally healing to herself, and at the same time was infinitely more effective than intellectual arguments could have been in persuading voters to defeat a state ballot measure.

Tiffany Campbell is a churchgoing Republican and mother of two from South Dakota. She was pregnant with twin boys in 2006 and looking forward to welcoming the new additions to her family when the doctor told her the bad news. Her twins had one functioning heart between them. One twin was doomed. If she carried the pregnancy to term, they would almost certainly both die. But a selective reduction—an abortion of the weaker twin—would save the life of its sibling.

The backdrop to this devastating, and intimately personal, diagnosis was virulently political. At the time, the South Dakota voters were about to vote on a complete ban on abortion. So-called "pro-life" activists were touting the measure as a way to save "unborn babies." From her own experience, she knew that the opposite could be the case. Because abortion has been made to seem such a taboo topic, most of us have little idea why people choose abortion.

Campbell recognized that her personal story could unsettle people's ingrained notions. "I knew I had the power to change people's perception on abortion," she told me.

It wasn't easy for her to share such intimate details of what was, after all, a personal tragedy as well as a personal triumph, a story of death and survival. I am humbled by her courage. But she says she knew that if she did not speak up, other women whom she might never know—women who found themselves in her situation, at the doctor's office hearing terrible news—might not have the options that she had, and might not be able to welcome a new baby into the world.

Her story helped defeat South Dakota's proposed abortion ban in 2006, and she told her story again when the ballot measure reemerged in 2008. Both times it was soundly defeated by more than ten points. "Women and men of all ages thanked me," she told me, describing the ultimate satisfaction that she derived from her difficult decision to share her story. "I knew that I had helped future generations of women be able to make their own medical decisions without government interference."

"I am often told that I am very 'brave,'" she continues. "I don't think it was bravery, it was rage felt deep inside me that someone whom I had never met, who didn't know my situation, felt they had the right to make medical decisions for me and my family."[26]

Tiffany Campbell's story demonstrates the power of telling stories, and nothing could illustrate this power tool better. People resonate to authenticity. Your story is your truth and your power. It defines you as much as you define it. Other women and men need to hear your story, too, and you need to hear theirs. It's how we learn best, and how we connect best to other people. Because no one can tell your story but you, I can't add more advice. As the well-known Nike slogan says, and it applies to all the power tools I've suggested and the thousands more I anticipate you have in your kit and will generously share with others, "Just do it."

# no excuses:
# don't follow your dream—lead it!

*"If the first woman God ever made was strong enough to turn the world upside down all alone, these women together ought to be able to turn it back and get it right side up again."*

**—SOJOURNER TRUTH**
in her "Ain't I a Woman?" speech to the 1851 Women's Rights Convention in Akron, Ohio[1]

- Was there a moment when you knew you had the power to (fill in the blank)? If yes, please tell me about it. If no, tell me about that, too!

- Go to www.gloriafeldt.com to share your stories and read others.

When I began writing *No Excuses* over a year ago, I put forth my belief that women are at an amazing moment; that the doors are open but women aren't walking through them in numbers and with intention sufficient to lead us to parity in work, politics, and personal life. And I set out to show how we could and why we should lead ourselves forward so that each individual woman can flourish and society as a whole will be well served as a result.

Every day since I started this book, I have encountered another inspiring woman's story I wanted to highlight, or a new-to-me fact that sets me exploring one more angle of this endlessly fascinating topic of women's relationship with power. I am now even more certain in my heart, and feel in my soul, that this is our moment. It's our turn. The time has come. The Oscar is ours. The keys are in our hands.

I confess, though, that writing these closing words has caused me much anxiety because I care deeply about the women who will read them. Because I want so passionately for the girls and women and, as a consequence, the boys and men of the future to be free from the constraints that have kept individuals of both genders from reaching their full potential. Because I've worked so hard for so long to bring about the changes that need to be set in place for women to hold their heads high as equals in a just world.

The possibilities are here in abundance.

But I also know from experience that possibilities are only seedlings, and they die unless we tend them. Our actions—individually and collectively—are the soil and sunshine that can coax a bud into flower. This is a time of opportunity, yes, but it is more profoundly a moment of choice. It's up to us to choose affirmatively to embrace our power and live unlimited. And never to step back from the brink of power again.

*Power-to* won't walk over to shake your hand and gather you in its warm embrace. Each of us has to step up and claim it. And each of us must envision and insist upon the new definition of power-to as a nonfinite resource with expansive capability, rather than the limiting, traditional, oppressive idea of *power-over*.

That's why I consciously choose not to use the term *empower* as something one person can do for another. No one can put power into you. And if you are unable or unwilling to use your power—whether because the deep memory of gender violence is paralyzing, or because you have been co-opted by the inevitable forces of inertia and backlash, or because of the fear of not being liked—then whatever capabilities you have in the abstract lose their meaning and value in the application. More than that, you lose the incredibly gratifying opportunity to know your actions are improving the lives of others around you, and others who will follow you.

Power doesn't come from a narcissistic focus on self-congratulation for having it. When all choices are framed as radically individual ones, not only are women less likely to perceive their own power to determine the course of their lives and the quality of others' lives, but they are also less likely to seek the recourse and strength that can be found in a collective movement united in Sister Courage.

Power, as we have seen exhibited in the many stories in this book, comes from the doing, the acting, the being, the caring beyond oneself and narrow self-interest. Power carries with it great responsibility and demands enormous courage.

And it takes effort to reach out, to engage, to break down barriers. We tend to filter into small groups of people who look like us, in part because of the entrenched race and class boundaries that have yet to crumble. Being mindful of Kristal Brent Zook's admonition not to overgeneralize experiences, I would still declare that just because we have a right *not* to engage in the larger struggle for progress toward parity for women doesn't mean we're excused from the responsibility. I don't mean that everyone has to do everything; I do mean that each of us has the obligation to do something.

It's more than worth the effort to understand one another across the lines that seem to divide us. Take age boundaries, which, like racial and ethnic experiences, can be like a mountain range that stops the transference of information. When an older generation grew up tethered to a stationary post of external restraints, like those baby elephants in the story I told in the prologue, they may restrict their own movements because they have internalized the idea that they aren't powerful enough to escape long after the ropes are gone. The messages these women pass on to the next generation may seem constrained to younger women who have grown up being told they can do anything. And younger women may be baffled by talk of barriers they perceive to be imaginary. Mistakes were made by the suffragists who didn't use their votes to continue moving an agenda forward; and Rosie the Riveter, who relinquished her workplace gains; and women today who think because they have choices to go to work or stay at home they have no obligation to consider the impact of their choices on other women. Yet the only way to move on from these mistakes is for each generation to tell its story authentically in good faith so that each can see themselves in the other's story.

That's how values and leadership roles pass to the rising generation and they in turn can bring their own successors on board. And get ready for the next leadership wave to break the remaining barriers.

## SOJOURNER'S TRUTH

Sojourner Truth was a boundary breaker whose story holds lessons for every generation. She embraced her power to its full extent. A former slave who became an abolitionist, a women's rights leader, and a Methodist minister, Truth was born with less than no power. With the triple whammy of being a woman, black, and a slave who had to leave four of her five children with her former owner when she escaped, she recognized that the only way to get rights was to take them for herself. It wasn't likely that anyone else was going to give them to her willingly, or even help her get them. She approached life and the quest for social justice much like other movement leaders: Susan B. Anthony, Margaret Sanger, and Martin Luther King Jr. They did their work even when they had no money, no laws supporting them, and no powerful allies. They changed the world because they stood in their power and walked with intention. Undeterred by those who said it couldn't be done, they simply did it.

A powerful orator, Truth used the gifts she had to lead her own dreams. In 1865, when she was working in Washington, DC, for the Freedmen's Association (and almost a century before Rosa Parks's famous bus ride), she rode city trolleys to desegregate them. Though she met Presidents Lincoln and Grant, she was turned away when she tried to vote in the 1872 presidential election. Her journey to reach equality continued long after her death. On April 28, 2009, Nancy Pelosi, the first woman speaker of the U.S. House of Representatives, unveiled a bust of Truth in Emancipation Hall located in the Capitol Visitors' Center—the first African American woman to be so honored.[2]

I tell this history to emphasize that the road to justice is long. Women have rounded many bends toward equality since Sojourner Truth lived, to be sure. Yet there are, in every era, injustices to be rectified, some old and some new.

The greatest challenge today is to know what to do with those Oscars remarkable women are finally starting to win. Each new generation must speak in its own tongue, tell its story from its own unique perspective of the world. And yet we also must come together for a common goal. Despite our divergent perspectives, largely based on the fact that we each have differing starting points from which we enter life, I feel the feminist waves converging to finish the race together—the second wave broke molds, the third wave began to create new ones, and the youngest wave now cresting enters with astoundingly little fear and high aspirations, but is bringing us all together by asking for mentorship from their mothers, grandmothers, and other role models.

# **power**tool number nine

## TELL YOUR STORY: your story is your truth and your truth is your power. others need and want to hear it, as you need and want to hear theirs.

### WHEN DID YOU KNOW YOU HAD THE POWER-TO?

When I began this journey to explore women's relationship with power, I asked many women whether there was a moment when they realized they had the *power-to;* it was up to them to specify exactly what that was.

Many women shared intimate and personal stories. Denise Brodey, author of *The Elephant in the Playroom,* a book for parents with special needs kids that she wrote based on her own experiences with a special needs son, said, "There is a moment every day of my life when I know I have the power to laugh instead of cry."

Suzanne Mathis McQueen, businesswoman and author of a holistic health book for women called *Four Seasons in Four Weeks,* realized she could "walk her life path alone with joy."

For Serena Freewomyn, a freelance writer and founder of the blog Feminists for Choice, it came when she realized she had the power to speak out: "I used to be so shy that I just wanted to blend in with the wallpaper. After ten years of debate (in high school and college), you can't shut me up. It helped me find my voice."

And Women on Fire founder and inspiring leadership coach Debbie Phillips revealed that her moment came when, "Off the cuff, I told an audience that I was trying to be thinner by wearing Spanx. And the unintended consequence was that my waist was two inches smaller but my pants were now two inches longer and I was tripping over them. They laughed so hard—and the energy I felt from sharing that story inspired me to realize that all I ever need to do is just speak the truth!"

In each of these insights, there is a sense of liberation, of getting rid of that "baby elephant thinking" that keeps us immobilized even when we have clearly grown strong enough to break free.

Other women shared how their *aha* moments blossomed their awareness of the power of their influence.

When linguist Deborah Tannen's books on gender and communications first escalated in popularity, she was overwhelmed with speaking requests and inquiries from people asking her to promote their books. A professional colleague warned that her hardest challenge would be dealing with the power. "I thought, *Power?* I did not initially think of my success in terms of power. Gradually, I realized that with success does come a lot of power. I guess there is power in the books." Tannen chuckled when I pointed out to her that the language she'd just used was in effect downplaying her own power. "Oh, that's so typical of women," Tannen commiserated.

Ellen Snortland, author of *Beauty Bites Beast,* began to focus on women's physical empowerment after an experience that profoundly altered the way she perceived herself during a self-defense class. "I was confronting a single, unarmed, padded assailant, and *then* another mock assailant snuck up behind me and attacked. My body knew exactly what to do; I knew in my bones that I was a potentially dangerous mammal," she said. The experience also made her realize how much energy she spent being careful, not provoking unwanted attention, not taking up too much space, not pissing anyone off, to all of a sudden "understanding that if push came to shove, I could be dangerous."

Snortland believes violence in general, and male violence toward women in specific, is to the globe what HIV/AIDS is to the body: It creates an unhealthy host that makes it susceptible to other diseases. "Therefore, empowering women and girls to stop an assault in the moment, and also raising children to see that females are not inherently victims of male violence, could allow the planet to recover sufficiently to take on other areas of violence."

Andrea March, a founder of the Women's Leadership Exchange, said her moment was when she appeared in front of the audience at the first WLE conference: "Women said what a difference it had made in their lives. First I thought what I was doing was just giving entrepreneurs advice, just giving the tools, but it's also allowing them to see that someone else just like them can do it; it gives them the impetus to go on and follow their dreams."

Or, as I'd prefer to say, they see they can lead their own dreams.

Former Secretary of State Madeleine Albright, the first woman to hold that venerable position, responded that she knew she had the power-to the first time she ever taught a class: "At Georgetown University in 1982, I realized that I could make a real difference for the next generation. I was charged with transmitting information to our future leaders. As I have watched some of my oldest students transform into successful professionals in a variety of fields, I take pride in the fact that they learned to define their place through hard work and a willingness to match their best against the best of others."

I was curious how Albright, who held one of the world's most powerful positions from 1997 to 2001, would answer because one of my own power-to moments involved her. It came during the April 25, 2004, March for Women's Lives in Washington, DC, the largest protest march in U.S. history. On the frontlines as one of the principal organizers, I could feel the energy of over 1.2 million women, men, and young people behind us, a whoosh of physical energy so immense that we had to start the march a half hour ahead of schedule or we would literally have been trampled by the enthusiasm we had generated. Next to me, like a little tank determined to keep moving forward, her steely grip holding her section of the giant "March for Women's Lives" banner that stretched the width of the Washington Mall, walked Albright, all four feet ten inches of her.[3]

I don't think it was simply because of her diplomatic skills that Albright replied to my query with a story of passing her leadership skills forward. In fact, at the 2009 New York opening of her "Read My Pins" exhibit, where she talked about how she uses her signature pins as a unique way to express subtle messages to her peers who might not be accustomed to dealing with women in powerful roles, she observed that three of the last four U.S. secretaries of state have been women. She made a point of reminding the audience that though she was the first, she has not been the only woman to hold the nation's top diplomatic position. That sense of intentionality about shaping the future by influencing others is one mark of a powerful and authentic leader.[4]

## CHANGE THE NAME, CHANGE THE GAME

"So where do we go from here?" That's a question I am often asked now that I have become one of the more senior leaders in the movement for women's equality. I always give the same answer: "Where do you want to go?" We have seen ample evidence throughout this book that women have no excuse for shying away from making the future one of our choice and walking through the doors to parity together. So the real question becomes, "How do we get there from here?"

Looking at the full picture allows us to map where we want to go and what we'll need for the journey. To take advantage of a moment of opportunity, we have to be ready to take on risk, to upset the applecart, to have the courage to "see your moment and seize it, honey," to quote one of Kathleen Turner's life lessons in *Send Yourself Roses*. We have our power tools at the ready.

But change always requires catalysts, people who pull things together and make it all happen. These catalysts are our leaders. Men would probably call them game changers. I'm calling them name changers because the power of naming is so critically important that it defines the game.

In that sense, power is amorphous, neither inherently good nor bad. We decide how it will be used. If you have a hammer, you can use it to bash someone's head in or you can use it to build a house. So let us, as women, lead the way to building social, political, and economic structures that enable humanity to thrive.

Women are more visibly present everywhere than we've ever been. We have a voice and we are or can use our voices to insist that we be acknowledged in all spheres of life, even in places where we have been previously invisible. As the next generation comes of age, our culture will be profoundly altered by the extent to which women step up to roles in leadership and by the ways women choose to embrace and utilize their power. Dramatic change is in the air. We've seen how the chaos of our turbulent world today can be an extraordinary opportunity, and how the dynamics of change are similar in work, politics, and love.

Change is inevitable, but the direction of change is not. So let's draw the map. Let us choose to lead it in the direction of our dreams instead of merely responding to circumstances—what do you say?

## LEAD YOUR BIGGEST, BOLDEST DREAMS

Okay, I'll start. This is a short set of examples of the thinking that will be needed to give that final push to the fulcrum so women can change how we think about power and lead unlimited lives. Let your imagination soar and your intention lead your dreams to even greater heights as you create more.

## Make Equality Visible

When young people grow up seeing more or less equal numbers of women and men who are deemed important enough to have their faces on these public representations of honor and glory, imagine how it will change their perceptions so that talents and accomplishments are valued regardless of gender.

Women's voices, just like women's faces on the statuary in the town square, have always been the alternative, the other, rather than being on a par with men in the central narrative of our culture and history. EVE (Equal Visibility Everywhere)[5] is a new nonprofit organization that decided to change that. They're working to achieve gender parity in U.S. symbols and icons—like statues (currently nine of one hundred in the Capitol's Statuary Hall are of women, and how many women so honored can you think of in your town?); currency (no woman ever on paper bills); national holidays (no women); and stamps (25 percent women). Changing that ratio would be a leap forward in teaching people about the many women who have accomplished important things.

Similarly, the media needs to do serious name changing by placing women in equal roles throughout the story lines, the faces and voices delivering the story, and placement on the news page, not the style section, that signals the importance of stories. As long as women occupy just 3 percent of the top decision-making positions within media, war and not peace will remain the central story and conflict rather than nurture or problem solving will frame the story. This is also why it's not sufficient for women to compose over half of journalism school students or to be increasingly seen in news reader roles.

And if you are as tired as I am of Rush Limbaugh's tirades about "feminazis" and want to see more Rachel Maddows on your screen, you'll be as glad as I am that the Women's Media Center is changing that name and changing the media game by training a generation of Progressive Women's Voices to lead the media conversation in the future. But it's also time for more women who care about advancing women to get together to create new media entities like the BlogHer founders did and for those who can to become majority investors in large media companies.

## Shape the Faith

What powerful group has traditionally been more responsible for doctrines that diminish women than clergy? Yet for this very reason, they are the same group that could be among the most influential in creating a culture in which women's full humanity is respected. Now that an increasing number of women are entering the clergy and other faith-based occupations, it's time for them to do some serious name changing. As just one example, a conference dubbed "United by Faith: Building a Better Future for Women and Girls" was convened by the Women's Funding Network to "congregate their power" behind the work of investing in girls and women. In a *Women's e-News* article, the Reverend Dr. Claudette Copeland was quoted as having said in her closing remarks—in fine Sister Courage mode—"You are on the right path, know your own authority, stick your breasts out, and seek solace and support in your allies. You are not alone."[6]

Many cultural historians, such as Riane Eisler in her classic book *The Chalice and the Blade,* and artist-archaeologist Merlin Stone who wrote *When God Was a Woman,* have documented that gender role-differentiation and so-called war of the sexes is not divinely ordained and that religion itself was female-centered in its origins.[7]

It's time modern theology shaped more egalitarian ideas about power from a feminist perspective.

## Create Wealth

Women are no longer the question; women are the answer—if we use our power.

So have an edge. Think big. Be an insurgent. Look at where the next great challenge is. Drawing a paycheck is fine, and aspiring to the corporate boardroom is great. But it's not enough. Be the next Bill Gates who creates wealth by creating new technology. The next Warren Buffett who owns the means of influencing the financial system. And, if you choose to be within an organization of any sort, be part of the change to put women into at least half of the upper management and board positions. Why stop at 30 percent, the suggested "critical mass" number? As the late New York congresswoman and intrepid feminist leader Bella Abzug used to say, "We want it all but we'll take half."[8]

The U.S. Women's Chamber of Commerce's groundbreaking Women's Ownership Movement has launched a dramatically name- and game-changing way for women to approach their work and financial lives. By strategically shifting their ambition and intention to "wealth building rather than merely wage earning" in a new "women-led economy," the USWCC is claiming ground that goes far beyond micro-credit programs, helpful as they are to women who want to become entrepreneurs, and even far beyond those efforts to put more women onto the boards and executive management staffs of the Fortune 500 companies.

"We're working hand in hand with women all across the United States on how to establish a strong, secure future. And we are focusing the women's economic market transforming women from a ripe target market into a mature market force," announces USWCC president Margot Dorfman on the group's website. It's the quantum leap beyond thinking of women as "undervalued assets," a project that instead is aimed boldly at putting women into the economic development driver's seat—a.k.a., having the "power-to" guide the direction of economic development.[9]

## Parity Politics

Women are advancing even faster in other countries. So we have role models to emulate: Forty-seven percent of the Swedish parliament, and 43 percent of Iceland's, are made up of women, as compared to our paltry 17 percent.[10]

Meanwhile, American women are stepping up to a wider array of political roles. Sonia Sotomayor joined the U.S. Supreme Court in 2009 as its third ever female and first Latina justice. As this book goes to print, Elena Kagan has been nominated to the U.S. Supreme Court. If she is confirmed, the highest court in the land will instantly hit that critical mass of 30 percent women, the number leadership experts claim shifts group dynamics for the good of all.

Numerous polls have shown that women are more trusted by voters than are male politicians. Hillary Clinton's presidential campaign demonstrated that women can aspire to the top and might well win, and even if they lose, they can still win big. Sarah Palin has demonstrated the same on her side of the aisle.

Apparently so many women took this message to heart in the 2008 elections that record numbers are lining up to run for office at all levels in 2010. The White House Project alone has trained ten thousand women thus far through its Vote, Run, Lead program[11]; the Women's Campaign Forum has amassed over two thousand online "She Should Run" nominations[12]; the 2012 Project of the Center for American Women and Politics is targeting women over forty-five as the age group most likely to run for office and making a nationwide push to increase the numbers of women running for both federal and state offices.[13] The cumulative effects from these alone—and they are just a few of many such endeavors—will have a dramatic impact.

The only question is how patient we can stand to be. In my opinion, the answer should be "not very." Taking this goal out of the realm of ambition and into intention, let's commit to a laserlike focus on results.

So why not set a goal that women hold half of all elected offices at all levels by 2020? It's a start toward parity in policy-making overall, and could assure passage of needed legislation that would eradicate the last vestiges of pay and employment discrimination, as well as passing the Freedom of Choice Act, which would guarantee reproductive justice for all women—and that, in the wake of 2010's healthcare reform legislation and President Obama's subsequent executive order banning coverage of abortion in even many private pay plans, is more needed than ever.[14]

## 50/50 at Home

Getting to equality and shared power between intimate partners is a critical quality-of-life issue. And men have been captive to power of the toxic kind as much as women have borne the brunt. I was deeply moved by Dale Allen's exhaustive study, *In Our Right Minds*. She lays out the case for rebalancing the masculine and feminine parts of our thinking and therefore our perceptions of how power should be used: "We call war human nature, and peace an impractical ideal," she observes. And yet, "We sing praises of women's traditional work of nurturing. Yet those who do the work of caring for children or the infirm or elderly are relegated to the lower economical, social, and political rungs." And further, she says, as a result, "We can hardly view sex and sensuality as holy expressions, for we have come to perceive sexuality through the lens of the left brain with its themes of dominance, power, and ownership."[15]

With women in the workplace, changes inevitably come in the home. And as more men become involved in caregiving at home, more traits that have been historically sorted into false masculine and feminine binaries become rebalanced into healthier human beings. As I have seen more and more men struggling with strollers in subways and carrying their babies in their Bjorns on the street, I find the trends heartening to witness, and very hopeful.

When George Stephanopoulos was announced as the new *Good Morning America* anchor to succeed Diane Sawyer (Sawyer's move to anchor the *ABC Evening News,* thus joining Katie Couric at CBS to make women anchors a two out of three majority on prime network evening news shows, is yet another gender-significant part of this tale) in December 2009, he rejected the suggestion that he also keep his Sunday morning show, *This Week.* Stephanopoulos, according to the *New York Times,* "expressed regret that he would not be able to keep both jobs permanently. 'I just can't do both jobs for long and also help raise a family,' he said." This is another example of the ways in which men and women can work together toward parity.[16]

There are rewards for men as well as women who are willing to say no to grueling schedules in order to honor their family time. Sharon Meers and Joanna Strober, authors of *Getting to 50/50,* a book chockful of advice about how couples can share the load at home as well as financially, cite a 2006 survey of 360 married men that found that men who did more chores at home had better sex. According to the survey, "The more satisfied a wife is with the division of household duties, the more satisfied a man is with his marital sex life."[17] Previous studies had already found that women with more egalitarian attitudes about gender roles have better sex. The time is ripe for a great feminist wave of women and men determined to change the workplace so both can achieve balance in their lives and have more fun while they do it.[18] Go for it.

## CHANGE NEEDS A CATALYST, AND A CATALYST NEEDS TO LEAD

It's time to unstick the dial of equality and move it to full parity; it's women's moment to embrace our power and live unlimited in order to make that happen. But change doesn't often happen organically. The balance isn't tipped nor is the dial moved merely because of an excess of *potential* power.

And as we've seen over and over, making change isn't a one-time fix-it-and-forget-it kind of endeavor. Change needs a catalyst, and a catalyst is a leader. Much of everything I've written about leading up to this point supports the fact that women's traditional aversion to power has also manifested itself as an aversion to leadership. Well, it's time to get over that, too.

In 2009, I attended an engaging lecture, "Women's Visions for the Nation: What's It Going to Take?" sponsored by the Elizabeth A. Sackler Center for Feminist Art at the Brooklyn Museum. As the program unfolded, so did a paradox: how to deconstruct a dysfunctional hierarchical model of leadership without leaving ourselves bereft of the leadership necessary to make the changes we're calling for.

The founder and, yes, leader, of a nonprofit organization told us, "We're not here to lead, but to spark." The questions from the floor following the panel addressed lots of problems, but no fire-in-the-belly solutions. I felt my hackles rising. After all, feminists have fought so hard, so courageously, against the injustices of patriarchal leadership, and yet we have not created our own effective leadership models.

I stood up and asked, "What in the world is wrong with leading?" But no one wanted to take that one on. That moment was truly a turning point for me. A movement has to move. Power and energy come from moving into new places, from taking action. There were incredible leaders at that panel discussion, and yet there we were, talking about sitting in a circle and sparking, not leading.

To be sure, there are still legions of social conservatives, gender essentialists, and chauvinist standard-bearers who are intent on restoring "traditional" relationships between men and women. Yet even absent the malevolent ranting from this fringe, patterns of inequality repeat themselves, raising internal roadblocks that keep us from going for what we deserve or getting our due. That's demoralizing at worst and uninspiring at best.

The challenge is to take leadership into our own hands, to accept the responsibility. We have the power, but power has to be mobilized. If indeed this is a moment for women, and if we truly, fiercely, deeply want that systemic change, we are going to have to embrace the concept of leadership for the common good.

What many women react to, and rightly resist, are leaders who abuse power by enforcing the outmoded hierarchies and power-over mode. We need to understand there's nothing inherently negative about being a leader or leading. We need to develop and implement new models of transformational leadership and use the ones that lead to greater justice. In rejecting domination, we mustn't also reject effective and definitive action; we must have the intention necessary to get the results we want. To lead our own dreams boldly forward, not just to follow them.

Understand that when you go forth to change the world, you will rattle cages, and some people will not be happy. But you are doing exactly what needs to be done. For in the end, it's all about courage. The human courage to overcome oppression, unfairness, bigotry, and hate and to advance justice, freedom, equality, respect, and peace. The courage to stand in your power and walk with intention.

So let us release our spirits to soar, our minds to envision unlimited vistas, our hands to create, and our hearts to engage. It is noble work. And let us be cognizant that the present we create will one day be someone else's history; our actions, someone else's inspiration.

Let us honor this moment, flush with the promise of transformation, by embracing our power to push the fulcrum, finally, to abundant justice and full equality so that women can at last lead unlimited lives.

I invite you to join me in conversation on my website at www.GloriaFeldt.com because there is so much more to say and to do.

# notes

## PROLOGUE: YOUR LIMITLESS MOMENT (AND WHY THERE ARE NO EXCUSES FOR NOT EMBRACING IT THIS TIME)

1. Harriet Beecher Stowe, "Sojourner Truth: The Libyan Sibyl," April 1863, www.sojourn-ertruth.org/Library/Archive/LibyanSibyl.htm, accessed March 7, 2010.
2. See www.youtube.com/watch?v=e-DPBOTISWk&feature=related, accessed March 29, 2010.
3. See http://benchmarks.thewhitehouseproject.org/page/the-white-house-project-re-port, accessed March 29, 2010.
4. Maria Shriver, "The Shriver Report," http://awomansnation.com/index/php, accessed March 7, 2010.
5. Nicholas D. Kristof, "Mistress of the Universe," www.nytimes.com/2009/02/08/opinion/08kristof.html, accessed March 7, 2010.
6. McKinsey and Company, "Women Matter: Gender diversity, a corporate performance driver," www.catawit.ca/files/PDF/Mckinsey_women_matter.pdf, accessed March 7, 2010.
7. The report, from 2001, is called "Engendering Development." A copy of the full re-port (and a summary) can be downloaded here: http://web.worldbank.org/WBSITE/EXTERNAL/TOPICS/EXTGENDER/0,,contentMDK:20186672~menuPK:489201~pagePK:148956~piPK:216618~theSitePK:336868,00.html. An overview of the report's findings can be found here: http://web.worldbank.org/WBSITE/EXTERNAL/NEWS/0,,contentMDK:20035009~menuPK:34459~pagePK:34370~piPK:34424~theSitePK:4607,00.html.
8. See www.emergeamerica.org/, accessed March 7, 2010.
9. See www.amazon.com/Womenomics-Write-Your-Rules-Success/dp/0061697184, accessed March 7, 2010.
10. The National Council for Research on Women, "Women in Fund Management: A Road Map for Achieving Critical Mass—and Why It Matters," www.ncrw.org/hedge-fund, accessed March 7, 2010.
11. Council on Contemporary Families, "Men's Changing Contribution to Housework and Childcare," www.contemporaryfamilies.org/marriage-partnership-divorce/men-change.html, accessed March 7, 2010.
12. Ellen Goodman, "My Ending, But Women's Beginning," www.miamiherald.com/opin-ion/other-views/story/1398433.html, accessed March 7, 2010.

13. Gloria Feldt, "Lilly Ledbetter, a Real War Hero, Could Help Obama Win," www.gloriafeldt.com/heartfeldt-politics-blog/2008/9/22/lilly-ledbetter-a-real-war-hero-could-help-obama-win.html, accessed March 7, 2010.

14. Anne Doyle, "Pass Your Power Forward," www.annedoylestrategies.com/OnAnnes-Mind/Entry.aspx?ContentItemID=11110, accessed March 6, 2010.

## CHAPTER 1: UNDERSTAND: YOU'VE COME A LONG WAY, MAYBE

1. See http://en.wikipedia.org/wiki/Frances_Perkins, accessed March 7, 2010; see http://womenshistory.about.com/library/qu/blquperk.htm, accessed March 7, 2010.

2. Lisa Belkin, "The Opt-Out Revolution," *New York Times,* October 26, 2003, www.nytimes.com/2003/10/26/magazine/26WOMEN.html?pagewanted=all, accessed March 7, 2010.

3. Linda Hirshman, "Why Opting Out Still Hasn't Been Proven False," *Double X,* October 26, 2009, www.doublex.com/blog/xxfactor/why-opting-out-still-hasnt-been-proven-false, accessed March 7, 2010.

4. Betsey Stevenson, "Beyond the Classroom: Using Title IX to Measure the Return to High School Sports," www.nber.org/papers/w15728, accessed March 7, 2010.

5. WeNews staff, "Seven Who Stake Our Claim to the Future: Bernice Sandler, Title IX Godmother," January 3, 2007, http://womesenews.org/article.cfm/dyn/aid/3006#Sandler, accessed March 7, 2010.

6. "Gender Roles—Interviews with Kids," www.youtube.com/watch?v=pWc1e3Nbc2g&feature=related, accessed March 7, 2010.

7. Tara Parker-Pope, "As Girls Become Women, Sports Pay Dividends," *New York Times,* February 15, 2010, www.nytimes.com/2010/02/16/health/16well.html?ref=science, accessed March 7, 2010.

8. Mary Pipher, *Reviving Ophelia: Saving the Selves of Adolescent Girls* (New York: Ballantine, 1995).

9. Dr. Louann Brizendene, *The Female Brain* (New York: Broadway, 2007) 46–47.

10. "Letters Between Abigail Adams and Her Husband John Adams," www.thelizlibrary.org/suffrage/abigail.htm, accessed March 7, 2010.

11. "'The Rule of Love': Wife Beating as Prerogative and Privacy," http://womhist.alexanderstreet.com/vawa/prologue.htm, accessed March 7, 2010.

12. The Seneca Falls Convention, July 19–20, 1848, www.npg.si.edu/col/seneca/senfalls1.htm, accessed March 7, 2010.

13. The American Association of University Women, "Bewitched, Battered, and Bewildered: A History of Domestic Violence" (Illinois: March 2009).

14. See http://wiki.answers.com/Q/What_was_the_conflict_between_women%27s_suffrage_and-African-American_issues, accessed March 7, 2010.

15. Inter-Parliamentary Union, "Women in National Parliaments," http://www.ipu.org/wmn-e/classif.htm#2, accessed August 30, 2011.

16. See http://en.wikipedia.org/wiki/Year_of_the_Woman, accessed March 7, 2010.

17. Quotes from interview by the author with Arizona Representative Gabrielle Giffords, January 5, 2007.

18. Taped interview notes with Hillary Clinton for research in Gloria Feldt, *The War on Choice: The Right-Wing Attack on Women's Rights and How to Fight Back* (New York: Bantam, 2004) 6.

19. Trends over Time for Women Candidates (1944–2008), http://www.cawp.rutgers.edu/fast_facts/elections/historical_trends.php, accessed March 7, 2010.

20. Elissa Haney and Beth Rowen, "Groundbreaking Women Quiz," http://quizzes.family-education.com/womens-history/62819.html?&detoured=1, accessed March 7, 2010.

21. "The Sveriges Riksbank Prize in Economic Sciences in Memory of Alfred Nobel 2009," http://nobelprize.org/nobel_prizes/economics/laureates/2009/, accessed March 7, 2010.

22. "Women Scientists Want Reconition," http://newsblaze.com/story/20100128082230 iwfs.nb/topstory.html, accessed March 7, 2010.

23. Vivian Gornick, "Why I'm Proud to Be a Feminist," www.doublex.com/section/news-politics/why-im-proud-be-feminist, accessed March 7, 2010.

## CHAPTER 2: REDEFINE: NOT POWER-OVER, POWER-TO

1. Linda Hirshman, "A Recipe for Disaster," http://scribe.doublex.com/blog/xxfactor/recipe-disaster, accessed March 9, 2010.

2. Ibid.

3. Merle Hoffman, "Flo Kennedy and Irene DaVall: Forever Activists," www.ontheissues-magazine.com/1985vol5_1985.php, accessed March 9, 2010.

4. See www.economyprofessor.com/theorists/johnstuartmill.php, accessed March 9, 2010.

5. J. P. R. French Jr. and B. Raven, "The bases of social power," in D. Cartwright and A. Zander (eds.), *Group Dynamics* (New York: Harper and Row, 1968), 607–23; see www.nwlink.com/~donclark/leader/leadled.html, accessed March 9, 2010.

6. See http://americanhistory.about.com/cs/lyndonbjohnson/a/quotelbj.htm, accessed March 9, 2010.

7. See http://answers.google.com/answers/threadview?id=289592, accessed March 9, 2010.

8. See www.goodreads.com/author/quotes/794023.Roseanne_Barr, accessed March 9, 2010.

9. See http://en.wikipedia.org/wiki/Florynce_Kennedy, accessed March 9, 2010.

10. See http://womenshistory.about.com/library/qu/blquKenn.htm, accessed March 9, 2010.

11. See http://en.wikiquote.org/wiki/Boss_Tweed, accessed March 9, 2010.

12. See www.theopedproject.org/cms/index.php?option=com_content&view=article&id=57&Itemid=63, accessed March 9, 2010.

13. Tory Johnson, "How to Ask for a Raise: Women Have to Be Confident When Making Their Case," April 28, 2006, http://abcnews.go.com/GMA/TakeControlofYourLife/story?id=1898808&page=1&page=1, accessed March 9, 2010.

14. Jessica Arons, "Lifetime Losses: The Career Wage Gap," December 8, 2008, www.americanprogressaction.org/issues/2008/lifetime_losses.html, accessed March 9, 2010.

15. See www.reuters.com/article/pressRelease/idUS199397+27-Apr-2009+PRN20090427, accessed March 9, 2010.

16. Linda Babcock and Sara Laschever, "Women Don't Ask: Negotiation and the Gender Divide," www.womendontask.com/stats/html, accessed March 9, 2010.

17. See www.homepagedaily.com/Pages/article6550-in-the-office-nice-girls-finish- last.aspx, accessed March 10, 2010.

18. Paula Maggio, "Get Smart: Get Trained to Help Women Negotiate Salary," http://ablogofourown.wordpress.com/2009/08/13/get-smart-get-trained-to-help-women-negotiate-salary, accessed March 9, 2010.

19. "Mad Men: Changing the Culture," http://nymag.com/daily/entertainment/2009/08/changing-the-conversat.html#1xaa0awP1yd8k, accessed March 9, 2010.

20. See www.homepagedaily.com/Pages/article6550-in-the-office-nice-girls-finish-last.aspx, accessed March 10, 2010.

21. McKinsey and Company, "Women Matter," October 2007, www.mckinsey.com/locations/paris/home/womenmatter.asp#Women, accessed March 9, 2010.

22. James MacGregor Burns, *Leadership* (New York: HarperCollins, 1978).

23. See www.onrec.com/news/the_role_of_gender_in_transformational_1.

24. Lin Coughlin, et al., *Enlightened Power: How Women Are Transforming the Practice of Leadership* (New York: Jossey-Bass, 2005).

25. See www.politico.com/news/stories/0909/27152_Page 2.html.

26. See www.forbes.com/lists/2009/10/billionaires-2009-richest-people_Warren_Buffett_C0R3.html, accessed March 9, 2010.

27. David Hawkins, *Power vs. Force: The Hidden Determinants of Human Behavior* (New York: Hay House, 2002), 133.

## NINA SIMONS PROFILE

1. See www.bioneers.org, accessed March 21, 2010.

## CHAPTER 3: UNBLOCK: POWER UNUSED IS POWER USELESS

1. Rafaella Barker, "A woman who knows her power has the keys to her happiness," June 1, 2008, http://women.timesonline.co.uk/tol/life_and_style/women/families/article4019936.ece, accessed March 10, 2010.

2. Gloria Steinem, *Revolution from Within: A Book of Self-Esteem* (New York: Little, Brown, and Co., 1993).

3. Personal interviews, both in New York City: Nedeau, September 20, 2009; Bennetts, September 2, 2009.

4. "Katie Couric Picks the Seven Most Powerful People in New Media," November 9, 2009, www.forbes.com/2009/11/09/google-couric-facebook-leadership-power-09-media_slide_5.html, accessed March 10, 2010; Lisa Stone, "About BlogHer," January 26, 2006, www.blogher.com/about-blogher-0, accessed March 10, 2010.

5. Elisa Camahort, "iVillage enters strategic partnership with BlogHer," July 16, 2008, www.blogher.com/ivillage-enters-strategic-partnership-blogher, accessed March 10, 2010.

6. 2009 Women and Social Media Study by BlogHer, iVillage, and Compass Partners, www.blogher.com/files/2009_compass_BlogHer_Social_Media_Study_042709_FINAL.pdf, accessed March 10, 2010.

7. Courtney Martin, "Does Being a Feminist Mean Voting for Hillary?" February 26, 2007, www.alternet.org/story/48390, accessed March 10, 2010.

8. Politico, "Exit polls: How Obama won," November 5, 2008, www.politico.com/news/stories/1108/15297.html, accessed March 10, 2010; "White Men Are Not Very Progressive," November 1, 2009, http://yglesias.thinkprogress.org/archives/2009/11/white-men-are-not-very-progressive.php, accessed March 10, 2010; William A. Galston, "The White Male Problem," July 12, 2001, www.dlc.org/ndol_ci.cfm?contentid=3564&kaid=127&subid=171, accessed March 10, 2010.

9. "Support the Paycheck Fairness Act," http://capwiz.com/aauw/issues/alert/?alertid=12819746, accessed April 15, 2010.

10. "Sen. Barack Obama's RH Issues Questionnaire," www.rhrealitycheck.org/blog/ 2007/12/21/sen-barack-obamas-reproductive-health-questionnaire, accessed April 15, 2010; "Obama and the Hyde Amendment," motherjones.com/mojo/2010/03/ obama-and-hyde-amendment, accessed April 15, 2010; "Obama's Failed Promise," www.thedailybeast.com/blogs-and-stories/2010-03-21/obamas-failed-promise, accessed April 15, 2010.

11. "About Us: Small, Young, Different," www.naissancecapital.com/NC/index.php, accessed March 10, 2010.

12. See www.womensconference.org/the-womens-conference-2009/video/katie-couric, accessed March 10, 2010.

13. See www.nytimes.com/2009/10/27/business/global/27fund.html?_r=1&dbk.

14. See http://en.wikipedia.org/wiki/Jenny_Shipley, accessed March 10, 2010.

15. See www.lauraliswood.com, accessed March 10, 2010; see http://www.cwwl.org, accessed March 10, 2010.

16. See www.85broads.com/janet_hanson, accessed March 10, 2010.

## KELI GOFF PROFILE

1. David Paul Kuhn, "Exit polls: How Obama won," November 5, 2008, www.politico .com/news/stories/1108/15297.html, accessed March 21, 2010.

2. See http://keligoff.com/meet.html, accessed March 21, 2010.

## CHAPTER 4: BE UNAFRAID: OPT OUT OF BEING CO-OPTED

1. See http://creativequotations.com/one/1593.htm, accessed March 10, 2010; see http:// in.integralinstitute.org/contributor/aspx?id=75, accessed March 10, 2010.

2. See www.alicepaul.org/alicepaul.htm, accessed March 10, 2010.

3. D. R. Hekman, et al., "An Examination of Whether and How Racial and Gender Biases Influence Customer Satisfaction," http://journals. aomonline.org/inpress/main .asp?action=preview&art_id=610&p_id=1&p_short=AMJ, accessed March 10, 2010.

4. James Chartrand, "Why James Chartrand Wears Women's Underpants," www .copyblogger.com/james-chartrand-underpants/?utm_source=feedburner&utm_ medium=feed&utm_campaign=Feed%3A+Copyblogger+%28Copyblogger%29, accessed March 10, 2010.

5. See www.eliewieselfoundation.org/nobelprizespeech.aspx, accessed March 10, 2010.

6. Amanda Hess, "James Chartrand's Constructed Masculinity Goes Far Beyond the Pen Name," www.washingtoncitypaper.com/blogs/sexist/2009/12/15/james-chartrands-constructed-masculinity-goes-far-beyond-the-pen-name/, accessed March 10, 2010.

7. See http://answers.yahoo.com/question/index?qid=20070501022431AA66KBW, accessed March 10, 2010.

8. Harriet Evans, "Don't patronise popular fiction by women," November 11, 2009, www .guardian.co.uk/books/booksblog/2009/nov/11/dont-patronise-popular-fiction-women, accessed March 10, 2010.

9. Laura Miller, "Why can't a woman write the Great American Novel?" www.salon.com/ books/review/2009/02/24/elaine_showalter, accessed March 10, 2010.

10. "10 Questions for Madeleine Albright," January 10, 2008, www.time.com/time/ magazine/article/0,9171,1702358,00.html, accessed March 10, 2010.

11. Author phone interview with Keli Goff, March 15, 2008.

12. Keli Goff, *Party Crashing: How the Hip-Hop Generation Declared Political Independence* (New York: Basic Civitas Books, 2008).

13. See www.observer.com/2007/coulter-culture; also see www.guardian.co.uk/media/2003/may/17/pressandpublishing.usnews.

14. Mickey Meece, "Backlash: Women Bullying Women at Work," May 9, 2009, www.nytimes.com/2009/05/10/business/10women.html, accessed March 10, 2010.

15. Katrin Bennhold, "Where would we be if women ran Wall Street?" February 1, 2009, www.nytimes.com/2009/02/01/business/worldbusiness/01iht-gender.3-420354.html, accessed March 10, 2010; Michael Fitzgerald, "Women Make Better Managers Than Men," March 5, 2008, http://blogs.bnet.com/business-books/p=159, accessed March 10, 2010.

16. Gail Collins, *When Everything Changed* (New York: Little, Brown and Company, 2009), 26.

17. Molly Ivins, in a speech given at the University of California, Berkeley, October 6, 2004.

18. Conversation with E. J. Graff on a private email listserv, March 22, 2010, quoting her part of it with her permission.

19. Author interview with Rosalind Hinton, October 1, 2008.

20. Matt Stearns, "Will U.S. voters elect a woman as president?" August 21, 2007, seattletimes.nwsource.com/html/nationworld/2003845865_clinton21.html, accessed March 10, 2010.

21. Laura Miller, "Touched by a vampire," July 20, 2008, www.salon.com/books/review/2008/07/30/Twilight/index.html, accessed March 10, 2010.

22. See http://kar3ning.livejournal.com/545639.html, accessed March 10, 2010.

23. Christine Seifert, "Bite Me! (Or Don't)" 2008, www.bitchmagazine.org/article/bite-me-or-dont, accessed March 11, 2010.

24. Peggy Orenstein, "What's Wrong with Cinderella?" December 24, 2006, www.nytimes.com/2006/12/24/magazine/24princess.t.html?_r=1&ref=magazine&oref=slogin, accessed March 10, 2010; Cathy K. Donovan, "When a princess costume becomes a culture,"February6,2008,http://news.rutgers.edu/focus/issue.2008-02-05.0513554387/article.2008-02-06.0314453901, accessed March 10, 2010; Mary Hoffman, "The princess problem," October 12, 2007, www.guardian.co.uk/books/2007/oct/12/booksforchildrenandteenagers.gender, accessed March 10, 2010.

25. See http://us.macmillan.com/BookCustomPage.aspx?isbn=9780571211852#Excerpt.

26. See www.chessbase.com/newsdetail.asp?newsid=5567.

27. Katha Pollitt, "Is Michael Connelly really a better writer than Lorrie Moore? Really?" November 13, 2009, www.shewrites.com/profiles/blogs/is-michael-connelly-really-a, accessed March 10, 2010.

28. James Chartrand, "Why James Chartrand Wears Women's Underpants," www.copyblogger.com/james-chartrand-underpants/?utm_source=feedburner&utm_medium=feed&utm_campaign=Feed%3A+Copyblogger+%28Copyblogger%29, accessed March 10, 2010.

29. From the 2009 Women Business Owners and Their Enterprises report, see www.nwbc.gov/ResearchPublications/keyFacts.html, accessed March 10, 2010.

## CHAPTER 5: UNFETTER: SECURE £500 AND A WOMB OF YOUR OWN

1. "Behind the Scenes with Dr. Jill Biden," December 11, 2009, www.cbsnews.com/stories/2009/12/11/sunday/main5966810.shtml, accessed March 13, 2010.

2. See www.answers.com/topic/newton-s-cradle, accessed March 13, 2010.

3. The Economist, "Womenomics," December 30, 2009, http://wo.ly/SEHi, accessed March 13, 2010.

4. Robert Thompson, "Barefoot and Pregnant: The Education of Paul Van Dalsem," The *Arkansas Historical Quarterly*, vol. LVII, winter 1998.

5. http://en.wikipedia.org/wiki/Coverture.

6. Ibid.

7. http://en.wikipedia.org/wiki/Spousal_rape.

8. www.mincava.umn.edu/documents/ffc/chapter5/chapter5.html.

9. Jean Reith Schroedel, *Is the Fetus a Person: A Comparison of Policies Across the Fifty States* (Ithaca, NY: Cornell University Press, 2000). Also see Sarah Kliff, "Coerced Reproduction," January 26, 2010, www.newsweek.com/id/232542, accessed March 13, 2010; Eli H. Newberger, et al., "Abstract: Abuse of Pregnant Women and Adverse Birth Outcome," www.midwiferytoday.com/reviews/abuse.asp, accessed March 13, 2010.

10. Sara Anzia and Christopher Berry, "Why Women in Congress Outperform Men," September 13, 2009, http://orgtheory.wordpress.com/2009/09/15/why-women-in-congress-outperform-men/, accessed March 13, 2010; also see Liz O'Donnell, "Women on Corporate Boards: The New Economic Stimulus," August 18, 2009, www.theglasshammer.com/news/2009/08/18/women-on-corporate-boards-the-new-economic-stimulus, accessed March 13, 2010.

11. Sara Anzia and Christopher Berry, "Why Women in Congress Outperform Men," September 13, 2009, http://orgtheory.wordpress.com/2009/09/15/why-women-in-congress-outperform-men/, accessed March 13, 2010.

12. See www.forbes.com/2009/11/11/worlds-most-powerful-leadership-power-09-people_slide_2.html, accessed March 13, 2010; also see Jacqueline Bell, "Women Make Few Inroads into Firm Leadership: Study," October 26, 2009, http://www.law360.com/articles/130156, accessed March 13, 2010.

13. Katty Kay and Claire Shipman, *Womenomics* (New York: HarperBusiness, 2009).

14. See http://washington.bizjournals.com/washington/stories/2006/03/06/smallb.html.

15. See http://ebooks.adelaide.edu.au/w/woolf/virginia/w91r/chapter2.html, accessed March 13, 2010.

16. Nicholas Kristof, "Mistresses of the Universe," February 7, 2009, www.nytimes.com/2009/02/08/opinion/08kristof.html, accessed March 13, 2010; Nicholas Kristof, "Pregnant (Again) and Poor," April 4, 2009, www.nytimes.com/2009/04/05/opinion/05kristof.html, accessed March 13, 2010.

17. See www.10000women.org/what.html, accessed March 13, 2010.

18. See www.helenlakellyhunt.com, accessed March 13, 2010.

19. See www.swaneehunt.com/bio.htm, accessed March 13, 2010.

20. See www.womenmovingmillions.net, accessed March 13, 2010.

21. "Anonymous donors support women students, college presidents," June 22, 2009, www.rankinfoundation.org/blog/9/Anonymous-donors-support-women-students-college-presidents, accessed March 13, 2010.

22. See http://thinkexist.com/quotation/for_most_of_history_anonymous_was_a_woman/146647.html, accessed March 13, 2010.

23. See http://womensvoicesforchange.org/gloria-steinem-it's-not-a-man's-world-or-a-woman's-nation.htm.

24. Michelle Goldberg, *The Means of Reproduction: Sex, Power, and the Future of the*

*World* (New York: Penguin, 2009), 223.

25. Kristin Luker, *Abortion and the Politics of Motherhood* (Berkeley, CA: University of California Press, 1985). See also www.mothersmovement.org/books/reviews/05/politics_of_motherhood.htm, accessed March 13, 2010.

26. Rachel Lehmann-Haupt, "Why I Froze My Eggs," May 2, 2009, www.newsweek.com/id/195691/page/1, accessed March 13, 2010.

27. Alex Kuczynski, "Her Body, My Baby," November 30, 2008, www.nytimes.com/2008/11/30/magazine/30Surrogate-t.html?_r=2, accessed March 13, 2010.

28. Richard Fry and D'Vera Cohn, "New Economics of Marriage: The Rise of Wives," January 19, 2010, www.pewresearch.org/pubs/1466/economics-marriage-rise-of-wives, accessed March 13, 2010.

## MARIA TERESA KUMAR PROFILE

1. See www.votolatino.org/mariateresakumar/, accessed March 21, 2010.

## CHAPTER 6: UNLIMIT YOURSELF: STAND IN POWER, WALK WITH INTENTION

1. Anna Fels, *Necessary Dreams: Ambition in Women's Changing Lives* (New York: Anchor, 2005), xvi.

2. See www.ipu.org/wmn-e/classif.htm, accessed March 13, 2010.

3. "Women Mayors in U.S. Cities 2009," www.cawp.rutgers.edu/fast_facts/levels_of_office/Local-WomenMayors.php, accessed March 13, 2010.

4. Jennifer Lawless and Richard Fox, *It Takes a Candidate: Why Women Don't Run for Office* (Cambridge: Cambridge University Press, 2005).

5. Author interview by phone, March 7, 2008; see also sheshouldrun.org/index.php?/pages/ask_a_woman_to_run, accessed March 13, 2010.

6. Jennifer Lawless, "Why Are Women Still Not Running for Office?" research.brown.edu/pdf/10066.pdf, accessed March 13, 2010.

7. Jessica Valenti, "The Sisterhood Split," March 6, 2008, www.thenation.com/doc/20080324/valenti, accessed March 13, 2010.

8. Author interview by phone, March 25, 2008.

9. Author interview in person in New York City, May 7, 2008.

10. Eric Lichtblau and Eric Lipton, "Senator's Aid After Affair Raises Flags Over Ethics," October 1, 2009, www.nytimes.com/2009/10/02/us/politics/02ensign.html?_r=1, accessed March 13, 2010.

11. "WCF Foundation Releases Vote with Your Purse Update," June 2, 2009, www.wcfonline.org/sn/2009_VWYP_update_release, accessed March 13, 2010.

12. Author interview by phone, May 4, 2006.

13. Author interview in person in Scottsdale, Arizona, March 27, 2008 and by phone, April 4, 2008.

14. Author interview by phone, April 21, 2008.

15. "Shirley Chisholm," womenincongress.house.gov/member-profiles/profile.html?intID=42, accessed March 13, 2010.

16. See murray.senate.gov/about, accessed March 13, 2010.

17. Author interview by phone, January 7, 2010.

18. See murray.senate.gov/about, accessed March 13, 2010, and www.whorunsgov.com/Profiles/Patty_Murray, accessed March 13, 2010.

19. Author interview by phone, May 28, 2008.

20. See www.house.gov/pelosi/biography/bio.html, accessed March 13, 2010.

21. From a speech to AFL-CIO reprinted in Emerge California newsletter, November 2007.

22. See https://litigation-essentials.lexisnexis.com/webcd/app?action=DocumentDisplay&crawlid=1&crawlid=1&doctype=cite&docid=10+Am.+U.J.+Gender+Soc.+Pol%27y+%26+L.+233&srctype=smi&srcid=3B15&key=f90c29ee6c4fd7a084891a-f79a3aedb2.

23. See http://andreas.com/poems.html, accessed March 13, 2010.

24. Author interview by phone, March 15, 2010. See also www.womenssuccesscoaching.com, accessed March 13, 2010.

25. See http://womengirlsladies.blogspot.com, accessed March 13, 2010.

26. Author interview by email, September 15, 2009.

27. See www.freepress.net/files/off_the_dial_summary.pdf, accessed March 13, 2010.

28. Derived from several interviews with MIW members by phone, September 2007.

29. Center for Women's Business Research, "Economic Impact Measured for the First Time," October 2, 2009, www.nfwbo.org/newsroom/pressreleases/2009pressreleases/economicimpactmeas/, accessed March 13, 2010.

30. "Take Our Daughters and Sons to Work," http://ms.foundation.org/about_us/our-history/take-our-daughters-and-sons-to-work, accessed March 13, 2010.

31. Jennifer Keil, "Women, the Recession, and the Impending Economic Recovery," 2009, http://gbr.pepperdine.edu/094/women.html, accessed March 13, 2010.

32. "Women and Equity Capital: An Exploration of Factors Affecting Capital Access," www.babson.edu/entrep/fer/XI/XIA/html/xi-a.htm, accessed March 13, 2010.

33. See www.makemineamillion.org, accessed March 13, 2010.

34. See www.empowher.com and http://www.ourbodiesourselves.org, accessed March 13, 2010.

## BARBARA LEE PROFILE

1. See www.barbaraleefoundation.org, accessed March 26, 2010.

## CHAPTER 7: UNLEASH: SISTER COURAGE

1. "Speak Truth to Power: A Quaker Search for an Alternative to Violence," www.quaker.org/sttp.html, accessed March 14, 2010.

2. Response to Twitter post, February 24, 2010.

3. Kristal Brent Zook, WomenGirlsLadies speech, June 30, 2009.

4. Kristal Brent Zook, "A Manifesto of Sorts for a Black Feminist Movement," *New York Times Magazine,* November 12, 1995.

5. See http://www.radiomiw.com, accessed March 14, 2010; see also http://talkers.com/online/?p=267, accessed March 14, 2010.

6. Matt Pressman, "Hate Sells: Why Liberal Magazines Are Suffering Under Obama," February 23, 2010, www.vanityfair.com/online/daily/2010/02/hate-sells-why-liberal-magazines-are-suffering-under-Obama.html, accessed March 14, 2010.

7. Kendra Tollackson, email and in-person interviews (various, Arizona); see also http://kendraforkids.com, accessed March 14, 2010.

8. See http://starwars.com/databank/character/yoda/index.html, accessed March 14, 2010.

9. See www.womensleadershipexchange.com, accessed March 14, 2010.

10. See http://en.wikiquote.org/wiki/Arthur_Schopenhauer, accessed March 14, 2010.

11. Aaron Zelinger, "Op-Ed: A Woman's Body Is Her Private Property," www.notunderthe bus.com/?p=406, accessed March 14, 2010.

## JULIE GILBERT PROFILE

1. See www.wolfmeansbusiness.com, accessed March 26, 2010.

## CHAPTER 8: JUST DO IT: YOUR POWER TOOLS

1. See http://seejanedo.typepad.com/see_jane_do/2010/01/the-story-behind-see-jane-do-and-the-future-of-extraordinary-janes.html, accessed March 24, 2010.

2. "Who Rules the Social Web?" October 2, 2009, www.informationisbeautiful.net/2009/who-rules-the-social-web, accessed March 24, 2010.

3. Jone Johnson Lewis, "August 26, 2010: The Day the Suffrage Battle Was Won," http://womenshistory.about.com/od/suffrage1900/a/august_26_wed.htm, accessed March 24, 2010.

4. See http://greetings.aol.com/display.pd?path=62352&bfrom-3&prodnum=3079182, accessed March 24, 2010.

5. See http://en.wikiquote.org/wiki/william_faulkner, accessed March 24, 2010.

6. "2010 Theme: Writing Women Back into History," www.nwhp.org/whm/index.php, accessed March 24, 2010.

7. Devin Dwyer, "Liz Cheney Group Defends Itself Against Criticism by Conservatives," March 11, 2010, http://abcnews.go.com/Politics/liz-cheney-group-defends-attack-holder-justice-department/story?id=1006523, accessed March 24, 2010.

8. Interview with Jenna Marie Mellor, Jen Nedeau, Brittany Dillman, and Nicola Wells in New York City, September 20, 2009.

9. See www.quotationspage.com/quote/27184.html, accessed March 24, 2010.

10. Deborah Tannen, "Can't We Talk?" http://raysweb.net/poems/articles/tannen.html, accessed March 24, 2010.

11. Author interview by phone, January 11, 2010.

12. See http://ballotpedia.org/wiki/index.php/Arizona_Initiative_to_Ban_Abortion_%2319 92%29, accessed March 24, 2010.

13. interview with Jenna Marie Mellor, Jen Nedeau, Brittany Dillman, and Nicola Wells in New York City, September 20, 2009.

14. See www.praythedevilbacktohell.com/nonflash/about.htm, accessed March 24, 2010; also see http://en.wikipedia.org/Ellen_Johnson_Sirleaf, accessed March 24, 2010; also see www.irinnews.org/IndepthMain.aspx?IndepthId=24&ReportId=66280, accessed March 24, 2010.

15. See http://creativethink.com, accessed March 24, 2010.

16. See www.quotationspage.com/quote/2901.html, accessed March 24, 2010.

17. Author interview by email, February 4, 2010.

18. See http://en.wikipedia.org/wiki/Jeremiah_Wright, accessed March 24, 2010.

19. "Vatican paper: Washing machine liberated women most," March 9, 2009, www.reuters.com/article/idUSTRE5282ME20090309?loomia_ow=t0:s0:a49:g43:r1:c1:000000:b30325542:z0, accessed March 24, 2010.

20. See http://microsoftontheissues.com/cs/blogs/mscorp/archive/2010/02/12/technology-at-the-margins-social-innovators-and-innovations.aspx, accessed March 24, 2010; see also http://answer.canadatop.com/Work/microsoft-bill-gates-company, accessed March 24, 2010.

21. Sophfronia Scott, "The Year of Living Fearlessly," January 1, 2010, www.thebook sistah.com/blog/writing/the-year-of-living-fearlessly, reprinted with permission, accessed March 24, 2010.

22. See www.fromfat2fit.com, accessed March 24, 2010; also author interview by email, February 6, 2010.

23. See www.amplifyyourvoice.org/u/Kirbygirl87/2010/2/26/Healthcare-Summit-Representative-Louise-Slaughter-Represents-Women-Everywhere, accessed March 24, 2010.

24. Annenberg Public Policy Center, "The Glass Ceiling Persists," 2003, www.annenberg publicpolicycenter.org/Downloads/Information_And_Society/20031222_Glass_Ceiling/20031222_glass_ceiling_report.pdf, accessed March 24, 2010.

25. "US Women Are More Present in Social Networking Sites," October 3, 2009, http://ontheweb.kimvallee.com/2009/10/women-rules-the-social-media-in-usa/, accessed March 24, 2010.

26. Peter Slevin, "S. Dakota Readies Again for Abortion Fight," September 21, 2008, www.washingtonpost.com/wp-dyn/content/article/2008/09/20/AR2008092002144.html, accessed March 24, 2010; and email interview by author of Tiffany Campbell.

## EPILOGUE: NO EXCUSES: DON'T FOLLOW YOUR DREAM—LEAD IT!

1. See http://thinkexist.com/quotation/if_the_first_woman_god_ever_made_was_strong/182811.html, accessed April 2, 2010.

2. See http://en.wikipedia.org/wiki/Sojourner_Truth#cite_note-Sojourner_TruthInstitute-1, accessed April 2, 2010; see www.sojournertruth.org/History/Biography/BC.htm, accessed April 2, 2010.

3. See www.absolutenow.com/features/height271.html.

4. Author's notes from events: Museum of Art and Design, New York City.

5. See http://equalvisibilityeverywhere.org, accessed April 2, 2010.

6. Deborah Richardson, "Women of Faith Called to Invest in Women, Girls," March 29, 2010, www.womensenews.org/story/religion/100326/women-faith-called-invest-in-women-girls, accessed April 2, 2010.

7. See www.rianeeisler.com/chalice.htm, accessed April 2, 2010; see www.amazon.com/When-God-Woman-Merlin-Stone/dp/0880295333/ref+sr_1_1?ie=UTF8&s=books&qid=1270068571&sr+1-1, accessed April 2, 2010.

8. See http://womenshistory.about.com/cs/quotes/a/qu_bella_abzug.htm, accessed April 2, 2010.

9. See www.uswccnewdeal.com, accessed April 2, 2010.

10. See www.ipu.org/wmn-e/classif.htm, accessed April 2, 2010.

11. See http://thewhitehouseproject.org/voterunlead/trainings, accessed April 2, 2010.

12. See www.wcfonline.org/sn/she_should_run, accessed April 2, 2010.

13. See www.cawp.rutgers.edu/education_training/2012Project/index.php, accessed April 2, 2010.

14. See www.thedailybeast.com/blogs-and-stories/2010-03-02/she-ate-his-lunch/2/, accessed April 2, 2010.

15. See http://daleallenproductions.com/iorm_index.htm, accessed April 2, 2010.

16. See www.nytimes.com/2009/12/11/business/media/11abc.html?ref=media, accessed April 2, 2010.

17. See www.gettingto5050.com/book/htm, accessed April 2, 2010.

18. See www.livescience.com/health/071017-feminism-romance.html, accessed April 2, 2010.

# index

child mortality rates, 57

child rearing: anti-choice views on, 200; and business ownership, 235–236; vs. career, 194–195; legislation allowing work and, 280; shared, 351–352; socialization in, 213–214; by women, 47–48, 196–197

children, planned, 201

Chisholm, Shirley, 221–222

choice: vs. expectation, 101–102; fear of, 100; to finish women's movement, 12; as goal of feminism, 140; to "opt out", 27, 54, 279; power-to as facilitating, 81; privilege of, 198–199, 234; vs. responsibility, 115; status quo adopts language of, 145; teen pregnancy as, 156–157

Circle Financial Group, 189–190

civil rights movement: and black feminism, 255; generational issues, 125, 142–143; internal debates in, 35

Civil War era, 36–37

Clinton, Bill, 111

Clinton, Hillary: attacks on, 223; co-option of, 151–153; cracks the glass ceiling, 10; Feldt supports, 110; Palin as dependent on, 149–150; as a role model, 223–224; as Secretary of State, 48; women oppose, 114; on the women's movement, 46–47

clothing: bloomers, 29; and credibility, 305–306

Cocco, Marie, 102

Code Pink, 92

coercive power, 69

Collins, Gail, 87, 317

communication, tips for effective, 306–307

Compass Partners, 108

competence, 229

Comstock, Anthony, 57

Condren, Debra, 252

confidence, 313–314

connectedness, 93

consumer power: and decision-making, 117–118; Julie Gilbert on, 285–287; of radio listeners, 261; squandered, 106–109; women as measured by, 119–120, 131

"Contract with America", 45

controversy: as fuel for change, 161; missed opportunities for, 162–163; as a power tool, 153; use of, 158, 311–316

Convention on the Elimination of All Forms of Discrimination Against Women (CEDAW), 279

co-option: of "choice", 145–146; controversy as protection against, 312; defined, 132; of girls, 157–158; of Hillary Clinton, 151–153; historic examples, 130; individualism and, 140–141; of James Chartrand, 132–139; of sex, 154–157; vs. speaking up, 286; strength as resistance to, 148–149; in the *Twilight* series, 155

Copeland, Reverend Dr. Claudette, 348

corporal punishment, 34

Coulter, Ann, 143–144

Council of Women World Leaders, 118

Council on Contemporary Families, 11

Count Me In, 238

courage: to assume power-to, 86, 102, 104; to follow passion, 232; injustice as fueling, 222; to lead, 319; to make change, 259, 266–267; Sister Courage, 250–252, 268, 283, 325; to tell your story, 335; vision of women's, 21; in young women, 148

coverture marriage, 175–176

Crick, Francis, 51

Cullison, Paula, 298

cultural narratives: buying into, 132; of catfights, 144; contradictory, 31–32; of diminished value, 103; male/female imbalance in, 92; as pressure, 271–272; of sexy Latinas, 208; surplus of, 213; women as helpless in, 137

Curie, Marie, 51

"Cutting Loose" (Kempton), 131

## D

Dawson, Rosario, 207

daycare, 224

debate, setting terms of, 74

decision-making, 82, 117

Dennett, Mary Ware, 59

difference, strength in, 275

Dillman, Brittany, 308

discrimination, gender: as banned from athletics, 29; confronting, 162–163, 191; as a generational issue, 217–219; in the healthcare system, 164–165, 327; legislation against, 43; in the workplace, 133–134, 146, 197

Disney princess myth, 101

divorce, 50, 100

domestic violence. see abuse

domination, 68

Dorfman, Margot, 349

*Double X*, 65

# gloria**feldt**

is a nationally renowned activist and author whose passion for social justice has propelled her life's work. Previous books include the *New York Times* bestseller *Send Yourself Roses,* coauthored with actress Kathleen Turner, *Behind Every Choice Is a Story,* and *The War on Choice.*

Gloria's popular Heartfeldt blog can be found at her website, GloriaFeldt.com. As a commentator and newsmaker, she has appeared in virtually all major national media. She teaches "Women, Power, and Leadership" at Arizona State University and is formerly president and CEO of Planned Parenthood Federation of America.

Gloria was named to *Vanity Fair* magazine's "Top 200 Women Legends, Leaders, and Trailblazers," *Glamour* magazine's Woman of the Year, and *Women's e-News* "21 Leaders for the 21st Century." She is a social media addict; you can find her on Facebook, Twitter, and LinkedIn. She and her husband, Alex Barbanell, share six children and fourteen grandchildren and live in New York City and Scottsdale, Arizona.

# acknowledgments

Ryan Fischer-Harbage of the Fischer-Harbage Agency reached out to me and believed from the start that I should write this particular book. His good counsel has been invaluable.

Brooke Warner, executive editor at Seal Press, is truly the best of the best. She immediately understood the importance of engaging women in this conversation at this moment in history. An extraordinarily skilled editor for whom I am supremely grateful, Brooke has also been a superb coach. Her insightful questions sharpened my thinking, and her confidence in the project buoyed my spirits. I owe her big-time gratitude for her patience.

I knew from the moment I first spoke with Brooke that Seal was the place I was meant to be with this book. They live up to their promise, "Groundbreaking books by women, for women." Donna Galassi, director of marketing, has taken a personal interest that means so much to me and to our ability to reach out to readers. And everyone, from publisher Krista Lyons to Christy Phillippe, who did such terrific copyediting, has been delightfully encouraging.

I believe in feeding the hands that help me. Many special people contributed; I'll name them according to the meal involved: First, there was the dinner party. Thank you, Gloria Steinem, for generously offering to suggest titles, which led to a most wonderful dinner at my apartment where she, Rachel Lehmann-Haupt, Kristal Brent Zook, and Deborah Siegel brainstormed dozens of title possibilities and talked candidly about their own relationships with power.

Second, the brunch: Jen Nedeau organized a fabulous group of young women, including Nicola Wells and Brittany Dillman, to talk with me about what women's power looks like from their vantage point. Jenna Mellor joined in, as well as magnificently transcribing many of my interviews (often over lunch) with other women whose stories enliven the book. The latter group constitutes a virtual banquet of women passionate about helping advance their sisters, including Cherie Blair, Jacki Zehner, Deborah Tannen, Leslie Bennetts, Michelle King Robson, Elisa Parker, Andrea March, Maria Teresa Kumar, Keli Goff, Carol Jenkins, Jennifer Buffett, Ellen Gustafson, Nicole Sexton, Lauren Bush, Barbara Lee, Gina Bianchini, Julie Gilbert, Marcia Reynolds, James Chartrand, and Marie Cocco. I also want to thank the many who responded to my incessant queries via email, Facebook, and Twitter, including Madeleine Albright, Bonnie Marcus, Linda Hirshman, Sophfronia Scott, Nina Simons, Jenn Pozner, and so many others I cannot even try to name you all—I can only say thank you, thank you, thank you for your munificent information and advice. You *are* Sister Courage.

To my beloved WomenGirlsLadies panel colleagues, Courtney Martin, Kristal Brent Zook, and Deborah Siegel-Acevedo, thank you for the chance to learn and grow from our public and private conversations about communication across the generations of women. My writing group, Lori Vadala Bizzoco, Jennifer Wortham, Janet Lombardi, and Kristi Berner, read sections I was struggling with and offered sage advice and encouraging words. Thanks to *On the Issues* for allowing me to use the piece I wrote for them on Margaret Sanger's leadership lessons.

Kamy Wicoff and the wonderful women at SheWrites.com all get giant kudos. Kamy shared invaluable insights about concepts and chapter structures. Sarah Saffian, Gala Delmont, and once again Deborah Siegel-Acevedo helped me wrangle the mass of data that I am prone to overcollect into ideas that made sense.

It takes a big village to write a book. I cannot thank Nadia Berenstein sufficiently. Nadia is a brilliant writer with whom I could hash out ideas, a remarkable editor who improved every chapter she put her hands on, and a cheerfully intrepid friend whom I simply adore. Laurie MacDonald pitched in with her amazing organizational abilities. Gregory Jackson skillfully helped create the powerful individual profiles. Debjani Chakravarty researched many of the academic studies cited and was a perceptive sounding board for ideas. Students in my Women, Power, and Leadership course at Arizona State University have also broadened my thinking about where the women's movement must go to be of service to this rising generation, but more important, they have given me huge confidence that the work will go on and the world will be in excellent hands.

My husband, Alex Barbanell, is my best cheerleader and the love of my life. Thank you for cooking for me, putting up with the many nights I worked late, yet being present when I needed a hug or a pep talk. To my children, who have truly made me what I am today, thank you—I love you.

Finally, *No Excuses* marks a significant juncture in my life. The first time I was introduced as simply a feminist author, I cried with happiness. I want to thank everyone who has stood with me and encouraged me along this path. I hope that by sharing my experiences and the knowledge I've gained from a lifetime of leadership and activism for women, along with the rich and varied stories of the many women who so generously allowed me to chronicle their power-to moments, I have provided inspiration and practical tools that will help you lead your own dreams.

# questions
# **for**discussion

1. Have you ever waited politely to speak during a meeting only to hear a male colleague offer the very idea you had planned to suggest? Taken on the major burden of household duties in part because you know it'll get done that way—and then you felt resentful?

2. Of all the leadership lessons from Margaret Sanger, which one resonates with you the most? What other women leaders have you learned from and how have they helped you?

3. Have you ever experienced a time in your life where you consciously defined your own terms and it made a difference in the course of events? How did you do that and what did you learn?

4. What would the world be like if women held most of the positions of power and leadership? What do you think would be different? What do you think would be the same? If you ran the world, how would you define power?

5. What is your relationship to money? How has it intersected with sex and power in your life? Can you have money and use it as a power-to rather than a power-over?

6. What's the difference between falling into a good job situation and actively seeking out a good situation? Is your passion your vocation? If not, why?

7. What's something that's ticked you off enough to get you politically involved? What would you like to see change and how do you think that change should be accomplished?

8. Think about mentors you have had in your life. How did they influence your career, public service, or personal life choices?

9. How can you have Sister Courage (be a sister and have courage to create a movement)?

10. How do you consume media? Where do you get your information? What percent of your media time is spent with traditional media versus social media and newer digital modes of media delivery?

11. Was there a moment when you knew you had the power to _____ (you fill in the blank)? Describe it and its meaning to you.

Continue the conversation at www.GloriaFeldt.com /9Ways